Daya Krishna and Twentieth-Century Indian Philosophy

Bloomsbury Introductions to World Philosophies

Series Editor

Monika Kirloskar-Steinbach

Assistant Series Editor

Leah Kalmanson

Regional Editors

Nader El-Bizri, James Madaio, Sarah A. Mattice, Takeshi Morisato, Pascah Mungwini, Omar Rivera, and Georgina Stewart

Bloomsbury Introductions to World Philosophies delivers primers reflecting exciting new developments in the trajectory of world philosophies. Instead of privileging a single philosophical approach as the basis of comparison, the series provides a platform for diverse philosophical perspectives to accommodate the different dimensions of cross-cultural philosophizing. While introducing thinkers, texts and themes emanating from different world philosophies, each book, in an imaginative and path-breaking way, makes clear how it departs from a conventional treatment of the subject matter.

Forthcoming Titles in the Series

A Practical Guide to World Philosophies, by Monika Kirloskar-Steinbach and Leah Kalmanson

Li Zehou and Twentieth-Century Chinese Philosophy, by Andrew Lambert

Māori Philosophy, by Georgina Tuari Stewart

Philosophy of Science and The Kyoto School, by Dean Anthony Brink

Samkhya and Classical Indian Philosophy, by Marzenna Jakubczak

Tanabe Hajime and the Kyoto School, by Takeshi Morisato

The Philosophy of the Brahma-sutra, by Aleksandar Uskokov

Daya Krishna and Twentieth-Century Indian Philosophy

A New Way of Thinking about Art, Freedom, and Knowledge

Daniel Raveh

BLOOMSBURY ACADEMIC
LONDON • NEW YORK • OXFORD • NEW DELHI • SYDNEY

BLOOMSBURY ACADEMIC
Bloomsbury Publishing Plc
50 Bedford Square, London, WC1B 3DP, UK
1385 Broadway, New York, NY 10018, USA

BLOOMSBURY, BLOOMSBURY ACADEMIC and the Diana logo are trademarks
of Bloomsbury Publishing Plc

First published in Great Britain 2021

Series design by Louise Dugdale
Cover image © Benjamin Toth / Getty Images

A catalogue record for this book is available from the British Library.

Library of Congress Cataloging-in-Publication Data
Names: Raveh, Daniel, author.
Title: Daya Krishna and twentieth-century Indian philosophy : a new way of thinking about art, freedom and knowledge / Daniel Raveh.
Description: London ; New York : Bloomsbury Academic, 2020. | Series: Bloomsbury introductions to world philosophies | Includes bibliographical references and index. |
Summary: "Daya Krishna and Twentieth-Century Indian Philosophy introduces contemporary Indian philosophy as a unique philosophical genre through the writings of one its most significant exponents, Daya Krishna (1924-2007). It surveys Daya Krishna's main intellectual projects: rereading classical Indian sources anew, his famous Samvad Project, and his ardent attempt to formulate a social and political theory that can better fit India's needs and challenges. Conceived as a dialogue with Daya Krishna and contemporaries, including his interlocutors, Krishnachandra Bhattacharyya, Badrinath Shukla, Ramchandra Gandhi and Mukund Lath, this book is an engaging introduction to anyone interested in contemporary Indian philosophy and in the thought-provoking writings of Daya Krishna"– Provided by publisher.
Identifiers: LCCN 2020019584 (print) | LCCN 202001958 (ebook) |
ISBN 9781350101609 (paperback) | ISBN 9781350101616 (hardback) |
ISBN 9781350101630 (ebook) | ISBN 9781350101623 (epub)
Subjects: LCSH: Krishna, Daya. | Philosophy, Indic–20th century.
Classification: LCC B5134.K73 R38 2020 (print) | LCC B5134.K73 (ebook) | DDC 181/.4–dc23
LC record available at https://lccn.loc.gov/2020019584
LC ebook record available at https://lccn.loc.gov/2020019585

ISBN: HB: 978-1-3501-0161-6
PB: 978-1-3501-0160-9
ePDF: 978-1-3501-0163-0
eBook: 978-1-3501-0162-3

Series: Bloomsbury Introductions to World Philosophies

Typeset by Deanta Global Publishing Services, Chennai, India

To find out more about our authors and books visit www.bloomsbury.com
and sign up for our newsletters.

For Mukund Lath, Yashdev Shalya and Rajendra Swaroop Bhatnagar

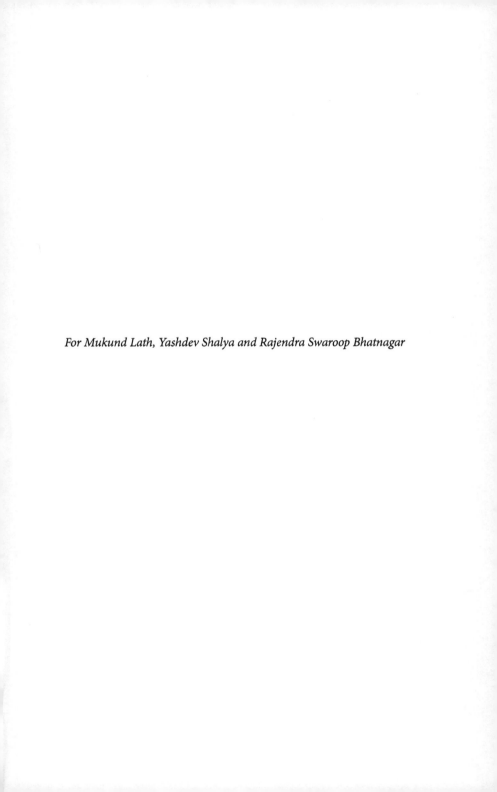

Contents

Preface

The introductions we include in the World Philosophies series take a single thinker, theme or text and provide a close reading of them. What defines the series is that these are likely to be people or traditions that you have not yet encountered in your study of philosophy. By choosing to include them you broaden your understanding of ideas about the self, knowledge and the world around us. Each book presents unexplored pathways into the study of world philosophies. Instead of privileging a single philosophical approach as the basis of comparison, each book accommodates the many different dimensions of cross-cultural philosophizing. While the choice of terms used by the individual volumes may indeed carry a local inflection, they encourage critical thinking about philosophical plurality. Each book strikes a balance between locality and globality.

Daya Krishna and Twentieth-Century Indian Philosophy offers a unique window into the mature thinking of Daya Krishna (1924–2007), one of the most original voices of twentieth-century India. It reiterates Daya Krishna's call for calibrating contemporary Indian philosophy to abet India in taking up its place in our decolonized world. For this purpose, Daya Krishna not only consciously strove to set the past in relation to India's present, and future, thus enabling a richer blending of tradition and innovation. He also partook in a lively exchange with some contemporaries like Badrinath Shukla, Ramchandra Gandhi and Mukund Lath. Together, they sought to find an appropriate (philosophical) place for a decolonized India.

—Monika Kirloskar-Steinbach

Acknowledgments

Mukund Lath, Bhatnagar Saab, Shalya-ji, Shlomo Biderman, Yoav Ariel, Yohanan Grinshpon, Arindam Chakrabarti, Jay Garfield, A. Raghuramaraju, Bhuvan Chandel, Bhagat Oinam, Murzban Jal, Heeraman Tiwari, Mathur Saab, Mercy Helen, Sri Kumaran, Neelima Vashishta, Ramesh Chandra Shah, Mrinal Miri, S. R. Bhatt, Ravindra Muley, Devasia Antony, Prasanjit Biswas, David Shulman, Balaganapathi Devrakonda, Ben Okri, Agastya Sharma, Ambika Datta Sharma, Hagi Kenaan, Galia Patt-Shamir, Alex Cherniak, Rafi Peled, Ronie Parciack, Roy Tzohar, Godavarish Mishra, Asha Mukherjee, Bijoy Mukherjee, Bhaskar Kowshik, Achia Anzi, Mikey Ginguld, Christopher Titmuss, Benzion Ghosalkar, Muzaffar Ali Malla, Ishwar Singh, Francis Arakal, Yogesh Gupta, Rashmi Patni, Rachana Sharma, Anha Osimlak Tsypin, Shaked Eshach, Randhir Singh, Rustam Bhai, Dima Shevchenko, Shalini Goswami, Dan Cordova, Gajendra Singh, Yam Maayan, Bheeshm Narayan Singh, Nir Feinberg, Itamar Ramot, Liat Grumberg, H. S. Shekhawat, Doron Peisik, Amir Appelbaum, Hgait Avidan, Sudarshan Singh and the Coffee House Parliament, Sohan Singh, Ravindra Singh Rawat, Rolan Crawford, Lyndelle Flintoft, Rakesh H. Singh, Lior Perry, Ouvi Lifshitz, Neeraj Sharma, Arvind Mayaram, Neerja Lath, Banwarilal Rao, Shanti Devi Rao, Sushil Joshi, Panchhi Bhatnagar, Shankar Singh, Premji, Ramdayal Dassji Maharaj, Ganeshji Maharaj, Lia Weiner, Ruth Raveh, Salu Pathania, Yoav Danziger, Timru Devi, Michal Magnes, Hava Magnes, Jonathan Magnes, and, always, Nina.

Special thanks to Sonia Nadine Weiner.

I wish to thank Shail Mayaram for her unique contribution.

I wish to thank G. J. V. Prasad, Rawat Saab, and Panditji of the Jawaharlal Nehru Institute of Advanced Study, JNU, for their warm hospitality.

I wish to thank Elise Coquereau-Saouma and Dor Miller, who together created "Daya Krishna: The Open Library" at dayakrishna.org, a website that provides open access to almost all of Daya Krishna's philosophical oeuvre.

I wish to warmly thank Shea Arieli, a vital member of the Daya Krishna Circle.

I wish to thank Monika Kirloskar-Steinbach, the architect behind the series of Introductions to World Philosophies, for the invitation to take part in this worthy project.

Finally, I wish to mention the contribution of N. K. Chaudhary of Piccadilly Book Stall, Connaught Place, Delhi, an old friend and an institution, who passed away in March 2018 and is dearly missed by the Bhaktas of his Pustak Mandir.

The research for this book was supported by THE ISRAEL SCIENCE FOUNDATION (grant No. 937/15)

Abbreviations

BG:	*Bhagavadgītā*, also *Gītā*
"Bondages":	Daya Krishna's paper "Bondages of Birth and Death: Emerging Technologies of Freedom on the Horizon and the Hope of Final Release from the Foundational Bondage of Mankind" (2006)
BU:	*Bṛhadāraṇyaka-Upaniṣad*
CU:	*Chāndogya-Upaniṣad*
DK:	Daya Krishna
"Encounters":	Daya Krishna's paper "Encounters between Civilizations: The Question of the Centre and the Periphery" (1997)
Eighteenth Century Onwards:	Daya Krishna's book *Developments in Indian Philosophy from the Eighteenth Century Onwards: Classical and Western* (2002)
Illusions:	Daya Krishna's book *Towards a Theory of Structural and Transcendental Illusions* (1998/2012)
KU:	*Kaṭha-Upaniṣad*
JICPR:	*Journal of Indian Council of Philosophical Research*
KCB:	Krishnachandra Bhattacharyya
Man, Society, and Polity:	Daya Krishna's book *The Problematic and Conceptual Structure of Classical Indian Thought about Man, Society and Polity* (1996)
New Perspectives:	Daya Krishna's book *New Perspectives in Indian Philosophy* (2001)
Prolegomena:	Daya Krishna's book *Prolegomena to Any Future Historiography of Cultures and Civilizations* (1997)

SK:	Īśvarakṛṣṇa's *Sāṃkhyakārikā*
"Socio-Political":	Daya Krishna's paper "Socio-Political Thought in Classical India" (1997)
"The Cosmic":	Daya Krishna's paper "The Cosmic, Biological and Cultural Conditionings, and the Seeking for Freedom" (2006)
"The Shock-Proof":	Daya Krishna's paper "The Shock-Proof, Evidence-Proof, Argument-Proof World of Sāmpradāyika Scholarship of Indian Philosophy" (2000)
"The Undeciphered":	Daya Krishna's paper "The Undeciphered Text: Anomalies, Problems and Paradoxes in the Yogasūtra" (2006, 2012)
"The Varṇāśrama Syndrome":	Daya Krishna's paper "The Varṇāśrama Syndrome of Indian Sociology" (1992)
"Thinking Creatively":	Daya Krishna's paper "Thinking Creatively about the Creative Act" (1999)
"Thinking vs. Thought":	Daya Krishna's paper "Thinking vs. Thought: Strategies for Conceptual Creativity" (1988)
"Three Myths":	Daya Krishna's paper "Three Myths about Indian Philosophy" (1966)
TU:	*Taittirīya Upaniṣad*
"Vedānta in the first Millennium":	Daya Krishna's paper "Vedānta in the First Millennium A.D.: The Case Study of a Retrospective Illusion Imposed by the Historiography of Indian Philosophy" (1996)
YS:	Patañjali's *Yogasūtra*

Transliteration

Whenever I use a term or quote a phrase, sūtra, or paragraph in Sanskrit, they are transliterated into English (Roman) letters. I follow the standard transliteration as (roughly) the following:

a as in c**u**t
ā as in c**a**r
i as in s**i**t
ī as in sw**ee**t
u as in f**u**ll
ū as in p**oo**l
ṛ pronounced ri as in **ri**ch
ṇ as in u**n**der or u**n**real
ñ as in i**n**ch or a**n**gel (both ṇ and ñ are different
from n as in a**n**d or a**n**t)
c pronounced as ch as in **ch**ain
ś pronounced as sh as in **sh**eep
ṣ pronounced as sh as in **sh**y

Introduction

Questions give birth only to other questions.
Vikram Chandra, *Red Earth and Pouring Rain*

1 Prologue

In the late 1990s, I came upon a book by Daya Krishna (henceforth DK) at the Tel Aviv University Sourasky Library. It was his *Indian Philosophy: A Counter Perspective*. I was totally captivated by the book. It was not just the intriguing content, comprising of a new reading of classical Indian philosophy, but the way it was written. A postgraduate student of philosophy at the time, I could feel that something was "happening" in the book. In retrospect, this "happening" can be formulated through DK's own distinction between "thinking" and "thought," in his essay "Thinking vs. Thought: Strategies for Conceptual Creativity" (1988). Here he makes a distinction between "thinking" as a dynamic, continuous, living process and "thought" as the tentative product of "thinking." For him, books and essays are just stops on the thinking journey. Or, to use another metaphor, they are like a window through which the reader can look into the author's creative thinking process. They work as an open invitation for the reader to "come on board" and take active part in this process, which according to DK is neither "mine" nor "yours," but is a collective striving.

After reading the book, I decided to travel to Jaipur to meet the author. I knocked on his door one steamy August evening. An old man in white kurtā-pāyjāmā opened the door and said "Yes?" This initial "Yes" led to an almost decade-long relationship, with endless hours of philosophical discussion, which continued until his last day in October 2007. The present monograph is part of my ongoing dialogue with Dayaji.

My focus in the following chapters is primarily on the last decade of DK's life and work, from his book *Indian Philosophy: A New Approach* (1997) to his final project, *The Jaipur Edition of the Ṛgveda*, completed in 2007 but unpublished as yet. As the Bibliography indicates, it was DK's most prolific decade. I concentrate on the final years, first, because these are "my DK years," having had the privilege of discussing with him many of the ideas that find expression in his writings during this period. And second, since his earlier writings, from *The Nature of Philosophy* (1955, born of his dissertation) to *Indian Philosophy: A Counter Perspective* (1991), have already been reflected upon. In fact, a whole volume, titled *The Philosophy of Daya Krishna* (1996), is dedicated to these earlier writings, with an intriguing section in which he responds to the papers written on his work by friends, colleagues, and students (several of the writers belong to more than one of these categories), including scholars such as Sibajiban Battacharyya, J. N. Mohanty, Yashdev Shalya, and D. P. Chattopadhyaya. One of the purposes of the present monograph is to introduce some of the central figures of twentieth-century Indian philosophy, such as these four, at least by name, if not more broadly through their correspondence and philosophical interface with DK. Other contemporaries of DK to be discussed in the following chapters include Krishnachandra Bhattacharyya (henceforth KCB), whom I consider the "founding father" of contemporary Indian philosophy, Pandit Badrinath Shukla, Mukund Lath, Ramchandra Gandhi, G. R. Malkani, and R. Balasubramanian, among others. "The enterprise of thinking," DK writes in "Thinking vs. Thought," "is usually supposed to be a solitary exercise. Similar is the feeling about creativity. But this is a mistake. When people gather together, something new emerges" (1988, 54). Dialogue, then, is the string that binds the following chapters together. I will spotlight the dialogic and often polemic dimension of DK's writings, with equal interest in the voices and the philosophical stance of his interlocutors.

I decided to focus on DK's last decade, but will certainly not confine myself to these years alone. There is a clear sense of continuity in DK's writings, an internal connecting thread, in accord with his vision of "thinking" as perennial and continuous. To use a Jaipurite illustration, visiting DK's writings is like entering the famous Śīśa Mahal, the Hall of Mirrors at the Amer Kilā. If one lights a candle, the flame is reflected simultaneously in all the mirror mosaics and colored glasses all around. Such is also the case in DK's oeuvre. If you light a candle, as I aim to do in each of the following chapters (this monograph is a "Daya Krishna Dīpikā"), one can see DK's pivotal thinking trajectories and philosophical concerns reflected in all of his writings.

Contemporary Indian philosophy is a unique genre of philosophy. On one hand, it corresponds with classical Indian sources, with the tradition. On the other, it is in constant dialogue with Western materials, classical and modern. The dialogue is mostly with the West, less with China and Japan, because of the language issue. British colonialism brought to India both the English language and European philosophy. Contemporary Indian philosophy was conceived in the face of "the British intrusion," as DK puts it. One of my discoveries while writing this monograph was the sharp political edge of DK's work, from the preface of his magnum opus *The Art of the Conceptual* (1989), to be discussed a few paragraphs down the road, to his subversive, cutting-edge yet hardly known textbook "Indian Philosophy: A New Approach" (1997). My hope is that through the discussion to be offered here, chapter after chapter, of central junctions of DK's corpus and his main projects, the spirit and orientation of Indian philosophy in the twentieth century will be revealed. Speaking of spirit and orientation, I think of the eclectic nature of this philosophical genre, born of the abovementioned inbuilt dialogue with Indian classics and Western sources, and of the pertinent question of identity in the face of colonialism and within the matrix of so-called globalization, and consequently the ever-present challenge of decolonization, of "svarāj in ideas," as KCB famously puts it, which is constantly bubbling under the surface and between the lines of contemporary Indian philosophy.

And speaking of DK's main projects, two of them will be discussed here in detail. First, his eager attempt to reread classical Indian texts through a new lens—eclectic, questioning, and uncommitted to old frames—from the Veda and the Upaniṣads, through the sūtras, to Śaṅkara and the Bhagavata-Purāṇa. DK's reading of the Veda is reflected in a series of papers, "The Vedic Corpus: Some Questions" (1985), "Where Are the Vedas in the First Millennium AD?" (1997), "Ṛgveda: The Mantra, the Sūkta and the Maṇḍala or The Ṛṣi, the Devatā, the Chanda: The Structure of the Text and the Problems Regarding It" (2006), "The Formative Period of Indian Civilization: The Vedic, the Śramaṇa, the Āgamic Traditions; the Interactions between Them and the Reflexive Reflections on Them" (2007), "The Sources, the Texts, the Subsidiaries, the Supportive, the Exegetical Literature: The Puzzle and the Problem of the Veda in the Indian Tradition" (2007), and "The Yajurveda Text—The Heart of the Veda Yajña: One, Two, or Too Many?" (2007), and culminates in his final ambitious experiment, *The Jaipur Edition of the Ṛgveda* (2007). DK's reading of the sūtra literature gave birth to papers such as "The Vedic Corpus and the Two Sūtra Texts Concerned with it, the Mīmāṃsāsūtra and the Brahmasūtra" (2006), and "The Undeciphered Text: Anomalies, Problems and Paradoxes in the Yogasūtra" (2006), and to his book *The Nyāya Sūtras: A New Commentary on an Old Text* (2004). I mention these titles to illustrate the vastness of DK's corpus. His second project to be discussed in detail is the Saṃvād Project, which he initiated in the 1980s with colleagues such as M.P. Rege, R.C. Dwivedi, and Mukund Lath. The idea behind this project, DK explains in the preface of his book *Discussion and Debate in Indian Philosophy* (2004), was to bring together "active practitioners of the two philosophical traditions, the Indian and the Western, in a dialogical situation where each was forced to existentially face the living tradition of a different way of philosophizing" (2004, xiii). Every phrase here is interesting:

active practitioners, dialogic situation, forced to existentially face, living tradition, and ways of philosophizing. This project, or "experiment" as DK often refers to it, established a dialogue between pandits and professors, that is, philosophers thinking and writing in Sanskrit, and their brothers and sisters trained in the parallel tradition of European or Western philosophy, on a variety of philosophical topics, from issues in philosophy of language to philosophical exploration of the emotions. In a letter dated February 2006, DK speaks of the meeting of these two intellectual traditions as "something like the Saṅgam at Prayāg Rāj," the famous confluence of Gaṅgā and Yamunā near Allahabad (here the phrase citta-nadī, "the river of the mind," from the *Yogasūtra-bhāṣya* comes in handy). This meeting of these two rivers/goddesses reveals a third goddess/river, namely, Sarasvatī. "Saraswati," Sri Aurobindo—not just a yogi, guru, and poet, but an argumentative philosopher and inspiration to DK in his initial years—writes in *The Secret of the Veda* (originally published in his monthly journal *Arya* between August 1914 and July 1916),

> means she of the stream, the flowing movement [. . .] Saraswati possesses and is the flood of the Truth. [. . .] Truth comes to us as a light, a voice, compelling a change of thought, imposing a new discernment of ourselves and all around us. (1998, 211)

Except for the Capital-T Truth, which is foreign to DK's thinking, Aurobindo's poetic account explains the Saṃvād Project as envisioned by DK. It was a matter of discovering a "flowing movement" in Indian philosophy, an attempt toward "a change of thought" and "new discernment." Moreover, it was a new instance of comparative philosophy, a new type of East-West exchange.

2 Two Letters

DK was an enthusiastic correspondent. Besides writing regularly to a circle of close friends, a large portion of his correspondence revolved around the *JICPR*, *Journal of Indian Council of Philosophical Research*, which he edited from August 1990 until his death in 2007. He responded personally to many of the papers received for publication, encouraged colleagues and experts in different areas of philosophy to contribute to the journal, responded to other publications, elsewhere, of the *JICPR* community, and answered, with full eagerness, to all those who wrote to him in response to his numerous writings and projects. After he passed away, DK's correspondence between

2003 and 2007 was preserved by Mathur Saab, his secretary and ally for many years. For DK, a philosopher without borders, philosophy was not confined to articles and books, or to the university classroom. His correspondence shows that for him, the philosophical and the personal, or philosophy and the lifeworld, are inseparable. DK's letters, especially to close friends, often resemble a captain's log. In these letters, he keeps a record of his philosophical voyages, and explains in which direction his ship is heading or what his present philosophical concerns are. In this respect, the letters can often work as a commentary to DK's published writings. I wish to quote from two letters, written by DK to his friend novelist-poet-thinker Ramesh Chandra Shah in 2006, to illustrate DK's "philosophy in the first person":[1]

> Dear R.C. Shah,
> *Ancestral Voices*[2] reached me a few days ago just as I, along with many others, was trying to "close" my ears to them in order to "hear" and "listen" better the voices from the "FUTURE" beckoning us and challenging to "think" and "act" in a new way.
>
> Ancestors are alright, but one is to "remember" them only once a year during the Śrāddha period and then forget them for the whole rest of the year.
>
> Their achievement is well-known, as we shall not be what we are without them. But their "failures" are equally obvious as we ourselves illustrate them in our life perpetually. And so did they, if the stories about them in the sacred texts themselves, are to be believed.
>
> Still it is good to be reminded and I look forward to reading what you have written on the subject. [. . .]

> My dear Shah,
> I hope your worry about my illness is over, though "illness" seems to be a "natural" condition of life at all its stages and ages. [. . .] The stranger problem is that there are not only "diseases" of life, or what may be called the "body" but also of "mind" and "reason" and "intellect" and even of the "spirit." Mental illnesses are fairly well-known, but not so the diseases which "reason" itself is prone to. As for the "spiritual illnesses," one hardly hears about them.

> But what about imagination? Does it play an important role in diseases at all these levels? and, if so, what is the "cure" for those diseases which are rooted in imagination and, at another level, in consciousness itself?
>
> If consciousness is a "disease" that has affected life, then could not "life" be considered a "disease" that has affected matter?
>
> Matter itself does not seem to have any diseases, though there is such a thing as "rusting" or "radioactive decay" which, in any case have not been seen as such. At one time, the story of the Black Hole seemed to suggest something analogous to what may be called "disease" at the heart of matter, but as Stephen Hawking has gone back on his earlier theory as recently reported in the newspapers, we can hardly see them as such.
>
> You are a writer; why not write on this? Is literature a disease of language just as, according to Wittgenstein, philosophy is a disease which language suffers from when it takes a holiday from its daily use? [. . .]
>
> Imagine, writing to you like this; but it is the person to whom the letter is written that provokes a thought current appropriate to him or her. [. . .]

The first thing one notices when reading DK is his extensive use of quotation marks. To "close," to "hear" and "listen," "FUTURE," to "think" and "act," "body," "mind," "reason," "intellect," the "spirit," "spiritual illnesses," the "cure," and the "person" are just a few illustrations of this distinctive feature. This is the case both in his letters and elsewhere. These quotation marks convey, or so I wish to suggest, DK's delicate "handling" of language. David Foster Wallace opens his famous essay "This is Water," delivered as a commencement speech at Kenyon College in 2005, with this short allegory:

> There are these two young fish swimming along, and they happen to meet an older fish swimming the other way, who nods at them and says, "Morning, boys, how's the water?" And the two young fish swim on for a bit, and then eventually one of them looks over at the other and goes, "What the hell is water?"[3]

Language is the water that we all swim in, and DK is the older fish. Whenever he uses quotation marks, he shows awareness, and calls our attention to the water. When you are a fish in water, it is easy to forget the water, to take it for granted. Like water, language can become transparent, too obvious to be noticed. The task of the philosopher is to ask "how's the water?" DK's quotation marks disclose his sensitivity to language-use, and a continuous reflection about choosing "the right word" (from among many "right words") to convey his ideas. Moreover, many words and notions carry with them a long history of use (or misuse): take for instance the word "reason" that DK quote marks. But by marking a notion, he does not merely remind us the history of the word, the baggage that it carries along, and the shackles of the context; my hunch is that DK's quotation marks are also endowed with a redeeming quality. They release a word or notion from the weight of history and context, that DK is aware of but refuses to be determined by.

The first letter to Shah Saab emphasizes DK's future-facing, rather than nostalgic, philosophical gaze. He writes "FUTURE" with capital letters and quotation marks. Capital letters to urge his old friend, and others, not to think, write, and look again and again into the past, the classical texts, "the wonder that was," but to think, write, and look into something new, to sail toward new destinations. I will discuss the intricacies of DK's repeated insistence on "something new" in philosophy in Chapter 1, "Toward a New Picture of Indian Philosophy," and in Chapter 3, "Freedoms," where I touch on DK's concept of "Knowledge without Certainty" which is "pregnant with the future." DK's quotation marks on the word "future" remind us that the future, as the word anāgata, future in Sanskrit, literally indicates, is something that "has not yet arrived." In the same way, the past, atīta, is literally "gone by, dead." The Sanskrit terms chosen here are from Patañjali's *Yogasūtra* (YS 4.12). For Patañjali, the past and the future exist in the present in the form of saṃskāras, that is, merely as "mental impressions or recollections" (it is interesting to think of the future as recollection, and of recollection as something that pertains not just to the dead past but also to the unborn future). The twist, namely, the future as "existing" in the present in the form of seeds, karmic seeds, recollection seeds, which are yet to ripen, or in other words, the future as both existing and not existing, is marked by DK's quotation marks.

When DK writes to his friend that he is trying hard to "close his ears" to the "ancestral voices" and listen to "voices from the future," I recall DK's Shimla Lectures (2005, published in 2012 under the title *Civilizations: Nostalgia and Utopia*). Here he speaks of the role of philosophy in the present "futuristic" era of cloning, genetic engineering, and "budgeted knowledge" (see my discussion in Chapter 3), and the need of philosophy to calibrate itself to the present, lest it becomes a prehistoric dinosaur. One of his listeners in Shimla, a classical pandit, made an attempt to defend the glorious past from DK's preposterous concept of "Knowledge without Certainty." In response to DK, he quoted passionately from memory, in Sanskrit, Bhīṣma of the *Mahābhārata*, the voice of tradition. "Bhīṣma uvāca" ("Bhīṣma said"), the pandit repeatedly uttered. "Why don't we forget Mr. Bhīṣma," DK retaliated (namely, "close our ears" to "ancestral voices," Bhīṣma being "the ancestor of ancestors"), "and concentrate instead on contemporary physics, technology, cloning, internet etc.?" The heretic phrase "Mr. Bhīṣma" was intended to work as a wake-up call for his listeners, like the capital letters (FUTURE) in his letter to Shah Saab. Incidentally, as DK spoke in Shimla and wrote to Shah, he was working on his last project, *The Jaipur Edition of the Ṛgveda*, "editing" (my quotation marks aim to convey his hardly traditional methodology), and hence contemplating on, being absorbed in, and devoting most of his time and intellectual energy to rethinking the Veda, the oldest text of the Indian tradition. A free traveler in time, DK was working with the past and the future together, bringing the FUTURE to his reading of the Veda.

The second letter, the illness letter, speaks for itself. DK is more interested in the notion of illness, in illness as such, than in his own illness. Even under severe illness, he finds the "right distance" without which reflection is not possible. When you are too near, you cannot SEE (speaking of "illnesses," DK's quotation marks and capital letters are contagious). "The fundamental message of philosophy," Slavoj Žižek writes, "says that you can immediately participate in universality, beyond particular identifications" (2009, 72). This is exactly what happens here. DK "participates in universality," and thinks of illnesses of the mind, reason, intellect and even the spirit as also of rusting, radioactive decay, and "the story of the Black Hole" as forms of illness or disease. The illness letter ends with the power of dialogue. "Imagine writing to you like this," DK reflects on his equation with Shah Saab. It is the other, "you," "my dear Shah," as he addresses his old friend, and the latter's letter (which DK answers) and concern, and his "writing personality," which provoke, as DK puts it, this thought current.

3 Daya Krishna's Introductions

Writing an introduction to a monograph dedicated to DK's philosophical work is an occasion to look into DK's own introductions to several of his books, to find out how he uses his "front pages"; how he develops his ālāpa, his philosophical overture; and how he opens the dialogue with his readers, with other authors, thinkers, philosophers and texts, and with his own previous work. It should be noted that owing to his deteriorating eyesight, most of DK's work in the last decade and a half of his life was dictated, rather than handwritten (the keyboard remained beyond his comfort zone throughout). Like Vyāsa, he used the good services of Gaṇeśa, who in DK's case took the form of close colleagues and research students. I mention DK's oral transmission not just as an anecdote, but owing to the inbuilt dialogic dimension of such practice. A large part of DK's oeuvre was conceived in dialogue with his "writers." We live in an era of writing and reading. Oral transmission sounds ancient. This was the practice, for instance, in the Vedic and Upaniṣadic eras. In the Upaniṣadic literature, we find many repetitions, intended to enable the listeners (rather than readers) to absorb that which has been said (rather than written). This is not the place to discuss the fundamental difference between the speaking/listening and the writing/reading cultures of thinking. For DK, "writing" a paper, or a book, was a matter of thinking out loud, in the present, in the now, without the security net of the written word. It is my feeling that one can literally "hear" DK through his writings.

DK opens his book *New Perspectives in Indian Philosophy* (henceforth *New Perspectives*) with the following words:

> These essays on Indian philosophy continue the dialogue initiated in the earlier collection entitled *Indian Philosophy: A Counter Perspective*. The tradition of questioning continues and many of the beliefs accepted as unquestionably true, are subjected to a close scrutiny that reveals them to be totally unfounded. (2001, 1)

DK emphasizes the continuity between his writings, the dialogic aspect of his work, and the task that he has taken upon himself, to shoot question-arrows at "the beliefs," many of them "totally unfounded," that constitute the conventional picture of Indian philosophy. In the next paragraph of his introduction, DK mentions for example the "belief" or the "myth" about Śaṅkara's decisive role in the disappearance of Buddhism from the Indian scene (a "myth" that he aims to refute in his paper "Was Ācārya Śaṅkara Responsible for the Disappearance of Buddhist Philosophy from India?" included in this anthology). DK further speaks of "the injustice done to Buddhism by the historians of Indian philosophy," in the sense that the centrality of Buddhist philosophy in the first millennium, until the destruction of Nālandā by Bakhtiyār Khiljī in 1193 CE, has been undermined. "The myth of Vedic Hinduism swallowing up all the other non-Hindu religious traditions of India," DK writes, "so persistently propagated by certain vested interests, is really a myth, unsubstantiated by any evidence whatsoever." His choice of the word "injustice" is interesting. DK alludes to the politics behind the historical narrative, and breaks once again the already shattered reputation of history as "objective record." Along the same lines, in another introduction to another book, *Developments in Indian Philosophy from the Eighteenth Century Onwards: Classical and Western* (henceforth *Eighteenth Century Onwards*), DK bluntly writes that "the past is what the historian has created" (2001, 3).

Later in his introduction to *New Perspectives*, DK implies that no text is "immune" to philosophical scrutiny, which is of the capacity of revealing "problems" and "inconsistencies." But inconsistencies and problems, for him, are part and parcel of every text, a fact that does not necessarily detract from the strength and value of the text. DK is well aware that this textual approach is hardly accepted by the traditionalist, who prefers that the texts that he holds precious remain "untouched" by a sharp philosophical scalpel such as DK's. DK's attitude toward "tradition," or "religion," or "orthodoxy" is disclosed in his introduction to *Bhakti: A Contemporary Discussion—Philosophical Explorations in the Indian Bhakti Tradition* (2000). This book is a transcript of the proceedings of a Saṃvād, a dialogue between philosophers and traditionalists, or "theorists" and "practitioners" (some of the participants belonged simultaneously to both categories), which he was one of the main forces behind, and which took place in Vrindavan, "the heartland of Bhakti itself," as he puts it in this introduction. The theme of the discussion was the philosophical dimension of bhakti, which is often perceived as "anti-intellectual emotionalism" (DK's phrase). Of his own position at this philosophy/religion intersection, he writes:

> At times it almost seemed blasphemous to say the things we said, when the eternal flute of the Divine itself called to us every moment to give up the vain, empty, dry world of intellect, and the greetings "Rādhe Rādhe" reminded us of the ecstasy of divine love. But amidst these enticements and allurements, what sustained us was the unbelievably long, hardcore tradition of the ever-seeking, ever-doubting sāttvika quest for the ultimate truth by the buddhi in the Indian tradition, which has never been afraid of raising the most formidable pūrvapakṣas [objections] against one's own position. (2000, iii)

With all reverence to "the eternal flute of the Divine itself" (Vrindavan is god Krishna's abode), DK confesses that he is a bhakta, a devotee, of another temple, "the temple of reason." He reminds the readers that the "ever-seeking, ever-doubting quest by the buddhi," the intellect, is as deeply rooted in the Indian tradition as the "religious" strands of bhakti. He beautifully portrays "the free play of reason, imagination and intellectual sensibility" as "bauddhika yajña," an "offering" at the "intellectual altar" (2000, iv).

Back in his introduction to *New Perspectives*, DK writes that,

> a picture once built is difficult to dismantle, but the evidence and the argument slowly undermine it, and the younger generation which is not so indissolubly "wedded" to "orthodoxy" as the older one, begins to be more open and responsive to the critique as it finds some substance in it. (2001, 5)

His observation about the solidity of "a built picture" pertains to the conventional portrayal of Indian philosophy as mokṣa-centered, that is, oriented toward "ultimate freedom," hence as subordinated to the spiritual quest (on his battle against this portrayal, I will expand in Chapter 1). In his Shimla Lectures (2005), DK speaks of the parallel narrative of the Western civilization as "rational," as against the "spiritual" Indian civilization—a prevailing narrative both in India and in the West to this very day. His attempt is to refute this schematic and hardly accurate mirror-picture. The Western civilization, DK argues, sees and depicts itself as rational: rationality that stretches from Aristotle's "man is a rational animal" to Descartes's "I think, therefore I am," thus "forgetting and suppressing," as he puts it, everything in between, that is, "almost the whole of Christianity." The Indian civilization, according to DK, has adopted the inverted narrative, forgetting and suppressing rationality, and highlighting spirituality alone. "Has not India had a long tradition of science, astronomy, medicine, linguistics, everything?" DK asks his listeners. "No," he answers sarcastically,

> We have built temples. But temples cannot be built without knowledge of engineering, knowledge of materials, knowledge of metals, knowledge of everything. However, for some reason, we do not regard this knowledge as important. Have we not contributed tremendously in the field of mathematics? It is amazing that this [Indian] civilization does not think of itself in terms of knowledge of any kind. [. . .] Imagine! We are not interested in the millennia-long thinking which took place in this country on understanding language through language. I am sorry to say that we are simply uninterested. India's picture, as it has been built, is a picture of huge suppression. We are spiritual people, seekers of mokṣa and nirvāṇa. We are not interested in this world. This world is unreal to us; it is māyā [illusory], or līlā [Cosmic Play], and it does not really matter. [. . .] India is a land where reason and argumentation were so central to the civilization. And yet, we identify the West with reason; we think that the West is rational, that the West is reason-centric, whereas we are not. (2012, 95-96)

This passionate plea was made in 2005, but the picture of "we have built temples, the West is rational" is still intact. DK's concern was naturally the Indian perception, namely, the internalization of this picture in India. As these lines are written, I travelled to Pune to give a talk at the University of Pune on the philosophy of Ramchandra Gandhi (1937–2007), DK's contemporary, whose writings epitomize the potency of contemporary Indian philosophy. When I completed my talk, one of the listeners, an established professor, said in response (and in tune with my present discussion):

> Sartre was a great philosopher. His writings touched me deeply and effected my thoughts. But Ramchandra Gandhi? Do you really think that he left behind a significant philosophical legacy?

Greatness is of course in the eye of the beholder, and Sartre's place in the history of ideas is surely carved out. But this immediate skeptic response (the "really" in "Do you really think") is a reminder that Indian philosophy, classical and contemporary, is rarely accepted by practitioners of its Western counterpart, even in India, as "really philosophical," and certainly not as "equally philosophical." The respondent did not say "Dharmakīrti was a great philosopher," or Śrīharṣa, or Raghunātha Śiromaṇi, or KCB, or anyone else. He said Sartre. Therefore, I do not think that the critique was directed specifically at Ramchandra Gandhi, but conveyed "the picture" that DK was striving to dismantle.

In the preface of *Prolegomena to Any Future Historiography of Cultures and Civilizations* (1997, henceforth *Prolegomena*), DK writes that his present aim is to develop "a new understanding of man" in terms of śilpa, śāstra, saṃskāra, puruṣārtha, smṛti, svapna, and vāsanā (arts and crafts, science, the unconscious, ethics, memory, dreams, and archetypes). He explains that he attempts to construct, or to begin to construct, a theory, based on Indian terminology, which will be applicable "to any future historiography of cultures and civilizations," and not just the Indian civilization. The title of his book corresponds with Kant, but its conceptual heart is Indian (I think of Shailendra's immortal line, phir bhī dil hai hindustānī).[4] The translations I offered earlier, to the key terms used by DK in the *Prolegomena*, are obviously approximations and can hardly capture the essence of these terms. This is especially the case with the terms saṃskāra and vāsanā, both belonging to the "karma family," which I translated as "the unconscious" (Freud) and "archetypes" (Jung), in an attempt to find (with all caution) parallel Western notions as a starting point for a cross-cultural dialogue. But why build a "global theory" on classical Indian terms?

In his paper "Disgust and the Ugly in Indian Aesthetics" (2002), Arindam Chakrabarti reads Charles Baudelaire, the nineteenth-century French poet, or more precisely his poem "Carrion," through the Indian theory of Rasa aesthetics. "Is it legitimate," Chakrabarti wonders in tune with our discussion,

> to take an ancient or medieval Indian theory and try to explain in its terms the meaning of a European or modern work of art? Isn't the cultural baggage of the former totally incommensurable to the semiotic milieu of the latter? [. . .] I want to point out that the reverse has been done only too often. Thanks to epistemological colonization, Oriental practices have been "interpreted" through European theories, partly because it was regarded as a truism that any "theory" would have to be European. [. . .] didn't Husserl remark that the Oriental mind is too crude and practical to fashion pure theories? Right now, even the postcolonial experts apply Freud, Marx, Foucault, Walter Benjamin, Max Webber and Julia Kristeva to understand Indian art, mysticism, politics, poetry and purity-pollution taboos etc. I think it is time we tried the cross-cultural enterprise the other way. (2002, 7)

Chakrabarti does not merely speak about "trying the cross-cultural enterprise the other way," but shows us how this move is fruitful. A Rasa analysis of Baudelaire's poem reveals an interplay between two rasas, or "aesthetic emotions," the hideous (bībhatsa) and the tranquil (śānta). But the twist lies in the fact that the "stable sentiment" behind the tranquil rasa is vairāgya, "dispassion." "Carrion" is a love poem. The lover reminds his beloved of "that lovely summer day" when they saw a hideous carrion together, and imagines the day that she too will "rot underground kissed by worms." Love is usually equated with rāga (attraction or passion). Chakrabarti's Rasa-reading of Baudelaire shows that in the present case, in this poem, love is depicted as extending from passion to dispassion. Vairāgya is the antonym of rāga, attraction, a different type of antonym than dveṣa (repulsion or aversion). In truth, dveṣa is also part of the Rasa picture revealed before us, owing to its proximity to jugupsā, or disgust, which is the "stable sentiment" behind the hideous rasa. Vairāgya, Chakrabarti explains, conveys "a sense of vanity and fragility of earthly pleasures [. . . . It is] dispassion which embraces death without any sadness, and goes beyond pleasure and pain" (2002, 17). Indeed, the lover's love to his beloved in Baudelaire reaches from the beautiful to the ugly, and from the passionate to sheer dispassion.

Chakrabarti's experiment sits well with DK's program in the *Prolegomena*, and moreover with his broad vision of dialogue as a two-way interchange. This vision finds further expression in DK's preface to his work *The Art of the Conceptual* (1989). Here he speaks of the "I-It," rather than "I-You" relationship (if I may employ Buber's famous terminology) between the Indian and Western worlds of scholarship. "The story of Western thinkers' response to a basic criticism of their work," he writes,

> reveals a strange sort of resistance to come to terms with a foundational critique of their work, particularly from persons belonging to other cultures. (1989, xiii)

And he further argues that,

> until and unless the West becomes an object of study of non-Western social scientists to the same extent, and in the same manner, as the non-Western world has been studied by the Western students of the societies and cultures, not only no balance will be achieved in the comparative study of societies and cultures, but the puerility and perversity of much of what is being done shall not be exposed. The West of course is not prepared to welcome such a reciprocal enterprise to redress the balance, or even admit its feasibility or desirability. (1989, xv)

Chakrabarti works in the field of aesthetics. DK writes here about the social sciences, but the spirit and direction in both cases is one and the same. In this preface, DK recalls a lecture delivered by Claude Lévi-Strauss at the Smithsonian, and later published in *Current Anthropology* (April 1966) under the title "Anthropology: Its Achievements and Future."[5] According to the French anthropologist, the relationship between the West and the non-West can only work in a single direction. He suggests that "anthropology is daughter to this era of violence" in which "millions of innocent human beings have had their resources plundered and their institutions and beliefs destroyed, while they themselves were ruthlessly killed and thrown into bondage." The outcome of this historical state of affairs, Lévi-Strauss further writes, is that "the larger part of mankind" became "subservient to the other," and "one part of mankind treated the other as an object."[6] But instead of striving to rectify the situation, he argues that this unfortunate reality results in the "fact" that the West can study "exotic cultures" (his articulation) "as things" (again his articulation), and not vice versa. On the possibility of reversibility and reciprocity between the West and the non-West that DK and Arindam Chakrabarti demand (and yes, it is a demand, not a polite appeal), Lévi-Strauss writes that,

> well-meant as it undoubtedly is, this solution seems to me naïve and unworkable, as though the problems were as simple and superficial as

> those of children unaccustomed to playing together, whose quarrels can be settled by making them follow the elementary rule: Let me play with your dolls, and I shall let you play with mine.[7]

Much has been written on anthropology and colonialism, or anthropology as (almost) a synonym of colonialism.[8] Lévi-Strauss's position sounds utterly outdated in the present era of postcolonial theories of hybridity, or chutnification as Salman Rushdie beautifully puts it (1982, 459), and DK's furious response—natural, but outdated as well. Why, then, do I discuss it in such detail? First, since DK's fury is directed here not as usual at the blindness of the Western scholar, but at non-Western delegates who were present as he delivered his talk but did not rise up to challenge him. These included, to DK's dismay, two Indian delegates. Their silence, for him, is an illustration of the subservience of which Lévi-Strauss speaks, or what KCB refers to in his essay "Svarāj in Ideas" as "shadow mind" (1984, 385)—imitative, submissive, and slavish, rather than free. Second, since I feel that the lack of openness and interest among Western thinkers with regard to voices from the non-West, of which DK speaks, still prevails. And third, I mention the Lévi-Strauss saga because it again reveals the dialogic dimension of DK's writing. He does not write a conventional preface, or introduction, that spells out in the future tense the contents of the book. The contents will unfold anyway as the reader moves on to reading the book. The chapters, or essays, collected here are "products" of DK's thinking. They have been written in the near and far past. The preface is written now, and conveys DK's present concerns. "But a preface," he suddenly thinks out loud, "is perhaps not the place to go into such issues" (1989, xvii). My contention is that it is precisely the place for "such issues." This is where DK deviates from the standard academic assembly line.

4 Synopsis by Chapter

This monograph is made of four interlinked chapters, intended to work as jigsaw puzzle pieces that together open a vista of DK's broad philosophical oeuvre.

Chapter 1, "Toward a New Picture of Indian Philosophy," focuses on DK's critique of the conventional, "accepted by all" picture of Indian philosophy, which is based—he claims—on a series of "myths," from philosophy as subordinated to the spiritual quest through the inevitable rigid classification of Indian philosophy to "schools," to famous triplets and foursomes such as the Prasthānatrayī ("the three sources" of Vedānta) and the four Puruṣārthas ("human goals"). But DK does not merely take upon himself the role of the pūrva-pakṣin, "the opponent," who raises the unasked questions, but offers an alternative. This alternative picture is sketched in his alternative textbook *Indian Philosophy: A New Approach.* The tone of this textbook is different—questioning rather than definitive, interrogative rather than authoritative. The textbook highlights the place and significance of philosophy of language in the history of Indian philosophy, and focuses on debates, such as the "unending debate," as DK puts it, between the Advaitin and the non-Advaitin (the non-dualistic versus the dualistic approaches within the Vedānta tradition). Social and political philosophy is also given a central place in the new map drawn here by DK. But DK is not interested in replacing "picture A" with "picture B." By challenging the authority and questioning the axioms of "picture A," and sketching a tentative "picture B," he aims to show that an alternative is possible and encourage other alternatives, besides his. He strives to strip the conventional picture of its aura, and to expose its so-called axioms as mere postulates. An exponent of multivocality, he struggles to release the history of Indian philosophy from the monopoly of its conventional reading. Moreover, he keeps on reminding his readers that this "history" never reached its end, and he argues that Indian philosophy is not a matter of the past and that contemporary Indian thinking is not a footnote to Nāgārjuna and Śaṅkara, Abhinavagupta and Gaṅgeśa, but a significant chapter in a continuous text.

Chapter 1 also includes a discussion of the Saṃvād Project, DK's abovementioned attempt to bring together pandits and professors. I focus on one of DK's last rounds of Saṃvād, which opens with his paper "Vedānta in the First Millennium A.D.: The Case Study of a Retrospective Illusion Imposed by the Historiography of Indian Philosophy" (1996, henceforth "Vedānta in the First Millennium"). DK looks into two bibliographies, which cover every philosophical text known to us in the history of Indian philosophy, prepared parallelly by two pandits, Karl Potter and Thangaswami Sarma, and discovers that the first millennium is the millennium of Buddhism and Nyāya. He submits this discovery before an ensemble of "insiders" of the Vedānta tradition that claims for hegemony during this period, and wonders about the politics of history-making and about the hands that write the narratives that we are so used to. My extended visit in the Saṃvād Project further includes a short discussion of Pandit Badrinath Shukla's essay "Dehātmavāda or the Body as Soul: Exploration of a Possibility Within Nyāya Thought" (1988), projected by DK as paradigmatic to "the pandit way of thinking." Through Shukla's essay, I attempt to decipher the "pandit way," which for DK, a self-aware product of Macaulay's education system, was a matter of great discovery, almost "discovery of self." Speaking of Macaulay, I also touch on "the burden of English" in dialogue with Nalini Bhushan and Jay Garfield

(2011 and 2017), who raise the burning question: "Can Indian philosophy Be written in English?"

Chapter 2, "Thinking Creatively About the Creative Act: A Dialogue with Daya Krishna," is a dialogue with DK on art and aesthetics, through his talk-turned-paper "Thinking Creatively about the Creative Act" (1999). This chapter is a matter of "grafting." It includes the full text of his paper, with my "commentary" interwoven between the lines and paragraphs of his text. Explaining his mode of work, DK writes here that when he reads a text, any text, "I get into his work [the author's], into his thought process, and carry it in a direction where it was not taken." This is exactly what I am doing to/with DK's present paper. I am a guest and a host at the same time, a guest in his text and a host of the text in my chapter. Interestingly, DK's paradigmatic example for a work of art is the act of philosophizing. This chapter, then, is a contemporary collage, or if you wish, a śleṣa, a "bi-textual poem," comprising of a philosophical dialogue that deals with the broad questions of how "to meet" a work of art and how "to do" philosophy.

Chapter 3, "Freedoms," deals—as the title indicates—with the question of freedom. The plural S reveals DK's position. He is interested in different dimensions of human life and consciousness, hence in different types of freedom. Moreover, he takes issue with the notion of "ultimate freedom," unrestricted and unconditioned by anything worldly, expounded in every mokṣa-treatise, including Buddhist and Jaina texts. He is an exponent of "empirical freedoms"—overlapping, complementing one another, or conflicting—freedoms now and here, not in a remote, beatific "beyondness beyond." This stance connects with the activist dimension of DK as an intellectual, and with his work in social and political philosophy. This dimension and work will be discussed in Chapter 4. My discussion in Chapter 3 draws primarily on DK's papers "The Cosmic, Biological and Cultural Conditionings, and the Seeking for Freedom" and "The Undeciphered Text: Anomalies, Problems and Paradoxes in the Yogasūtra" (both from 2006), with constant reference to his early essay "An Attempted Analysis of the Concept of Freedom" (1952). Hence I create a dialogue between two Daya Krishnas, young and older, who think together on freedom as concept and seeking.

For DK, freedom and knowledge, knowledge and freedom, are inseparable. He sees a noetic quality in every instance of freedom and, moreover, perceives knowledge itself as an act of freedom. Both in the external sense that it should be open for all, rather than prohibited or limited, and internally, being the positive expression of the capacity of setting up and braking down, of connecting and disconnecting, of foregrounding and backgrounding at the conceptual level, in the realm of ideas. This capacity is a matter of freedom—freedom that for DK is both essential and potent. Since freedom and knowledge are closely related, I wish to discuss, still in Chapter 3, under the rubric of "Freedoms," a new concept of knowledge, Knowledge without Certainty (KWC), developed by DK in a series of articles, his "knowledge articles". KWC is DK's alternative to the conventional definition of knowledge as "justified true belief" (JTB). What happens to the concept of knowledge if it is disconnected, or stripped of, or freed from old "companions" such as certainty and truth? What are the implications of such a move? And which new companions can we assign to this new avatar of the age-old concept of knowledge? DK works with new companions such as uncertainty, ambiguity, probability, and even chance. The main incentive of DK's move was the giant leap that science underwent toward the end of his life, and the challenge of dealing with a new situation in which "new forms of matter are being created, with properties which question the old notions of matter, space, time and causality." Moreover, he adds, "the basic parameters on which the sciences of economics and sociology were based are [now] in jeopardy, as the notions of land, labour and capital have undergone a sea-change" (see full quote and discussion in Chapter 3).

A bird's-eye view of DK's corpus shows that after his first book *The Nature of Philosophy* (1955), a theoretic attempt at articulating what he sees as the crux of the activity called philosophy, he was preoccupied for about three decades, India's initial years after independence, with social and political philosophy, and even issues in economy, as his contribution to the crystallization of the new nation-state. During these years, he worked with crucial notions such as "development" and "welfare," often in dialogue with other thinkers (for instance, Fred Riggs, a scholar of public administration, in *Development Debate*, 1987). With age, both his and India's, DK's focus shifted more and more to Indian philosophy, from re-reading classical texts to the Saṃvād Project. But his contribution to social philosophy did not come to an end in the 1980s. His social and political sensitivity finds expression in his writings throughout. Chapter 4, "Concepts and Actions: Daya Krishna and Social Philosophy", highlights social and political threads in DK's oeuvre. I spotlight, for instance, his reading of the famous Upaniṣadic story about Satyakāma Jābāla, which he discusses in his paper "The Vedic Corpus and the two Sūtra-Texts: The Mīmāṃsāsūtra and the Brahmasūtra" (2006/2011). Here he suggests (or dares to suggest) that the text is "twisted and perverted" by Śaṅkara, its most authoritative commentator, "to suit narrow sectarian caste-interests of a society." Moreover, for DK, Śaṅkara's metaphysics, and for that matter any metaphysical or spiritual claim, is utterly empty unless it has an effect at the social level. I will depict DK, through his writings on social philosophy, as theorist and activist in one, emphasizing the interlacement of these two complementary dimensions of his work.

5 And Finally

Finally, I wish to remind the readers that the picture presented here of DK and twentieth-century Indian philosophy does not claim authority or precedence over other interpretations. The picture can be sketched otherwise, with other colors and other emphases. My picture is open-ended and full of questions, in tune with DK's own approach. Moreover, it is not a historical picture. I am not writing in the past tense. It is a philosophical inquiry in the present tense, a dialogue with DK on vital themes and issues that arise from his writings.

I opened this introduction with a quote from Vikram Chandra's novel *Red Earth and Pouring Rain* (1995). It is extracted from a dialogue between Sikander (Alexander of Macedonia) and an Indian sādhu, a wandering ascetic, as imagined by Chandra. "He wants to know why you're naked," says Sikander's translator to the sādhu. "Ask him why he's wearing clothes," the sādhu answers with a question (1995, 271). Sikander is power and authority, the sādhu is the ultimate outsider. I often imagine DK as a sādhu, wandering and wondering between philosophical traditions, texts, and ideas. He used to arrive in a text or a philosophical tradition, leave the specialists—the "insiders"—a pile of questions for consideration, turn the tables on their fundamental premises, provoke a philosophical hullabaloo, and drive his question-wagon onwards, to the next text, tradition, or discipline. Like Chandra's sādhu, who refuses to accept the emperor's premise that clothes make a person cultured and nakedness is a sign of primitivity, and dares to question authority and power, DK often stands all alone against capital-T Truths and capital-A Answers, a stubborn protestor with a question mark in hand. "He says he's asking the questions here," the emperor's translator tells the sādhu in Vikram Chandra. "Questions give birth only to other questions," the wise sādhu retaliates (1995, 272). At the narrative level, Chandra's sādhu is willing to participate in a dialogue between equals, or alternately to have no dialogue at all. But emperors, especially mahā-emperors like Sikander, are interested in dominance, not equality. The question is whether philosophical interactions between India and the West, the West and India, or more generally, the West and the non-West, are based on a dialogue between equals or just replicate old colonial patterns. Chandra's dialogue, or pseudo-dialogue, is imagined, but the colonial mindset is still here, real and tangible. DK was worried about colonial overtones that often accompany these academic encounters. This worry, and sometimes fury (as in his preface to *The Art of the Conceptual*, apropos Lévi-Strauss's dolls), find expression in many of DK's writings, and culminate in his paper "Comparative Philosophy: What It Is and What It Ought to Be" (1986). His fury, conveyed by the word "ought" in the title, is directed at the politics of comparative studies, at the one-sidedness, hypocrisy, and colonialism in the name of universalism that one finds under the promising rubric of "comparative philosophy." The failed promise is the promise of dialogue, since dialogue—DK believed—is the heart and soul of every genuine human interaction.

But the maxim "Questions give birth only to other questions" is much more than a protest against the colonial claim (from Sikander's translator to Lévi-Strauss): "He says he's asking the questions here." For DK, questions are perennial, and answers are tentative. He changes the balance of the question-answer scales. He seeks to show us that questions are "weightier," more crucial and far more interesting than answers. We are taught to value the answer. DK turns the tables, and invites his readers, us, to pay close attention to the question, to the power of the question, to the journey of the question.

I recently attended a talk by Sanjay Subrahmanyam at Tel Aviv University. He closed his inspiring talk ("Connected Histories of the Early Modern World") with these words:

> History is always an unfinished project, an ongoing conversation, if you are willing to partake in this conversation.

Replace the word "history" with "philosophy" and you will hear DK's voice. My hope is that the following chapters entice the readers to partake in a conversation with DK, as part of the broader conversation, ongoing and unfinished, as much as history is for Subrahmanyam, that DK called "philosophy." Moreover, I hope that these chapters will convince the readers that twentieth-century, and consequently twenty-first-century Indian philosophy, is worth looking into, with care and attention.

And a final note: a perennial traveler between texts and disciplines, DK wanders with ease between languages. Key philosophical notions are translated, explained, and discussed in the body of each chapter. Unless otherwise stated, all the translations from Sanskrit and Hindi are mine.

1

Toward a New Picture of Indian Philosophy

A picture once built is difficult to dismantle.
Daya Krishna, *New Perspectives in Indian Philosophy*, 5

But temples cannot be built without knowledge of engineering, knowledge of materials, knowledge of metals, knowledge of everything.
Daya Krishna, Shimla Lectures, 2005

Fences keep us safe, and fences hold us back.

Fences come to define us. They define our boundaries and limitations, our fears and our inhibitions, our hopes and our desires.

We come to rely upon fences. We get used to them. We fall in love with them. We take them for granted, and fail to realize that they exist.
Sonia Weiner, *f-e-n-c-e-s*

1 "Six Plus Three, What Else?"

In a recent visit to the department of philosophy of an esteemed Indian university, I met the professor in charge of Indian philosophy. The segregation of "Indian philosophy" is always a surprise, especially in Indian universities (in departments of philosophy in the West, non-Western philosophy is usually ignored altogether under the pretext that is not "really philosophy"). His colleagues do not teach "Western philosophy," but "ethics," "aesthetics," "epistemology," "phenomenology," etc., drawing solely on Western sources from Plato to Husserl. Why cannot Indian philosophical sources, or non-Western sources, become part of these philosophical themes? I was interested to know what was taught under the rubric of "Indian philosophy," imagining a blend of all these themes, drawing on Indian sources from the Upaniṣads to contemporary Indian philosophy. The professor whom I met seemed surprised when I asked what he teaches. "Six plus three, what else?," he said in reply, referring to the classical darśanas, or schools of Indian philosophy, "orthodox" and "non-orthodox" (his articulation, which is a common translation of the notions of āstika and nāstika, pertaining to the alleged acceptance or non-acceptance of the authority of the Veda, respectively). What about DK's critique of "sāmpradāyika scholarship," namely, default-thinking in terms of schools and, moreover, his critique of the inevitable classification of these schools into the rubrics of āstika versus nāstika, in a way that ensures that the former category wins over the latter (well, at least mathematically, six against three), I asked. And what about the appropriation of Patañjali of the *Yogasūtra* and Īśvarakṛṣṇa of the *Sāṃkhyakārikā*, who reject the authority of the scriptures, in YS 1.6-7 and SK 2 respectively, into the category of āstika that is about acceptance of the Veda, I continued to ask. The professor, friendly and pleasant, smiled. "Daya Krishna was a great man," he said (and spoke to me of his personal acquaintance with him), "but very provocative." I heard this excuse before, namely, the labeling of DK as "provocative," to justify the fact that his critique is brushed aside and the old narratives prevail. It reminded me of the presidential address delivered at the Indian Philosophical Congress at Magadh University, Bodhgaya, several years ago, which I attended with an audience of young students. The speaker—the president of the Congress for that year—projected Indian philosophy as spiritual, and its Western sister not just as worldly, but as materialistic and even hedonistic. It was a typical "Ātman, Brahman, Mokṣa" type of talk. The students around me were not interested. Connected to the internet through their cellular phones, bored by such dogmatic talks, and curious about "real philosophy," not empty slogans, they quench their thirst through services such as Google Books and YouTube. They are acquainted with current trends in philosophy (for the speaker at Bodhgaya there is no "current," only "past continuous"), and they hardly care about the spirituality/materiality distinction, realizing (they told me) that both exist together everywhere. However, they are doomed, still, to study the unavoidable "six plus three," and therefore prefer (they continued to explain) classes in Western philosophy, which they perceive as religion-free and hardly dogmatic. There are of course religious threads in Western philosophy also, but these threads are not presented to them as the crux of the matter. These students, my fellow listeners at Magadh University, are the appropriate readers for DK's writings, DK whom they probably did not even hear about, since their "six plus three" teachers do not include him in their syllabi. I think of them as I write these lines.

2 Emerging, Toward

In the opening paragraph of his paper "Emerging New Approaches in the Study of Classical Indian Philosophy" (1993), DK writes:

> Indian Philosophy by and large has been treated up to now in an antiquarian spirit, something belonging to past history which has no relevance to current concerns of philosophical thought in the world. [. . .] The intellectual and cultural domination of the West, as well as the establishment of educational institutions on Western models ensured that the paradigmatic model about philosophy and what is to count as philosophical are determined by the West. Also, as English is the language of both national [i.e., Indian] and international intellectual life [. . .] a scholar who cannot read, write or speak in English is invisible in the philosophical scene during the course of this century in India. [. . .] This has happened surprisingly even in such an area of study as Indian philosophy, where a large mass of significant material continues to be written in Sanskrit and other regional languages of the country. (1993, 69–70)

For DK, Indian philosophy does not belong to the past, to history, to antiquity. It is alive, dynamic, drawing on its past, and on other pasts of other thinking traditions, and is written in dialogue with contemporary philosophical voices and other materials. DK's grand project of reading classical Indian texts anew is all about rejecting the view that Indian philosophy belongs to the museum of ideas. The tradition itself acknowledges development and renewal in phrases such as Navya-Nyāya, "new reason," pertaining to the writings of thinkers such as Gaṅgeśa (twelfth century), Raghunātha Śiromaṇi (sixteenth century, to be spotlighted as we move on), Mathurānātha, Jagadīśa and Gadādhara (all of the seventeenth century). DK's monograph *Eighteenth Century Onwards* is dedicated to renewal and development in Indian philosophy in the last three centuries, with chapters focusing on new strands in Mīmāṃsā, Sāṃkhya and Yoga, Nyāya, Dharma-Śāstra, Alaṅkāra-Śāstra, and Jaina philosophy. Another chapter of this monograph is devoted to the controversy between the Advaitin and non-Advaitin within the framework of Vedānta during this period. Two other chapters are titled "New perspectives in looking at the classical traditions of Indian philosophizing in Indian terms" and "Developments in Indian philosophy since the coming of the British." The former is an attempt to become free from European definitions, frames, and concepts imposed on Indian philosophy, both by resurrecting old Indian terms and frames, and by creating new ones. This is a chapter in decolonizing knowledge, by creating a new (or reviving old) language for philosophizing. The latter includes a discussion, first of its kind, of twentieth-century Indian philosophy as seen by DK, including a unique analysis of the philosophical work of KCB. Commonly seen as a neo-Advaitin, interweaving Advaita with Kantian philosophy, KCB is portrayed here as a neo-Sāṃkhyan, striving toward "the pure subject" through "inverted Hegelian dialectic." "KCB," DK explains, "moves through what may be called a process of de-identification, where each step of de-identification reveals the earlier identification to have been both voluntary and mistaken" (2002, 297). However, DK does not merely depict KCB's philosophical endeavor as he sees it, but responds and takes issue with KCB. "KCB," DK writes,

> is in a hurry to reach the subject as freedom, forgetting that the real life of the subject as freedom is in the phenomenology of identification and de-identification, along with creation and dissolution of worlds, and not only in the complete withdrawal of the spirit into itself, without any correlate world at all with which to relate or to withdraw from. (2002, 298).

DK's move—and I use the word "move" since I imagine DK as a chess player, moving conceptual pieces on the philosophical board—in defense of the world and the worldly is illustrative of his broader attempt, throughout his oeuvre, to retrieve the phenomenal and objective, the corporeal, and the material, too often neglected for the sake of metaphysical pursuit. In this respect, KCB is no exception. As much as he is an inspiration for DK, in thinking old philosophical notions and texts afresh, at the bottom-line KCB is a mokṣa-thinker "in a hurry to reach the subject as freedom," privileging the subject over everything objective. DK's attempt is to show that there is more, much more to Indian philosophy than the metaphysical horizon of mokṣa, or "ultimate freedom."

3 The Political Cat

Two more issues are raised by DK in the opening passage of "Emerging New Approaches," which I quoted earlier. First, his claim that Western models and standards determine the conventional picture of Indian philosophy, and second, the over-dominance of English. The portrayal of Indian philosophy as mokṣa-centered, DK suggests, is too narrow to cover the multifacetedness of the age-long thinking traditions folded together under the umbrella of "Indian philosophy," and is Western through and through. In his Shimla Lectures, he explains:

> I suggest that this picture, taken by some as self-evident, is a build-up of the eighteenth century onwards. In the nineteenth century it was further built both by the West and by us. These so-called contrasts between

> India and the West are presented by Radhakrishnan in his book *Eastern Religions and Western Thought*. Imagine! We have no thought at all! What a condemnation of our civilization, what a suppression; India is full of thought! [. . .] He should have contrasted Western thought with Indian thought. There is power in Indian thought, and it has the capacity of confronting Western thought. It should! (2012, 99)

DK's lecture was delivered at the Rashtrapati Niwas, formerly the Viceregal Lodge, in Shimla, which served as the summer capital of British India, a symbolic site for a lecture culminating with the roar "There is power in Indian thought." This message echoes throughout DK's writings. Here he zooms in on Radhakrishnan's title, suggesting that the latter has internalized the Western picture that projects the West as rational, India as spiritual, or, to borrow a metaphor from Karl Popper (even though Popper used it in a totally different context in his famous Arthur Holly Compton Lecture, 1965), the West and India as "clocks" and "clouds," respectively. DK smashes this stigma by highlighting non-religious strands, texts, and thinkers in Indian philosophy, and by pointing out religious or spiritual elements in Western (Greek, European) philosophy. His emphasis on the non-religiousness of Indian philosophy finds expression in his extensive writing on Indian philosophy of language; for instance, in his monograph *The Nyāya Sūtras: A New Commentary on an Old Text*, and on Indian social and political philosophy, for example, in his major work "*Classical Indian Thought about Man, Society and Polity*" (1996). On the hidden, or even suppressed, religious features of Western philosophy, DK speaks in his Shimla Lectures (2005), where he shoots his arrows at the myth about rationality as the core of the Western civilization. Western philosophy—this myth, narrative, or agenda-driven picture implies—begins with the pre-Socratic "everything is ______" (water, air, or apeiron). The abstractization "everything" is perceived as the first instance of philosophical thinking, to be followed by Socrates/Plato, Aristotle, and Descartes. Yes, Aristotle and then Descartes: a gap of two millennia between these great philosophers is leaped over with a blink. "Mathematics and Aristotle's logic," DK writes,

> have become the paradigm examples of what the Western civilization considers itself to be rooted in. This is what the West puts in the foreground, and it forgets everything else. Imagine! The last four thousand years of the Western civilization have been built on a vast forgetfulness, a vast act of repression. This act of repression is not merely of the Greco-Roman history, of the Stoics and the Epicureans, of thinking after Aristotle, but also of almost the whole of Christianity.

> The whole thing has been sidelined by saying that this is theology. No other civilization in the past has put aside and suppressed so much of it. (2012, 94)

In his paper "Aristotle and the Roots of Western Rationality" (1992, presented at the at the *East-West Conference* at Mount Abu, Rajasthan, January 1990), Mukund Lath joins DK in refuting the myth about the rational West versus spiritual India. "There is a strange idea," Lath writes,

> which deserves to be called a cultural myth, though presented in a rational, scientific garb, that is dominant in the thinking of the West concerning society and culture. The idea is that the culture of the West is distinguished from all other cultures in being rational. [. . .] This idea has almost the status of a proved mathematical theorem for some, and is an unquestioned dogma for many, not only in the West, but also among the "educated" in other cultures too, who have been socialized into Western modes of thought. (1992, 55)

Lath lets the political cat, implicit in DK, out of the bag, speaking as he does of rationality as the feature that is supposed to distinguish the West from other cultures. It is rationality, Lath suggests, which grants the West—in Western eyes of course—a sense of superiority over "the other," which—in Western eyes again—is seen as irrational or at least less rational. "The whole scheme," Lath adds, "of stacking societies and cultures under the labels of 'modern,' 'traditional,' 'primitive' etc., so central to Western thought is based on this criterion." Here I recall Bryan Van Norden's recent book *Taking Back Philosophy: A Multicultural Manifesto* (2017), where he quotes Immanuel Kant, the Urim and Thummim of Western Rationality. "The Hindus," Kant writes,

> have a strong degree of calm, and all look like philosophers. That notwithstanding, they are much inclined to anger and love. They thus are educable in the highest degree, but only to the arts and not to the sciences. They will never achieve abstract concepts. (From Kant's *Lectures on Anthropology*, as quoted in Van Norden 2017, 22)

No comment is required here. For Kant's own sake, as a groundbreaking thinker, and for our sake, if we wish to appreciate his philosophical contribution, we should make the effort to distinguish between the lucid philosopher and his uninformed, if not straight-out racist views about non-

European or non-Western cultures,[1] which probably reflect the zeitgeist of his time and place.

Lath, in his paper, visits Aristotle's central writings, *The Nicomachean Ethics* and *Politics*, to figure out the context of his famous maxim "Man is a rational animal," and to ascertain the connection between the rational and the political, according to "the major guru of Western rational thought," as he puts it. In Aristotle's *Politics*, Lath finds a discussion of what he refers to as "two basic pairs among humans in which the one is incapable of existing without the other." These, he explains,

> are the pairs of man-woman and master-slave. [. . .] The man-woman is necessary for the continuance of mankind. Equally necessary is the other pair of maser and slave [. . .] the master is the man with intelligence, who can see ahead and decide what is to be done. The slave has bodily strength [. . . .] A single purpose unites them into a single, necessary whole. (1992, 58)

First, it is interesting to see that Lath, a Sanskritist, and (in his own way) a pandit and a traditionalist, goes as far as to read Aristotle's writings "first hand" (even if in English translation). It is of course an invitation for anyone rooted in Western philosophy to take a parallel visit to classical Indian texts. Second, as in the case of Kant earlier, one could argue that a distinction should be made between different "compartments" of the famous Greek philosopher, some still useful today, other representing the zeitgeist (I should have looked up a Greek term, I picked "zeitgeist" for Kant) of era and place, but hardly valid, interesting, or relevant today. It is implied in Lath that the master-slave narrative in Aristotle can be seen as contributing to the ideology that led to colonial excursions, from Alexander of Macedonia, Aristotle's alleged student, onwards. Along similar lines, it is implied in Jonardon Ganeri's paper "Why Philosophy Must Go Global?" (2016) that later European colonialism was (is?) driven by universalistic (Hegelian?) philosophical agendas, that the colonizers sought to fulfill de-facto, geographically, politically. Ganeri's move is both creative and effective. A student of Nyāya, he explains to the uninitiated that in classical Indian logic, "the most distinctive aspect is the fundamental importance given to the citation of an example, single cases said either to be similar or dissimilar to the topic at hand" (2016, 138). Hence the proverb "where there is smoke, there is fire" cannot be valid in Nyāya logic unless an example is given, "like in my kitchen," for instance. This is to say that, according to this logic, "the standards are context-sensitive and localized, not absolute and universal," as Ganeri accurately puts it. Now his move becomes clear: within logic hides ethics. If such is Nyāya logic, namely, sensitive to details, "to the body of every case," then it cannot be colonial logic—logic that supports and gives a tailwind to colonial approach and action.

Now to the issue of English, the over-dominance of English, pointed at by DK in the paragraph quoted earlier and in numerous other occasions. So much has been written on the subject. Should not an Indian thinker think-write in an Indian language? Or a Nigerian writer in a Nigerian language, as Ben Okri was straightforwardly asked at the Jaipur Literature Festival? This was his reply:

> If you write about Africa and you're African, you really should do it in an African language. And that's fair. It's really self-evident, and there is really not much to say after that, except for one small problem, which is the problem of history. You know, history is what happens to us. Most of us did not choose what happened to them. [. . .] We inherited the problem of language. The matrix of one's consciousness and its relation to reality was changed by the presence of this new language [English]. [. . .] So the language problem is important on the one hand, and is a false problem on the other. Because the more essential problem, whether you write in an African language and whether you don't, is how to bend language, to make it as it were transparent to reality. [. . .] The real problem is writing well; the real problem is to be able to see the richness and complexity of life itself, and then being able to translate that into stories, meditations, memoirs, long walks. The difficulty is writing well, and right now our job, as usual, is to write well. (Okri spoke at the session "The Afropolitans," in the 2012 edition of the JLF).

Every word here is accurate: "That's fair, self-evident," "one small problem, history," "the matrix of consciousness was changed," and Okri's conclusion "right now our job, as usual, is to write well." DK would fully embrace this conclusion. But as a product of Macaulay's education system in India, DK did feel "the burden of English," and in the paragraph I quoted earlier, he highlights the place and significance of philosophizing in Sanskrit and other regional languages. "If Sanskrit was dead like ancient Greek and Latin," DK writes to a friend in a letter dated February 2006, "there would not be thousands of persons in this country, young and old, whose language of intellectual discourse is Sanskrit even now." In the same letter, DK mentions the Saṃvād Project, which acknowledges and spotlights contemporary philosophizing in Sanskrit. In the next segment, I will begin to discuss this unique experiment.

4 Hospitality to Ideas

There is also intellectual hospitality: the hospitality to ideas, to dreams, to ways of seeing, to perception, to cultures. This is the most important hospitality of all, and it includes all other hospitalities.

(Ben Okri, *A Time for New Dreams*, 55)

A. Raghuramaraju, one of the few scholars who responded to and reflected on the Saṃvād Project, explains that "Daya Krishna and others have initiated Saṃvād to instill new life into contemporary Indian philosophy" (2013b, 56). Several meetings were conducted under the umbrella of the project, from the first meeting in Pune (July 1983), dedicated to Russellean logic through Naiyāyika and Mīmāṃsaka eyes, to meetings focusing on issues in Nyāya (at Sarnath), Mīmāṃsā (Tirupati), Kashmir Shaivism (Srinagar), Bhakti (Vrindavan), and Indian Muslim philosophy (Aligarh, Hyderabad, and Lucknow). DK speaks of the meetings with Ulema, classical scholars of Islam, "Muslim pandits" if you wish, as a rare occasion to figure out "the story of the transplantation of Arab philosophy into India and its independent treatment here" (1993, 80). The final Saṃvād, to be discussed as we move on, was conducted in writing on the pages of the *JICPR* and later published as *Discussion and Debate in Indian Philosophy: Vedānta, Mīmāṃsā and Nyāya* (2004). There is an advantage in the spontaneity of the direct face-to-face meeting. In this respect, Elise Coquereau-Saouma (in a dissertation dedicated to DK's Saṃvād Project, see Bibliography) speaks of "breaking the ice between thinking-communities, overcoming prejudices, letting go of frozen pictures." The ice metaphor connects with Sonia Weiner's fences (see epigraph). "Fences keep us safe, and fences hold us back," she lucidly writes. The merit of the "present personal" is that it has the capacity to cut through ice, or fences, both conceptual and psychological fences. But writing has its own merits. It allows more time to look deeper into the other's view, argument, or query, and to shape one's own response in detail. In *Discussion and Debate in Indian Philosophy*, the procedure was that a full-length paper, in each of the philosophical disciplines that the book covers, namely, Vedānta, Mīmāṃsā, and Nyāya, was sent to specialists, or insiders, or pandits in each of these disciplines, for discussion and debate. In each case, the initial paper, their elaborate responses, and a final word by the author of the initial paper, responding to their responses, were presented together before the readers. It was primarily the age factor that dictated the written form of this Saṃvād. DK could no longer travel far easily. It was a last round of Saṃvād for a unique generation of thinkers, rooted in their respective thinking traditions, but open to and eager for dialogue.

In retrospect, each of the Saṃvād-rounds is a conceptual journey. A conceptual journey, like any other journey, is driven by curiosity and brims with a sense of discovery. One leaves the familiar and the known, and explores new territories. Ramchandra Gandhi, DK's contemporary, suggests (in his essay "What is it like to be God?" 2011, 99–102) that hard philosophical questions, such as his title-question (an "impossible question" that he explores in his usual creative way), are to be looked into "trusting the authority of curiosity." That curiosity is powerful we all know, but Ramchandra Gandhi goes as far as implying that it has an authority of its own and, moreover, that this authority should be trusted in intellectual voyages to unknown regions, when one hardly knows whom or what to trust. I find Ramchandra Gandhi's articulation inspiring. His work on the concept of hospitality, primarily in the sense of hospitality to ideas and beliefs (see his essay "Sītā's Kitchen," 1992, which I read as a manifesto of hospitality), is also fruitful in our attempt to understand the Saṃvād Project. Ramchandra Gandhi speaks of a kitchen-type, or rasoī-type of dialogue. The metaphor draws on the warmth and intimacy of the rasoī (imagine cūlhe kā khānā cooked slowly on firewood), which makes it the perfect site for a long conversation without formality and ceremony. Hospitality is the heart of DK's Saṃvād Project, and the connotations of Ramchandra Gandhi's rasoī are fully applicable here. These meetings opened a space for conversation and dialogue, with uncommon tolerance to new tastes and textures, and the rare willingness to cook together across philosophical kitchens. As convener and participant of the Saṃvād Project, DK was both a guest and a host. As a guest, he visited the pandits in their own "place," both physically and philosophically. He travelled (with other colleagues trained in the Western tradition of philosophizing) and stayed with the Mīmāṃsakas in Tirupati, the Naiyāyikas in Sarnath/Varanasi, Swami Lakshmanjoo in Srinagar, Shri Shrivatsa Goswami in Vrindavan, etc. As a host, he invited the pandits to participate in a broader philosophical discourse, which as the editor of the *JICPR* he was in power to shape. To keep the dialogue with the pandits alive, DK was contemplating to broaden the scope of the *JICPR*, a journal of philosophy in English, as to also accept for publication papers in Sanskrit, an initiative that was never materialized owing to his premature death. His successors did not take this initiative forward. But DK was also a host in the sense that the meetings with the pandits, face-to-face and in writing, influenced and became part of his own thinking, writing, philosophizing.

"Saṃvād," I quoted DK in the Introduction, "brought the active practitioners of the two philosophical traditions, the Indian and the Western, in a dialogical situation" (2004, xiii). He repeats this classification in *Eighteenth Century Onwards*. Here he speaks of "Indian philosophy: classical and Western." The term "classical," he explains in his introduction, refers to the work of the pandits, in Sanskrit. The word "Western" refers to the work of "those who have written in the English language after the coming of the British, and have obviously been influenced by the Western traditions of philosophizing which they were exposed to by their education" (2002, 11). For DK, further reading in his introduction reveals, the category of "Indian philosophy: Western" includes Indian thinkers writing in English, whether they work on/with Indian or Western sources. The latter sub-category (Western sources), he further explains, "may be seen as a branching-off and an important development of the Western philosophical tradition in a new intellectual and cultural setting." But "it has not of course been seen in this way," at least in the West, he adds soberly (2002, 12). Under this category, take, for example, the contemporary work on Kant in India. "India's attitude towards Kant was always independent of Kant's attitude towards India," Arindam Chakrabarti writes in his paper "Kant in India," presented at the Eighth International Kant Congress. "The *Critique of Pure Reason*," he further writes, "and the *Groundwork of Metaphysics of Morals* have been absolutely central to the philosophy curricula all over India for at least 125 years" (1995, 1281). Chakrabarti further suggests that,

> no modern Indian philosopher understood and explained Kant and Vedānta more creatively than Krishnachandra Bhattacharyya. In his canonical paper (like Frege's "On Sense and Reference" and Quine's "Two Dogmas") "The Concept of Philosophy"—where KCB puts forward his Tractatus-like view that philosophy is self-evident elaboration of the self-evident, and not a body of judgements—Kant, once again, is his reference-point. (1995, 1283)

Chakrabarti further highlights the contributions of N. V. Banerjee, R. K. Gupta, P. K. Sen, and R. Sundara Rajan, all "first-class philosophers," to the study of Kant and to thinking with and from Kant. The merit of Chakrabarti is that he writes philosophy, not just about philosophy, hence his engagement with each of these five Indian Kantians is worth looking into, even if it is beyond my present discussion. In the few sentences that I quoted from him, Chakrabarti compares KCB to Frege, Quine, and Wittgenstein, as if to convince his Western audience that KCB is on a par with the major gurus of Western philosophy (if I may borrow Mukund Lath's phrase). As such, Chakrabarti implies, his reading of Kant deserves close attention. The special number of the *Indian Philosophical Quarterly*, "200 Years of Kant" (2004), edited by Sharad Deshpande, is again on Kant in India, and again illustrates what DK refers to as "important development" of Western philosophy "in a new intellectual setting." And along similar lines, A. Raghuramaraju dedicates a whole section of his book *Philosophy and India: Ancestors, Outsiders, and Predecessors* (2013) to what he refers to as "Indian solutions to Western Problems." The first part of this section, titled "Advaita to Kant," focuses on KCB's response (or Advaitic solution) to the issue of the unknowability of the subject/self in Kant. Jay Garfield takes a parallel and complementing route in his paper "Solving Kant's Problem: K.C. Bhattacharyya on Self-Knowledge" (2017), and explains the problem that KCB aims to untangle:

> In his *Critique of Pure Reason*, Kant argues that while we can think the transcendental subject—and indeed must think it as a condition of the subjectivity itself—we cannot know the subject or self. [. . .] From the perspective of Vedānta, knowledge of the self is the very goal of philosophical and spiritual practice, and the self, being that with which we are most intimately involved, must be knowable, if indeed anything is truly knowable. (2017, 355–56)

Moreover, Garfield writes,

> Bhattacharyya sees the Kantian view as committed to a series of claims about the self that undermine its own commitment to the self's unknowability. The first of these is the obvious claim that it is unknowable. To assert this is to assert something about it, and to know that it is unknowable is to know something about it. (2017, 356)

It is KCB's sensitive Advaitic eye that enables him "to handle" Kant the way he does. "Other philosophers," Raghuramaraju writes, "such as Brentano, Meinong and Husserl, who largely toed on the Hegelian line in understanding and overcoming the Kantian problematic, have not seen this problem in Kant the way that Bhattacharyya did" (2013, 5). KCB's solution, he further suggests, is based on "breaking open the equivalence between knowing and thinking assumed by Kant," a move derived from KCB's conviction that "there are ways of knowing outside the mode of thinking" (2013, 6). KCB reads Kant through an Advaitic prism, but at the same time, in dialogue with Kant, he wakes Advaita Vedānta from its philosophical slumber, using old formulations in a new discourse.

I made this detour to KCB and Kant to clarify DK's category of "Indian philosophy: Western." But KCB as an illustration shows that even when working on Western sources such as Kant, he has an open eye for India, that is, for Indian philosophy. In this respect, the category of "Indian philosophy: Western" is comparative in essence. In the next segment I will return to the question of language: Can Indian philosophy be written in English?

5 Indian Philosophy in English

This is the place to mention Nalini Bhushan and Jay Garfield's project on Indian philosophy in English under the British Raj, which unfolds in two books, *Indian Philosophy in English: From Renaissance to Independence* (2011) and *Minds Without Fear: Philosophy in the Indian Renaissance* (2017). The former book is a reader, consisting of essays by twenty Indian thinkers, from Rabindranath Tagore and Sri Aurobindo to KCB and A. C. Mukerji. The latter work consists of analysis and reflection on the texts included in the reader, and discussion of the subject matter at large, Indian philosophy under the colonizer in his own language. The project is eye-opening. Bhushan and Garfield illuminate what is often considered as the "dark age" of Indian philosophy. They do not merely argue but show (in their reader) that creative Indian philosophy was written during this period. In their introduction to each of these books, the authors quote from a conversation with DK, in Jaipur, sometime in 2006. In the introduction to the reader, beautifully titled "Whose Voice? Whose Tongue? Philosophy in English in Colonial India," Bhushan and Garfield write:

> Daya Krishna, one of the most eminent Indian philosophers of the 20th century, says of Indian philosophy: *Anybody who is writing in English is not an Indian philosopher*. . . . (2011, xiii, italics mine)

The same quote from DK appears in chapter 1 of *Minds Without Fear* (2017, 10). In their paper "Can Indian Philosophy Be Written in English? A Conversation with Daya Krishna" (2008), they quote DK as suggesting that "Philosophy written in English is not Indian Philosophy. Indian philosophy is not written in English, but in Sanskrit." Sharp, dramatic, clear-cut sentences are a wonderful starting point for a philosophical discussion. Bhushan and Garfield, just like DK, are well aware of it. But this quote from DK, in either version, hardly conveys his view of Indian philosophy in English.

DK dedicates a whole chapter, "Developments in Indian Philosophy Since the coming of the British," chapter 11 of *Eighteenth Century Onwards*, to an ensemble of thinkers—including Ram Mohan Roy, Dayananda Saraswati, Bankim Chandra, KCB, Kalidas Bhattacharyya, N. V. Banerjee, G. R. Malkani,

Ras Bihari Das, D. M. Datta, T. R. V. Murti, Ananda Coomaraswamy, V. Subramaniam, Swami Abhedanada, Bhagavan Das, P. T. Raju, N. K. Devaraja, S. Radhakrishnan, Surendranath Dasgupta, and his contemporaries M. P. Rege, D. Prahladachar, J. N. Mohanty, R. Sundara Rajan, D. P. Chattopadhyaya, Basant Kumar Malik, J. L. Mehta, B. K. Matilal, Sibajiban Bhattacharyya, K. Satchidananda Murty, Rajendra Prasad, G. C. Pande, and Yashdev Shalya. Most of these thinkers wrote mostly in English. "Most," since Yashdev Shalya, for instance, wrote only in Hindi. "Mostly," since many of them wrote not just in English. G. C. Pande, for instance, also wrote in Hindi and Sanskrit. DK's longest discussion in this chapter is dedicated to KCB. "His writing on Indian philosophy," DK suggests (I quote not from this chapter, but from a review article that he wrote when the first volume of KCB's collected works was published),

> marks, in my opinion, a distinct break in the history of writing on this subject. There seems to be far more insight into the nature of the problems discussed than in any of the voluminous works that I have read up till now. (1960, 1)

Speaking of "voluminous works," DK hints at Radhakrishnan's *Indian Philosophy* (in two volumes, originally published in 1923 and 1927) and Surendranath Dasgupta's *A History of Indian Philosophy* (in five volumes, originally published between 1922 and 1955). But DK adds to his appreciative analysis of KCB's work the remark, "It is a pity that KCB concerned himself mainly with Vedānta, Sāṃkhya and Yoga in Indian Philosophy. Had he devoted his attention equally to other systems of Indian thought, we might have had a real vantage point from which to view Indian philosophy as a whole" (1960, 1). This remark again conveys DK's critique of KCB's mokṣa-centeredness, and his plea for a broader vista of Indian philosophy. On Radhakrishnan and Dasgupta, DK writes (in chapter 11 of *Eighteenth Century Onwards*) that their books

> almost became the standard work on Indian philosophy, providing many of their contemporaries the support for the generally accepted view about the dichotomy between the West and the East, and the idea that most of Indian philosophy was essentially "spiritual" and "idealistic" in character. [. . .] One of the strange legacies of this presentation of Indian thought was the debate regarding the place of reason in Indian philosophy, and whether it could even be regarded as philosophy. [. . . For] most Indians trained in educational institutions modelled on the Western pattern it was a serious question as to whether Indian

> philosophy could be strictly regarded as an enterprise of reason, as it always seemed subservient to the trans-rational goal of seeking mokṣa. (2002, 305–6)

And in the same chapter, DK further explains that under the British Raj,

> the whole world of classical knowledge and those who pursued and practiced it became gradually invisible to those who came out of the new institutions modelled on the British pattern. [. . .] The two worlds developed in almost complete ignorance of each other, and had hardly any awareness of the other or interaction. (2002, 310)

This paragraph explains the crucial need for a project such as the Saṃvād Project. In another chapter, sharply titled "Development in classical Indian philosophy after the British intrusion and the creation of apartheid in the intellectual world of modern India," chapter 18 of DK's *Indian Philosophy: A New Approach*, DK again dedicates a thorough discussion to Indian philosophy under the British. The apartheid in the title refers to the "gradual invisibility" of the pandits and the pandit way of philosophizing, and the creation of two parallel intellectual worlds.

Jonardon Ganeri's monograph *The Lost Age of Reason: Philosophy in Early Modern India: 1450-1700* (2011) covers the historical period just before DK's *Eighteenth Century Onwards*. In his introduction, Ganeri—well-acquainted with DK's project[2]—prefers the term "bifurcation" over DK's harsh "apartheid." Ganeri blames "the disruption caused to established patterns for conducting and financing education by the British imposition of new fiscal arrangements and educational policies," for the discontinuity of the "age of reason" that his book portrays. "Work in new reason," Ganeri writes (and Navya-Nyāya, or "new reason," is the heart of this "age of reason"), "continued into the ninetieth and twentieth centuries in an educational setup now sharply bifurcated between low-prestige traditional networks and well-funded colonial colleges and universities." Ganeri closes his introduction, suggesting-speculating-regretting that "what was lost from this lost age of reason is the what-might-have-been had that bifurcation not taken place" (2011, 10).

Back in DK, he opens his "intrusion and apartheid" chapter, suggesting that,

> the most widely known and the most controversial development in the field of classical philosophy [in the historical period under discussion, namely after the arrival of the British] is the one given to Advaita Vedānta by Vivekananda, Rāmatīrtha and others. (1997, 197)

What catches the eye in this opening sentence is the fact that DK does not single out Swami Vivekananda. History (with the forces and agendas bubbling under its surface) often selects a single person as the ambassador of a certain idea, insight, or new turn. However, this does not mean that this insight or idea was not developed elsewhere, simultaneously, by others. It is DK's conviction that any development in the realm of ideas does not occur in isolation or "belong" to a single individual, even as great as Vivekananda. But who is Swami Rāmatīrtha, and in what way is his contribution to the universalization of Advaita (DK's articulation) and the inclusion of members of every caste, varṇa, jāti, race, and religion (DK's articulation again) in the spiritual quest parallel, similar, or complementary to Vivekananda's? This is exactly what DK, in his present capacity as author of an alternative textbook, invites his readers to find out. This chapter further consists of a philosophical discussion of Sri Aurobindo, with emphasis of his notion of evolution, of KCB and his comparative concept of the subject (on the scale between the Advaitic ātman and the Western history of the concept of the subject), Kalidas Bhattacharyya, Ramchandra Gandhi, N. V. Banerjee, J. L. Mehta, Sibajiban Bhattacharyya, and J. N. Mohanty. Anyone interested in Indian philosophy in English, both under the British and after independence, should read this chapter. DK's discussion also includes the philosophical contribution in Sanskrit by pandits such as Vasudev Shastri Abhyankar and Badrinath Shukla in the fields of Vedānta and Nyāya, respectively, and Yashdev Shalya's work in Hindi on philosophical intersections in Nāgārjuna, Śaṅkara, and Kant.

Since DK dedicates such a detailed discussion to Indian philosophy in English in two of his major publications, *Indian Philosophy: A New Approach* and *Eighteenth Century Onwards*, why would he claim in conversation with Bhushan and Garfield that Indian philosophy cannot be written in English?

It could be a matter of sharing his enthusiasm about the philosophical contribution of the pandits, in Sanskrit, both under the British and after independence, that he became aware of during the Saṃvād Project, and yet again, as he was working on *Eighteenth Century Onwards*. If this is the case, then DK was simply reminding Bhushan and Garfield that Indian philosophy in English is not the whole story, and that philosophizing in Sanskrit and other modern Indian languages must also be taken into account. Or it could be a pūrva-pakṣa, a "counter perspective" or "contrary thinking," which invites the interlocutor, in this case Bhushan and Garfield, to defend and justify his position, here the research project that they were embarking on. A provocative statement such as "philosophy written in English is not Indian Philosophy," is a perfect pūrva-pakṣa, as it triggered–urged–encouraged Garfield and Bhushan to defend their stance and refute the objection. The pūrva-pakṣin, namely, the opponent who raises the objection, is like the villain in a Bollywood movie. Without him, the hero, or the protagonist, cannot show, or even find in himself his hero-ness. Hence a pūrva-pakṣa is an effective point of departure for a fruitful philosophical discussion. This is indeed how Bhushan and Garfield depict DK's statement in their paper "Can Indian Philosophy Be Written in English?" "Daya-ji's challenge," they write here, "and it was meant very much as a challenge, not an oracular pronouncement, gave added urgency and point to our investigations."

In chapter 12 of *Eighteenth Century Onwards*, titled "Problems and issues still remaining to be explored in the intellectual history from the eighteenth century up to the present time," DK articulates the same invitation from the "positive angle." Here he speaks of "philosophy that has been written in English during the modern period" as a landscape that deserves "intensive exploration," since "hardly any attention has been paid to the work of most of these thinkers [who wrote in English]. K.C. Bhattacharyya and Sri Aurobindo are perhaps the only exceptions, but even their work has not received the critical attention it deserves, for providing a take-off point for subsequent thinkers to develop their ideas further" (2002, 338). And in appendix VI of the same book, titled "Eminent Indian Philosophers of Western Tradition in the 20th Century," DK provides his readers with a list of Indian philosophers who wrote mostly in English ("mostly," which also applies to many of the philosophers included in Bhushan and Garfield's project). From among the twenty philosophers included in Bhushan and Garfield's project, twelve appear in DK's list (Tagore, A. K. Coomaraswamy, Bhagavan Das, KCB, M. Hiriyanna, R. D. Ranade, A. C. Mukerji, Ras Bihari Das, P. T. Raju, Hiralal Haldar, G. R. Malkani, and N. A. Nikam). I mention the names, since each of these thinkers—and here I am in one mind with DK, Bhushan and Garfield—deserves to be read closely. Sri Aurobindo and Swami Vivekananda, who are part of Bhushan and Garfield's project, are not mentioned in DK's appendix but are discussed by him in *Indian Philosophy: A New Approach* and elsewhere (incidentally, DK's first published paper is "The Experiential Standpoint in the Philosophy of Sri Aurobindo," 1948). The two lists, then, DK's and Bhushan and Garfield's, are almost identical.

I wish to return to Bhushan and Garfield's conversation with DK, since it provides yet another glimpse into his master-project. I italicize what he told them. Their own analysis and evaluation is in regular print:

> [DK:] *What the British produced was a strange species—a stranger in his own country. The Indian mind and sensibility and thinking* [during the colonial period] *was shaped by an alien civilization.* [The British] *created a new kind of Indian who was not merely cut off from his civilization, but was educated in a different way. The strangeness of the species is*

> *that their terms of reference are the West . . . . They put* [philosophical problems] *in a Western way. . . . This picture of Indian philosophy that has been presented by Radhakrishnan, Hiriyanna and others . . .* [each of whom is an Indian, writing philosophy in English during the colonial period] *is not the story of Indian philosophy. We have been fed on the Western presentation of Indian philosophy, which hardly captures the spirit and history of Indian philosophy. . . . If I were not to know Indian philosophy myself, I would say that* [their presentation] *is wonderful, that it presents it clearly, with great insight and understanding. Now that I know a little Indian philosophy, I say that they did not . . . . They are not concerned with the problems that Indian philosophers were concerned with.*
>
> [Garfield and Bhushan:] The view to which Daya Krishna gives voice, despite its prevalence, is deeply mistaken. The intellectual agency and creativity in the domain of Indian philosophy in the 19th and early 20th centuries belongs to Indian thinkers; they sustained the Indian philosophical tradition and were the creators of its modern avatar. From the late 19th century through the middle of the 20th century, important and original philosophy was written in English, in India, by Indians. These philosophers were not cut off from Indian civilization; they were deeply committed to it. Their engagement with Western philosophy was an act of appropriation in the service of a modern, indeed cosmopolitan, Indian project. The problems they addressed were their own, raised by and for philosophers working in a tradition with roots in India, but who were cognizant of the Western tradition as well. Daya Krishna may indeed have been wrong about the state of philosophy under the Raj, but he gets something deeply right. He correctly characterizes the experience of Anglophone Indian intellectuals under colonial rule when he says in the same interview: . . . *The deepest anguish of the Indian intellectual is that he is unrecognized in the West as an equal, or as an intellectual at all.* This failure of recognition is tragic. These philosophers wrote in a context of cultural fusion generated by the British colonial rule of India. They were self-consciously writing both as Indian intellectuals for an Indian audience and as participants in a developing global community constructed in part by the British Empire. They pursued Indian philosophy in a language and format that could render it both accessible and acceptable to the Anglophone world abroad. In their attempt to write and to think for both audiences, they were taken seriously by neither. (2011, xiii–xiv)

DK sketches before Bhushan and Garfield the very picture of colonialism that I portrayed above through Ben Okri. "The matrix of [our] consciousness was changed by the presence of English," Okri said. DK's articulation, as quoted here, is reminiscent of KCB's "Svarāj in Ideas," his seminal lecture delivered at the Hooghly College sometime toward the end of the 1920s. KCB warns his listeners about the dangers of "cultural subjection," in which "an alien culture possesses one like a ghost" (1984, 383). He further speaks of "assimilated Western ideas fixed in language [English]," which induce "certain habits of soulless thinking which appear like real thinking [. . .] shadow mind that functions like a real mind, except in the matter of genuine creativeness" (1984, 384–5). Finally, KCB remarks that,

> under the present [British] system, we generally receive Western culture in the first instance, and then we sometimes try to peer into our ancient culture as a curiosity and with the attitude of foreign oriental scholars. [. . .] Many of our educated men do not know and do not care to know this indigenous nature of ours. When they seek to know, they do not feel, as they ought to feel, that they are discovering their own self. (1984, 384)

KCB's phrase "with the attitude of foreign oriental scholars" is strong. Along the same lines, DK speaks of the scholar produced by Macaulay's education system as "a stranger in his own country, cut off from his civilization." KCB's impression that many of his colleagues "do not know and do not care to know [. . .] their own self," again echoes in DK, despite the years that passed since KCB's lecture at the Hooghly College. KCB, and DK after him, fight for the resurrection of Indian philosophy and philosophizing in India. They are freedom fighters, striving to transform soulless thinking and shadow mind. KCB, a pandit in many of his writings (for instance, in his hardly noticed "Studies in Yoga Philosophy," based on a series of lectures delivered by him in 1937), rooted in classics, in the Sanskrit commentaries of the text (even though English has become his default medium of philosophical expression), is hardly politically naïve. He is aware of the political dimension of the task he has taken upon his shoulders. He is in search of a sense of selfhood that, according to him, has been lost. He strives to awaken his colleagues, "our educated men" as he puts it. DK (and others) continue this strive and pursuit. Bhushan and Garfield's attempt is to highlight those who remained awake, those who neither slumbered nor slept. Or perhaps, their argument is even stronger, implying that resurrection is hardly needed since these thinkers "were not cut off from Indian civilization; they were deeply committed to it." But KCB and DK lived among their people. They were acquainted with most of the texts included in Bhushan and Garfield's reader. But these texts, and the thinkers behind them, hardly resolve KCB and DK's concern and worry about the ricochets of Macaulay's education system in India.

In his conversation with Bhushan and Garfield, DK further suggests that the narrative written by the likes of Radhakrishnan and Hiriyanna is a colonized narrative, which reflects the mirror-picture of Western rationality/Indian spirituality and is deaf to the multivocality of Indian philosophy. "They are not concerned with the problems that Indian philosophers were concerned with," he says. I mentioned earlier Radhakrishnan's book *Eastern Religions and Western Thought* and DK's harsh critique of its title in his Shimla Lectures ("There is power in Indian thought!"). A quick visit to Hiriyanna's famous textbook *Outlines of Indian Philosophy* (originally published in 1932) reveals that it is a typical "six plus three" book—efficient and informative, but presenting and representing the "same old, same old" picture that DK strives to refute. In his introduction, Hiriyanna writes:

> In the words of Max Muller, philosophy was recommended in India not for the sake of knowledge, but for the highest purpose that man can strive after this life. The conception of mokṣa varies from system to system, but it marks, according to all, the culmination of philosophic culture. [. . .] Indian philosophy aims beyond logic. [. . .] Philosophy in India did not take its rise in wonder or curiosity as it seems to have done in the West; rather it originated under the pressure of a practical need arising from the presence of moral and physical evil in life. (1932, 18)

Max Muller as the voice of authority, the claim that philosophy in India (as against the West) neither aims for knowledge nor is born of wonder, mokṣa according to all, duḥkha or day-in-day-out-ness (my articulation) as evil (Hiriyanna's articulation that is deeply rooted in Christianity), and philosophy as the remedy for this so-called evil—DK would say QED. Everything that he argues against is included in this short paragraph from Hiriyanna. But Bhushan and Garfield, who estimate Hiriyanna's book as "excellent history of Indian philosophy" (2017, 285), suggest that "the view to which Daya Krishna gives voice, despite its prevalence, is deeply mistaken." And they argue that Indian philosophy in English under the British was full of "agency," "sustained the Indian philosophical tradition," was "important and original," its authors "were not cut off from Indian civilization," and "the problems they addressed were their own." I would counter-argue that DK's view, which rejects the picture of Indian philosophy as presented by Radhakrishnan and Hiriyanna, on the basis that it has internalized the Western claim for monopoly over rationality, is hardly a prevalent view. On the contrary: Hiriyanna's book, and similar books, are still printed, sold, and taught. DK's view is still a minority view. *Indian Philosophy: A New Approach*, his alternative to Hiriyanna and Radhakrishnan, is hardly known, read, or taught. I will look into this unconventional textbook as we move on.

There is one rock in Bhushan and Garfield's conversation with DK that I still left unturned, namely, the question of the reception of Anglophone Indian philosophy (DK's "Indian philosophy: Western") at the global level, or more precisely, in the West. Bhushan and Garfield hit the bull's eye when they suggest that their philosophers, the philosophers that they bring out to light, wrote in two simultaneous registers, both for Indian readership and for the West, but their work has not been duly acknowledged, certainly not in the West. The problem to my mind is not (just) the deaf Western ears, which hardly listen to voices from the non-West, but the constant yearning of the "slave" to be appreciated by the "master" (I use Mukund Lath's terminology from his Aristotelian voyages), in philosophy and every other field. The "terms of reference," as DK told Bhushan and Garfield (thirteen years ago, but I do not think that the situation today is any different), are still the West.

As I write these lines, a friend called my attention to a review article on Bhushan and Garfield's *Minds Without Fear*, recently published on the pages of the *Notre Dame Philosophical Reviews* (*NDPR*, August 2018). "A prevailing view among specialists," the reviewer writes,

> is that Indian philosophy proper can only be philosophy written in Sanskrit and a few other Prakrits (any of the several Middle Indo-Aryan vernaculars formerly spoken in India), in a doxographical style, and along more or less clearly drawn scholastic lines. As such, it encompasses the entirety of speculative and systematic thought in a doxographical style, and along more or less clearly drawn scholastic lines. [. . .] A case in point is Daya Krishna's infamously laconic and trenchant statement that "anybody who is writing in English is not an Indian philosopher" because the "Indian mind and sensibility and thinking [during the colonial period] was shaped by an alien civilization."[3]

We live in a world of one-liners. Descartes is known to have famously said "I think, therefore I am," Wittgenstein is remembered for the maxim "Whereof one cannot speak, thereof one must be silent," and DK, I now realize, is in danger of being remembered for his "infamously laconic and trenchant statement that "anyone who writes in English . . . ." Descartes and Wittgenstein deserve, of course, a much more serious look. The same is true for DK, but in his case, this one-liner-in-the-making hardly captures his position. The reviewer seems to have missed everything that DK stood for, and if this is not enough, he seems to have also missed the creativity of the pandits, which is hardly restrained (as I will show further) by the fact that they work "along more or less clearly drawn scholastic lines." The problem is, and in this respect I cannot blame the reviewer, that in the world of today, Bhushan and Garfield's work (and their harsh verdict, "Daya Krishna is deeply mistaken," which I totally disagree with) is far more available than DK's own writings, even in India, both because of its electronic accessibility and owing to their contemporary language and style of writing.

6 Ancestors and Predecessors

The title of this segment draws on A. Raghuramaraju's book *Philosophy and India: Ancestors, Outsiders, and Predecessors*. In chapter 4, "The Texts on Sabbatical," he discusses DK's Saṃvād Project, and offers an insightful reservation (limitation is the word he uses) with reference to the rationale behind the project. Raghuramaraju sees "temporal imbalance" between the parties brought together in the project, since "contemporary Western philosophy is compared or contrasted with classical Indian philosophy" (2013, 56). Raghuramaraju's observation pertains primarily to the first Saṃvād, in Pune, the proceedings of which were later published under the title *Saṃvāda: A Dialogue between Two Philosophical Traditions* (1991). The topic at the center of the discussion was Russell's theory of propositions, as presented in his *Principles of Mathematics*. In his introduction to the volume born of this meeting, M. P. Rege explains that this theory was selected for discussion with Naiyāyika and Mīmāṃsaka pandits "because it represents something like an attempt to make a new beginning in philosophical analysis," hence "its exposition would not demand many references to the tenets and arguments of earlier schools and thinkers, and the points of agreement and disagreement between them. Also Russell's realistic and analytical approach has an obvious affinity with that of Nyāya and Mīmāṃsā" (1991, xxv). Rege's explanation (less background is needed and affinity of approach) makes a lot of sense, as far as Russell's theory as an efficient launching point for the Project is concerned. But Raghuramaraju's objection (temporal imbalance) is still pending. I will try to answer it though DK, but first I wish to return to Raghuramaraju, who takes his objection even further. This is how he puts it:

> There is an antagonistic relation between modern and classical philosophy. So to make a plea, or propose to modern Western philosophers that they take into account classical Indian philosophy, would be too naïve an idea. Yet this is precisely what is proposed by the

> Saṃvād Project. What is, however possible, is to contest the antagonistic relation that presently obtains between the classical and the modern. This is what is undertaken by philosophers such as Swami Vivekananda, Sri Aurobindo and Krishnachandra Bhattacharyya. [. . .] they strove to connect the Indian and the Western, thereby avoiding the wholesale rejection of both. [. . .] Without preparing the ground, it would be unrealistic to make such a proposition [to bridge the gap between Western-trained philosophers and pandits . . .]. The opportunity that these modern Indian philosophers, such as Vivekananda, provide, and their immense contribution have escaped the attention of the authors of the Saṃvād Project. There is no mention in the Project to modern Indian philosophers. [. . .] The Project, in its enthusiasm for their ancestors, neglected their predecessors. (2013, 61–2)

The distance, or even break (antagonism is the word Raghuramaraju chose) between "modern Western philosophers" and "classical Indian philosophy" creates a situation, he suggests, in which reconciliation (synthesis is the term he uses) between these two is hard to accomplish. And here, Raghuramaraju comes up with an idea. Why not use as a bridge the work of thinkers such as Vivekananda, Aurobindo, and KCB? Later in this chapter, he adds, as another possible bridge, the work of Mahatma Gandhi. These thinkers, the "predecessors," "strove to connect the Indian and the Western, thereby avoiding the wholesale rejection of either," and "attempted to negotiate developments in the West, while making sense of classical philosophy in India" (2013, 63). They already worked, Raghuramaraju suggests, in same direction of the Saṃvād Project, mediating between classical and modern, Indian and Western. But DK and M. P. Rege, he further implies, architects of the project, insisted on starting from scratch, instead of drawing on the work that has already been done. Raghuramaraju further points out critically that whereas the Saṃvād Project hardly had any impact ("while the twentieth century is concerned with egalitarianism, the texts that the Saṃvād Project was recalling for discussion are elitist and exclusive," he suggests), the "predecessors" managed "to translate" classical sources and insights to the broad audience, "restating Advaita outside the confines of the pandits' circle" (2013, 64).

Interestingly, Raghuramaraju includes KCB in the same group with others whose influence reached way beyond the academic circle. Sri Aurobindo, Swami Vivekananda, and Gandhi were gurus (even Gandhi). They touched the masses.

If I am to extract from DK's reflection on the Saṃvād Project an answer to Raghuramaraju's observation and critique (imbalance and limited impact), I would say that for DK, the project is not about negotiating classical Indian philosophy with modern Western philosophy but about establishing a dialogue between two groups of contemporary Indian philosophers, which he refers to as "Western" and "Classical." The Saṃvād meetings enabled each group to become acquainted with the intellectual world and the philosophical toolbox of the other. For DK, as member of the "Indian Philosophy: Western" group, the Saṃvād Project is not about reaching out to classical sources in Sanskrit instead of Kant and Russell. It is about different methods of philosophizing. "Thought or reason," KCB writes in "Svarāj in Ideas," his manifesto that inspired the whole project, "may be universal, but ideas are carved out of it differently by different cultures according to their respective genius" (1984, 388). And a few paragraphs later, he adds:

> We condemn the caste system of our country, but we ignore the fact that we, who have received Western education, constitute a class more exclusive and intolerant than any of the traditional castes. Let us resolutely break down the barriers of this new caste. (1984, 393)

This is a very strong statement. It is exactly in order to break the boundaries of this "caste," that the Saṃvād Project came into being, as also to invite the pandits to examine their own boundaries and ways of seeing, and understanding, through their "other," namely, their brothers and sisters trained in Western philosophy. M. P. Rege, in his introduction, emphasizes this reciprocity—Raghuramaraju's "egalitarianism"—at the foundation of the project. The pandits are not "informants," but interlocutors, equal partners.

The Saṃvād Project, then, is not an encounter between "contemporaries" and "ancestors," but between two groups of contemporaries, with different training and tools, but nevertheless with a common denominator, a sense of "Indianness," and a mutual past preceding the "bifurcation." For the Western-trained participants, for DK after KCB, the project was matter of creating a new language for philosophical discourse. For them, it was a matter of aiming toward "svarāj in ideas." The political dimension lurks between the lines of the dialogue that focuses on issues in philosophy of language, epistemology, and metaphysics. The strive for decoloniziation in the realm of ideas is a political strive. The attempt to transform subjection into subjecthood is a political attempt. In this respect, the participants of the Saṃvād Project continued the endeavor of "predecessors" such as Aurobindo, Vivekananda, and KCB. But unlike the work of Aurobindo and Vivekananda, DK insisted on keeping the Saṃvād Project (even the Vrindavan meeting that focused on bhakti) religion free. We saw earlier that even KCB's mokṣa-centrism, at the horizon of his hardcore philosophical ventures, is seen by DK as a limitation on the scope of his work.

7 The "Pandit Way"

"I would begin to theorize the Pandit way of thinking," Arindam Chakrabarti wrote to me (personal communication, December 2018), "as involving the following four necessary conditions, but they are developed in different directions with additional features by different Pandits." Before enumerating these necessary conditions, he remarks that this is surely a schematization, since every pandit thinks in his own way. "Sibajiban Bhattacharyya," Chakrabarti illustrates, "was a Pandit in this loose sense in which you are calling me one, but not at all in Badrinath Shukla's sense. And B.K. Matilal surely thought like a Pandit, but not at all in Sibajiban's or Badrinath Shukla's way, and D. Prahladachar thinks in a yet fourth way." I quote him and mention the names, since all four are key players in twentieth-century Indian philosophy. From among them, I suspect that only Matilal, the Spalding Professor of Eastern Religion and Ethics at the University of Oxford for more than a decade, might be known to the Western intellectual community. Shukla wrote and Prahladachar still writes primarily in Sanskrit. The four necessary features of the pandit way of thinking, according to Chakrabarti, are (I continue to quote him):

1. Formulating a vipratipatti (a question with clearly two or more alternative answers) such as "Is there positive happiness/joy in the state of final liberation?" as clearly as possible.
2. Arranging the possible logically available answers from one's very wide range of learning of traditional texts (may include Aristotle, Spinoza, Kant, also, along with the six Indian orthodox schools and Buddhist, Jaina, and Cārvāka traditions) (a pandit has to be erudite without showing off the erudition).
3. Developing the strongest objections or opponents' positions against one's own view (if one has a settled view, or if one is committed to a particular tradition, e.g., Nyāya, or Sāṃkhya, or Empiricist).
4. Finally, in answering those objections, not just defend the tradition or sub-tradition one is committed to, but silently and subtly (without CLAIMING originality) change the classical position and make a small but dazzlingly insightful contribution. This last, in the context of Matilal, I called "the art of absence," or "reverse plagiarism," passing off one's own original new view to be already found in ancient or medieval texts.

The example Chakrabarti gives for vipratipatti is the title-question of his own paper "Is Liberation (mokṣa) Pleasant?" (1983). Interestingly, this is a paper on the logic of negation (abhāva). Does negation merely negate, or does it also consist of a positive horizon? Does mokṣa stand merely for "no-duḥkha" (non-suffering), or does the negation of duḥkha necessarily imply a positive sense of joy/happiness? Mokṣa for Chakrabarti is a case study through which he investigates the scope of negation, and vice versa, through negation he aims to reveal a new angle of the notion of mokṣa. His title-question is articulated as a riddle or puzzle that the reader is invited to crack. If cracked, a hidden connection between logic and metaphysics is to be revealed. Paragraph 2 of Chakrabarti's pandit way scheme emphasizes the vast scholarship without which the pandit cannot be a pandit. He speaks of learning in classics, and moreover, the philosopher without boundaries that he is, Chakrabarti mentions both Western and Indian sources. This connects with Mukund Lath's explorations in Aristotle discussed earlier. With reference to the pandit's vast learning, Chakrabarti mentions the "six plus three," that is, the schematization that DK strived to stir and shake. But the most interesting feature of Chakrabarti's scheme is what he refers to as "reverse plagiarism." I presume that this intriguing act, of adding a new bead to an old mālā without claiming originality, implying that it was there all along, hidden or hardly noticed as yet, is a sign of humbleness rather than attempt to bestow unjustified authority upon one's own work. In his paper "Identity through Necessary Change" (2013, 2018), Mukund Lath speaks, as the title implies, of identity, not as usual as that which remains the same despite change, but of identity that embraces change, identity that change is an indispensable ingredient of. Lath's case study is classical Indian music, or rāga-music as he puts it. He emphasizes the ālāpa, that is, the improvisatory overture of the rāga, the played or sung piece. The ālāpa is the "place" for novelty and innovation, without which, paradoxically, the rāga will not remain "the same" rāga. Similar paradoxicality I see in Chakrabarti's "reverse plagiarism."

In the next segment I will look into Pandit Badrinath Shukla's paper "Dehātmavāda," which DK, time and again, mentions as paradigmatic to what he sees as "the Pandit way of thinking."

8 The Body as Soul

As an illustration of "creative innovation within the tradition," DK highlights—both in *Indian Philosophy: A New Approach* and in *Eighteenth Century Onwards*—Pandit Badrinath Shukla's thought-provoking paper "Dehātmavāda," delivered in Sarnath at the Saṃvād with the Naiyāyikas

(1985) and later translated from the original Sanskrit by Mukund Lath as "The Body as Soul: Exploration of a Possibility Within Nyāya Thought."[4] In this paper, Shukla suggests that the ontological purpose fulfilled by the ātman in the Nyāya framework can be fulfilled instead by the physical body (deha) in a certain constellation with the mind (manas), which makes the ātman as the ninth substance (dravya) of this classical framework redundant (atirikta). The Nyāya framework is old, its method of philosophizing is traditional, but Shukla's move ("exploration of a possibility," as Lath gently puts it) is brand new. Shukla's argument unfolds through a series of thirty-two objections that he raises against the Dehātmavāda position, and thirty-two answers that he provides to defend this position against the objections. The philosopher, Shukla's paper demonstrates, is like a puppeteer, operating both the pūrva-pakṣin, the "opponent" or "objector," and the siddhāntin, the "assertor," who does not merely assert and affirm but has to defend his initial position against the opponent's objections. However, the latter is as much a voice of the philosopher as the siddhāntin. The role of the pūrva-pakṣin is not just to be finally defeated by the siddhāntin, hence to illuminate his unrefuted position. Through the pūrva-pakṣin, the philosopher can raise an issue, or reveal an angle that is not insignificant for him, even if he cannot endorse them through the siddhāntin. Some moves (the riskier ones?) can only be taken with the black pieces, when one plays chess against oneself. But who wins in such a game, or what does it mean "to win" if one operates both the white and the black pieces to the best of his ability? I would say that winning, in this case, has to do with the quality of the game, with what one succeeds in doing with each set of pieces, and whether the moves taken in the interaction between pūrva-pakṣin and siddhāntin are challenging and creative.

Shukla aims to show, then, that within the framework of Nyāya, it is possible to replace the ātman, the soul, with the body. It is a thought-experiment with an edge. The edge is that the reputation of the body in classical Indian philosophy is questionable, to say the least. The body conveys not just hedonistic connotations, but even worse: the author of the *Chāndogya-Upaniṣad* refers to whomever believes that the body is the ātman as "demonic" (āsuraḥ, CU 8.8.5). As noted earlier, Shukla works through a long series of objections to the Dehātmavāda ("the body as soul") position that he himself articulates, and answers them one by one. This is, for instance, objection #12:

> The attempt at repudiating the ātman and replacing it by the body and the manas [mind], in effect, elevates these two to the status of the ātman; it does not negate the ātman as such. (1988, 8)

The opponent (namely, Shukla with the black pieces) suggests that the whole experiment of replacing the ātman with body and mind is just semantic, a replacement of one word with a couple of other words, with just another name for the "same thing." But Shukla, in defense of Dehātmavāda replies:

> In our theory, the body is non-eternal, whereas the manas [mind] is eternal. If both together were to form the ātman, we shall have to conceive the ātman as having two contradictory qualities of being both eternal and non-eternal. This could give rise to ideas contrary to experience, ideas such as "sometimes I am eternal, but sometimes I am not." [. . .] Gautama in his *Nyāyasūtra* says: "Desire, revulsion, effort, joy, suffering and buddhi [the locus of knowledge], these are what characterizes the ātman." We have accepted all these characteristics as belonging to the body alone and not the manas. (1988, 8)

Shukla makes it clear that according to his Dehātmavāda, it is merely the body that replaces the ātman, not the body and the mind. The body as the ātman, Shukla explains, is not and need not be eternal. Continuity according to the principle of karma is nevertheless maintained through the mind, which travels from one bodysoul (dehātman) to another, after the death of the previous bodysoul to which it was associated. "Manas [mind], in our view, is the āśraya [receptacle] of adṛṣṭa [unseen karma], through which it acquires contact with a new body and is thus reborn" (1988, 14).

Another objection to the Dehātmavāda position, presented and replied to by Shukla, refers to the ātman in a dreaming state:

Objection #22:

> In certain states of consciousness, such as dreaming, the existence of outer objects including one's own body can become either doubtful, hazy or even controverted. But such a veil of doubt or negation never falls upon the existence of the ātman. If the body were the ātman, then such an experience should have been impossible in the case of the body too.

Shukla replies on behalf of Dehātmavāda:

> What happens in the above cases is not different from what happens in states of illusion (bhrama), when an object is not perceived in its true character. In a dream, the true character of the body as ātman becomes veiled by doubt. But this does not mean that we begin to perceive the body as non-ātman, and doubt its truth in the capacity of a non-ātman. (1988, 11)

In his objection, the pūrva-pakṣin suggests that dreaming experience refutes the move that claims that the body can replace the ātman. In reply, Shukla does not underestimate the power of dreaming to obscure, or even to negate, that which is known to us in the waking state. But even if the body as the ātman is negated in a dream, he argues, "this does not mean that we begin to perceive the body as non-ātman." We are back with Arindam Chakrabarti's implied question (in "Is Liberation Pleasant?") about the scope of negation. Here the question would be: If X is not Y (in a dream), does it make it a "Not-Y"?

Another interesting objection to "the body as soul" position is this (Objection #23, the translation all through is Mukund Lath's):

> The Dehātmavādin [exponent of Dehātmavāda] cannot but accept that the final goal of life (the parama puruṣārtha) is the achievement of physical comfort and material happiness. Yet we see that human beings are prepared to undergo personal sufferings for the good of others. How can this be explained in Dehātmavāda?

The first part of the objection suggests that if the ātman is the body, one can only aspire for "physical comfort and material happiness" (hedonism, which in the Upaniṣadic context we saw earlier equals demonism), instead of aspiring for other-centeredness (ethics), or other-worldliness (metaphysics). The second part of the objection offers an empirical observation that is supposed to prove that there is more to life than material happiness and physical comfort. But Shukla's Dehātmavādin strives for more, far more than what he is accused of. This striving will be revealed as Shukla unfolds his position by posing and answering objection after objection. For the sake of dismissing the present objection, it is sufficient for him to merely suggest:

> In truth, only a few altruistic persons give up their own happiness and devote themselves to performing actions that would lead to the happiness of others. Such people will continue to exist whether we believe in Dehātmavāda or in the ātman doctrine. [. . .] The Dehātmavādin, if he is a man of sympathy, culture and discernment, will devote himself to furthering the happiness of other bodysouls, giving up his own happiness and accepting pain in the process. (1988, 11–12)

This means that egotism and altruism, self-centeredness and other-centeredness, are not the conclusion of a comprehensive theory, but a matter of inclination ("if he is a man of sympathy"), education ("culture"), and a sense of clarity, or discernment, allowing one to see and to feel the pain of the other.

Shukla's stand in this paper as the "defense attorney" of the "body as soul" position does not mean that this is his own conviction and belief. In his work *Śataślokī* ("Hundred Verses on Emancipation," 1987), yet another example of contemporary Indian philosophy in Sanskrit, he speaks of seeing the body as the ātman, as a "great delusion which is the root cause of suffering" (duḥkhamūlaṃ mahāmoho dehādyātmaikyaniścayaḥ) [Verse 21]. And he further writes here that,

> the ātman is different from the body etc. This is the position of learned men (ātmā dehādito bhinna ityeṣā tattvadhīr matā) [Verse 22].

Shukla's "Dehātmavāda," then, as implied by the title of Lath's translation, is an "exploration of a possibility." But even if Shukla is not a Dehātmavādin, as his *Śataślokī* reveals, I would say that at least in his final two answers to the final two objections (#31 and #32), there is something of Shukla himself. Or to put it differently, the Dehātmavāda position enables him to point at the weaknesses and the risks involved in the position that he himself ascribes to, which sees the ātman as different from the body. Every position has its pros and cons. Adopting a certain position does not mean that it is free from flaws; it only means that one sees more virtues than flaws in it. The Dehātmavāda position, which Shukla represents in this experiment, enables him to expose and to deal with, rather than to ignore or suppress, the flaws, or risks, involved in his own position that the ātman is NOT the body. In objection #31, the opponent questions the novelty of Dehātmavāda as "a new doctrine." "For all this doctrine has to say," he argues, "is that the ever continuing (nitya) manas [mind] keeps transmigrating from one body to another," whereas the bodies serve merely for experiencing the results of previous karma carried into them by the manas, or mind (1988, 14). In reply, Shukla takes an unexpected ethical turn:

> The doctrine of a separate ātman cannot avoid taking an amoral stance regarding human action. Since, in that view, men are determined totally by their previous karmas and their adṛṣṭa, they are powerless against exploitation and tyranny. The [separate] ātman theory does not permit men to do anything about such things [. . .] they are not free to remove inequalities from any given social and economic setup, nor can they fight against a cruel government indifferent to the welfare of its subjects. Dehātmavāda is open to the idea that new action can be undertaken by a new bodysoul. No earlier karma is powerful enough to constrain a man to acquiesce passively in the exploitation of one man by another under the belief that this is an inevitable result of earlier karma.

> The community of Dehātmavādins is free to engage in actions aiming at changing the present conditions and creating a more just social and economic order beneficial to them all. They are free to create a more beautiful world. (1988, 15)

It is implied here that "the doctrine of a separate ātman" contributes to the neglect of the world and the worldly. Shukla goes as far as speaking of social stagnation, including exploitation and tyranny justified as being the inevitable consequences of past karma. In the separatist doctrine, the body is disposable, and the metaphysical beyondness of the ātman overshadows the now and here. As an alternative, Shukla envisions a "community of Dehātmavādins," engaging in action for the betterment of the world. Even if he is not a Dehātmavādin, this does not mean that fruitful insights from this stance and theory cannot be adopted by the "separate ātman" camp. Can the beyondness of the ātman and social justice in the world "live together" under the same roof? Shukla, as I read him, works in this direction. But his pūrvapakṣin, written by non-other than him, is a stubborn opponent. In his next objection (objection #32) he responds:

> This is mere wishful thinking, for Dehātmavāda will actually encourage people to seek their own selfish ends without caring for others. [. . .] If one is not made responsible for one's actions beyond death, then there will be no reason for a man to desist from seeking selfish ends. (1988, 15)

The opponent suggests that without the whip of "the next birth," or "next life," ethical conduct in the present life cannot be ensured. The migration of the mind from one bodysoul to another, when the former dies, is hardly seen by him as continuity strong enough to maintain the ethical level that the transmigration of the ātman safeguards. Moreover, he equates the "body as soul" approach with egotism, again portraying it as "demonic." "Dehātmavāda," Shukla answers,

> can influence people to improve themselves in this very life, since improvement in an afterlife is not possible. [. . . I]n the ātman doctrine, the temptation of postponing a good action and leaving it for another life is very strong. A man is more likely to pursue mean and selfish ends under that scheme than under dehātmavāda. Dehātmavāda is, consequently, not only more rational but also more moral. (1988, 15)

Again "the body as soul" position is projected by Shukla as moral and other-centered, and moreover as focused on the now, rather than relying on previous or future births. Like the opponent, he does not perceive the new bodysoul that the mind migrates to as a "new birth" of the previous bodysoul. Shukla's emphasis on the here and now corresponds with his plea in the *Śataślokī* for "enlightened engagement" toward "the annihilation of all types of suffering of all the people." Engagement in the world requires a body, even if the body is not presented in this treatise as replacement to the ātman. Hence Shukla writes:

> There have been a number of sages in this land of Bharat [India]. But they never desired disembodied emancipation. [*Śataślokī* Verse 77]

Here Shukla's *Śataślokī* and "Dehātmavāda" meet. He assigns the body a central role and a positive status even within the conventional framework that distinguishes between body and soul. It is the insistence on the body, born of the "body as soul" experiment, insistence on the physical body and the physical world it belongs to, which saves the ātmanist, or "soulist," from the ethical deficiency that his theory is at the risk of entailing.

I appealed to Shukla's "Dehātmavāda" to demonstrate "the pandit way" of philosophizing, even if as Arindam Chakarabarti and Mukund Lath rightly maintain, each pandit—in philosophy and music—has an ālāpa and a vision of his own. For me, Shukla's work is not about acceptance or rejection of the Dehātmavāda position, but about the freedom to travel between philosophical positions. If one can cross over and adopt, even for an instant, a different point of view, one is given a unique opportunity to view and review his initial stance as an "outsider," to see familiar landscapes with "new eyes." The parivrājaka, or wanderer between perspectives, is of the rare capacity to appreciate the other's position (cutting through stigmas and prejudices), and to reevaluate one's own position in light of his "out of the body" experience.

In the next segment I will continue to rethink the Saṃvād Project, through one of its last rounds. The theme under discussion is historiography.

9 The Shock-Proof, Evidence-Proof

This round of Saṃvād begins with DK's paper "Vedānta in the First Millennium A.D.: The Case Study of a Retrospective Illusion Imposed by the Historiography of Indian Philosophy." DK challenges the prevalent historical picture that highlights the dominance of Vedānta in this historical period, and wonders what are the agendas, revealed and concealed, behind it. DK's working method is this: he looks closely into two bibliographies that provide a list of every philosophical text composed in India, along with the name of the author and a line of information, if available, about text and author. These bibliographies are compiled respectively by Karl Potter (1970, 1983, 1995) and R. Thangaswami Sarma (1980, 1985, 1996). "Potter's *Encyclopedia of Indian Philosophies,*" DK justifies his choice,

> has by now become a standard reference work in the field of Indian philosophy, and its first volume devoted to the bibliography of the subject is the most exhaustive reference tool on what has till now published in Indian philosophy, or even referred to in catalogues of manuscripts. (1996, 162)

Alongside Potter's work, DK relies on Pandit Thangaswami Sarma's bibliography, covering texts that belong to the Advaita Vedānta, Nyāya-Vaiśeṣika, and Mīmāṃsā schools of thought. DK digs into these bibliographies and counts Vedānta texts, compared with texts belonging to other philosophical traditions. His findings are clear: most of the texts in the period under discussion are not Vedāntic, but Buddhist, Jaina, and Naiyāyika. The prevalent historical picture of Indian philosophy, which highlights Vedānta hegemony in the first millennium, is therefore inaccurate, to say the least. In another paper, published shortly after "Vedānta in the First Millennium," titled "Indian Philosophy in the First Millennium: Fact and Fiction" (1996), DK discusses his findings:

> It appears that the philosophical perception of the historians of Indian philosophy has been profoundly shaped by the situation as it obtained in the second millennium A.D. [. . .] disregarding the facts as they actually occurred. This seem to have been facilitated further by the emergence of Neo-Vedāntism in India in the late nineteenth and early twentieth centuries through works written mostly in the English language, which reinterpreted India's cultural past in a certain light to make it acceptable to the modern mind, primarily shaped by Western influence. [. . .] The historians of Indian philosophy, then, seem to have been not only greatly biased, but almost blind to the reality which stared them in the face. (1996, 133–4)

We live in an era in which each of us takes pictures on his cellular phone and easily edits them, bending reality as it were to one's needs and wants, goals, and agenda. In this paragraph, DK suggests that the situation is not essentially different in the case of the historical pictures and narratives that we have become used to thinking about as an "objective record" of the past.

DK not merely challenges the picture at hand but also—and for me this is the crux of the matter—invites us to view the pictures that our historical, philosophical, and in fact every other album consists of with a questioning eye.

The simple counting of texts in two bibliographies reveals that the standard picture magnifies the place of Vedānta in the first millennium, and undermines the significance of other philosophical players, primarily the Buddhists. As always, DK does not hesitate to let the cat out of the bag, and suggests that neo-Vedānta thinkers, in the late nineteenth century (Vivekananda's famous talks at the Parliament of World's Religions in Chicago, 1893, come to mind) and the early twentieth century (take, for instance, the writings of Radhakrishnan), are responsible for this picture, projecting Vedānta as the crown jewel of Indian philosophy from the Upaniṣads until this very day, without rupture. I recently revisited Radhakrishnan's abovementioned textbook *Indian Philosophy*, and found statements such as,

> Buddha is not so much creating a new Dharma as rediscovering an old norm. [. . .] Early Buddhism, we venture to hazard a conjecture, is only a restatement of the thought of the Upaniṣads. (2008, 303)

Or,

> The central defect of Buddha's teaching is that in his ethical earnestness, he took up and magnified one-half of the truth and made it look as if it were the whole. His distaste for metaphysics prevented him from seeing that the partial truth had a necessary complement and rested on principles which carried it beyond its self-imposed limits. (2008, 399)

These quotes show that for Radhakrishnan, Buddhism is hardly an independent school of thinking. It is rather a branch of Vedānta (I use the word here as another name for the Upaniṣads), emphasizing its ethical dimension but neglecting the complementary metaphysical horizon, a neglect born out of the Buddha's "distaste for metaphysics." For Radhakrishnan, the metaphysical horizon of the Brahman is unquestionable, even if the Buddha, as he depicts him, prefers to de-emphasize it. According to him, "every form of Hinduism is related to the common background of Vedānta" (this quote is from Radhakrishnan's *The Hindu View of Life*, 1954, as cited in Halbfass 1995, 245). And as we just saw, even Buddhism is considered by him as a "form of Hinduism." DK challenges this "common background." Moreover, Radhakrishnan takes it for granted that the Upaniṣadic corpus, vast as it is, speaks in a single voice and conveys a unified message. DK questions this unity, and the alleged cohesive structure of the corpus. In his paper "The Upaniṣads: What Are They?" (1983), he writes:

> It is well-known that many of the Upaniṣads are not independent works, but selections from pre-existing texts [i.e., the Brāhmaṇas and the Āraṇyakas]. But if that is so, someone must have made the selection. It is not quite clear what was the basis for the selection. It is also not quite clear why during the long period of time since the first selection was made, no one has made a different or alternative selection. (1983, 97)

DK is not just interested in the politics of the selection that created the corpus as we know it today, but wonders why a single selection has become fixated. He further suggests that if the Upaniṣads are seen as what they are, namely, an edited collection extracted from previous sources, "the way becomes open for a new selection, or even a number of selections" (1983, 107). In his Shimla Lectures (2005), DK asked the Sanskrit pandits in the audience why they would not compose new Vedic Sūktas (hymns) and Upaniṣads. After the session, I spoke with one of these pandits. "Did you hear what he just said?" he asked me with amazement, "He wants us to compose Sūktas and Upaniṣads, this is impossible!"

Back in the Saṃvād with the insiders of Vedānta, DK informs them that he could hardly find any Vedāntic text between the *Brahamasūtra* and Śaṅkara, and even several hundred years after Śaṅkara (besides his direct disciples). "Surprisingly," DK writes,

> the *Brahmasūtra* remained entirely unnoticed until the appearance of Śaṅkara, who wrote his commentary on it, along with several *Upaniṣads* and the *Bhagavadgītā*, which resulted in the famous myth of the Prasthānatrayī, that is, the view that the source of Indian philosophy lies in these three texts, when even the so-called different schools of Vedānta do not treat them in this way, as except for Śaṅkara and Madhava, no one else has commented on all the three. (1996, 202)

DK dares to suggest that there was limited interest in the *Upaniṣads*, the *Gītā*, and the *Brahmasūtra* between their composition and Śaṅkara, who wrote bhāṣyas (initial commentaries; the term "bhāṣya" referring to a commentary written by a commentator who read merely the source-text and does not know of any commentary prior to his)[5] on them. To this heretic speculation (at least in the eye of the Vedāntin), DK adds his skeptical remark about the status of these texts as the Prasthānatrayī, "the three sources" of Vedānta. He refers to the axiomatic view that these are the foundational texts of the

Vedānta tradition as a "myth," a notion that he often uses with reference to what he considers to be an unestablished belief that is commonly accepted. The very notion of Prasthānatrayī, which conveys a sense of elementary-ness and primordiality, grants these texts unique status and aura. But DK, a modern avatar of the child in Hans Christian Andersen's *The Emperor's New Clothes*, is hardly taken by auras and is ever-ready to point out that the emperor is naked. In the present case, he wonders about the prestige of this "textual trinity" in light of his discovery—through the bibliographies compiled by Potter and Thangaswami—that these texts did not have much impact, at least until Śaṅkara. And DK adds yet another feature to his critique, suggesting that among the great Ācāryas, the illustrious teachers of Vedānta, merely Śaṅkara and Madhva commented on all three texts. DK develops this critique on the authority of the Prasthānatrayī in a separate paper titled "The Myth of the Prasthānatrayī" (1998). Here he clarifies which Ācārya commented on which texts from among "the three source texts." Moreover, he underscores the overgrowing importance of the *Bhāgavata Purāṇa* for the later Vedānta tradition, or as he puts it, "the inclusion of this text by Madhva, and then by Vallabha, and still later by the followers of Caitanya, who gave up the whole Prasthānatrayī tradition altogether" (1988, 89).

In brackets (since this monograph deals with DK's contribution on the backdrop of twentieth-century Indian philosophy), I wish to mention Ramchandra Gandhi's creative reading of the notion of Prasthānatrayī in "Wardha, Pondicherry, Tiruvanamalai—Prasthāna Traya?," chapter 24 of his book *I am Thou* (2011, 103–04), dedicated to three of his protagonists: Mahatma Gandhi, Sri Aurobindo, and Ramana Maharshi. But it is the title that caught my eye. Wardha, Pondicherry, and Tiruvanamalai are the places identified with these three gurus, respectively. Referring to places as Prasthānatrayī (or Prasthāna Traya) is an unusual move. Ramchandra Gandhi deconstructs not just the notion of Prasthānatrayī (extracting it away from its traditional framework) but even the notion of text. A text is not always written on paper, or leaf, and bound between two covers. It can be inscribed in soil, and in the collective consciousness of a people. For Ramchandra Gandhi, the soil of consciousness and the consciousness of the soil, precede and transcend the written page.

Back in our Saṃvād, DK studies both bibliographies, Potter's and Thangaswami Sarma's, very closely. One by one, he identifies Vedānta authors, not too many of them, before and after Śaṅkara. On his journey, he challenges yet another myth—the myth according to which Śaṅkara is responsible for the disappearance of Buddhism in India, whether by defeating Buddhist thinkers in philosophical debate, or alternately (in another version of the same myth) through "absorption" of Buddhist elements into his philosophical system in such a way that Buddhism as an independent school becomes redundant. "The Buddhists," DK writes,

> are ahead of the Vedāntins, both in quantity and quality, even after Śaṅkara, thus nullifying the myth that they were defeated by Śaṅkara. (1996, 203)

He returns to the question of Śaṅkara and the Buddhists in a separate paper titled "Was Ācārya Śaṅkara Responsible for the Disappearance of Buddhist Philosophy from India?" (1999). "The disappearance of Buddhism from India is one of those enigmas which defies explanation," he opens this paper. And he further writes:

> For more than fifteen hundred years, Buddhism dominated the Indian scene and has left unbelievable marvels in the realm of sculpture, architecture and painting, that it is difficult to understand how the faith that created this ceased to function as a living force in the very country it originated. (1999, 127)

DK speaks of Buddhism first in sculpture, architecture, and painting. Whoever saw the mesmerizing murals of Ajanta, or had the occasion to visit the great Stupa at Sanchi, a gem of Buddhist art and architecture, to mention just two quick examples, would understand why DK mentions art first, before getting down to business and speaking of "the disappearance of Buddhist philosophy from the Indian scene, where it had a visible dominating presence for so long." "The myth of Vedic Hinduism swallowing up all the other non-Hindu religious traditions in India," DK continues to write, "so persistently propagated by certain vested interests, is really a myth, unsustainable by any evidence whatsoever" (1999, 127). Jaina philosophy, or Jainism at large, is DK's example for a tradition that is alive, independently alive, until this very day, despite this alleged "swallowing up." In reply to the twofold myth ("Śaṅkara refuted the Buddhists in such a decisive way that they could not hold their own after being defeated by him," and "through subtle diplomacy, he had assimilated all the crucial elements of their distinctive thought"), DK writes that,

> however widespread the theory, it does not even prima facie make any sense. Śaṅkara refuted not just the Buddhists, but in spite of his refutation, they continued to flourish in India. Philosophical schools do not die of criticism. Rather, they get a new life and rigour as they try to meet the challenge, usually introducing interesting modifications in

> their position, or different arguments in support of their position. The history of philosophy, in all traditions, is the history of argument and counter-argument. (1999, 128)

Most interesting is DK's remark that "philosophical schools do not die of criticism, they get a new life and rigour." He further writes that,

> the history of Buddhist philosophy after Śaṅkara completely refutes the claim that it disappeared from the Indian philosophical scene because of his decisive demolition of their position by his arguments. In fact, they did not disappear. They continued to flourish another five hundred years after Śaṅkara. Not one, not two, but literally scores of Buddhist thinkers flourished during this period, and if one compares them with those who followed in the steps of Śaṅkara's thought, one is amazed as to how such a contention could ever have been made by anyone. Potter's Bibliography of Indian Philosophy (3rd edition) lists at least forty-three important Buddhist thinkers from the 8th century to the first quarter of the 13th century, that is 1220 AD. The list includes such well-known names as Śāntarakṣita, Kamalaśīla, Dharmottara, Jitendra Buddhi, Yaśomitra, Prajñākara Gupta, Paṇḍita Aśoka, Jñānaśrīmitra, Atiśa, Ratnakīrti, Mokṣākaragupta and Aniruddha. (1999, 128–29)

What is interesting in this paragraph are the names. DK mentions these names not just to substantiate his argument that Buddhism thrived after Śaṅkara but to illustrate the richness of Indian philosophy, often reduced by the uninitiated to just a few "big names," such as Nāgārjuna, Vasubandhu, Dignāga, and Dharmakīrti in the Buddhist tradition. "Indian thinking is not anonymous," DK claims in his Shimla Lectures (2005), "it is varied to particular persons, and we must know their names, we must know their opinions, we must know their diversities. This country will never be known to itself unless it hears the diverse voices which are there; conflicting voices, but respectful voices. People respected others who were totally opposed." This is DK's attempt: to reveal the plurality, diversity, and multivocality of Indian philosophy.

Back in his paper on Śaṅkara, DK reaches his conclusion:

> Only one thinker is listed in the Bibliography after 1200, the date usually given for the destruction of Nālandā by Bakhtiyār Khiljī in the standard books on Indian history. There can be thus no ground for ascribing Śaṅkara the responsibility for the disappearance of the Buddhists from the philosophical scene in India. It is a myth like many other myths, and

> should be recognized as such. The cause of its disappearance lay in the destruction of Nālandā, the acclaimed intellectual center of Buddhism in 1200 A.D., though even that leaves many questions unanswered, such as why, unlike Jainism, it had only one centre in the whole country. (1999, 129–30)

DK's conclusion, "Bakhtiyār Khiljī, not Śaṅkara," urged me to dig a little deeper into the question of the decline of Buddhism in India. In my search, I came upon Frank Whaling's paper "Śaṅkara and Buddhism" (1979). Whaling provides several reasons for this decline, internal and external. His external category includes Bakhtiyār Khiljī's attack on Nālandā. He explains that during this period, the attitude of the Indian kings toward Buddhism had changed. The Buddhists could no longer rely on royal patronage and protection as before, and indeed, when Khiljī attacked, no one came to their aid. Whaling further explains that the Buddhist decline was a process over time: "The numbers of Buddhists were becoming less; thousands of monasteries that had been in use were abandoned; the decline was evident throughout the subcontinent, with a few honorable exceptions such as Nālandā" (1979, 32). The process argument, from the gradual loss of royal patronage to a growing rift between monkhood and laity, which Whaling points out, makes sense. But Whaling implies that a parallel process took place internally. In this respect, he suggests that,

> Śaṅkara did play his part in the demise of Buddhism in India, by his own attacks on the Buddhists, by his strengthening of Hinduism as a living force, and by his appropriating of monastic Buddhist ideals and Mādhyamika and Vijñānavāda insights. [. . .] By the time that the Muslim depredations added a new dimension to the situation, the Buddhism which by Śaṅkara's time was already declining had through him become weaker still. His work finds its place in a complex series of reasons for the retreat of the religion of the Buddha from the land of its birth. (1979, 37)

DK's discovery that Buddhist philosophy continued to be significant hundreds of years after Śaṅkara ("not one, not two, but literally scores of Buddhist thinkers"), especially compared with the scarce presence of Vedānta—Śaṅkara's own tradition—during this period, pulls the rug out from under Whaling's argument. Śaṅkara's part, if any, was hardly effective.

Before I return to our Saṃvād, I wish to make a small bibliographical note of my own. The development and decline, rise and fall, of a philosophical tradition is an interesting theme in itself. How is a philosophical tradition born, and what are the stages of its growth and drying out? These are exactly the questions dealt with by Karl Potter in his paper "The Development of Advaita Vedānta as a School of Philosophy" (2004), in which Advaita is taken as a case study. This paper was sent by DK to an ensemble of pandits, including G. C. Pande and Sibajiban Bhattacahryya, for response and discussion. It is the first Saṃvād in DK's worth-reading *Discussion and Debate in Indian Philosophy* (2004). The next Saṃvād in this volume is our Saṃvād, on Vedānta in the first millennium. The Saṃvād that revolves around Potter's paper paves the way to the Saṃvād discussed here.

Back in our Saṃvād, Daya Krishna summarizes his findings:

> There is practically no Vedānta in the first millennium A.D., and the idea of its dominant presence is a superimposition by the historiography of Indian philosophy. [. . .] The propounders of the theory of Adhyāsa have perhaps themselves imposed one on the history of philosophy in India. (1996, 207)

At a first glance, the last sentence looks like a sarcastic remark, a final blow to the common Vedānta–Vedānta–Vedānta picture of Indian philosophy. But DK uses here one of the essential concepts of Śaṅkara's Advaita Vedānta, the notion of adhyāsa, which he translates as "superimposition." Since this notion holds a central place in the interlocutors' response to DK, let us take a detour to see how it is shaped and molded philosophically by Śaṅkara, to be able to decipher the crux of their dispute with DK.

In his introduction to the *Brahmasūtra-bhāṣya*, his commentary on the *Brahmasūtra*, an introduction known as the *Adhyāsa-Bhāṣya* ("The Commentary that spotlights the concept of Adhyāsa"), Śaṅkara defines adhyāsa as,

> satyānṛte mithunī-kṛtya aham idaṃ mamedam iti naisargiko 'yaṃ loka-vyavahāraḥ. (Bansidhar Bhatt 1978, 350)
>
> The natural procedure (naisargika) of copulating the real and the unreal through phrases such as "this is me" and "this is mine," which roots (the human person) in the phenomenal world.

In Śaṅkara, adhyāsa occurs through and within language. The two examples he gives ("this is me" and "this is mine") convey not just separateness (or if you wish, egotism) as against the all-embracing Brahman, but confusion, or misidentification resulting from the mixture of components altogether different from each another. In both phrases, "the real me," which for Śaṅkara is the Brahman alone, is mixed or copulated with the "unreal" (or "less real," I cannot delve here into the unique ontological status of what Śaṅkara refers to as māyā), namely, with body, mind, and whatever other property or possessions one is used to identify with. It is worse than mixing apples and oranges, owing to the existential consequences of this epistemological error, namely, duḥkha, or phenomenal existence as suffering. The twist is that from a metaphysical perspective, adhyāsa is a fatal error, but at the phenomenal level, adhyāsa is the a priori condition for any cognition. "Adhyāsa," Śaṅkara further explains (in Georg Thibaut's translation),

> is the apparent presentation (avabhāsaḥ) in the form of remembrance, to consciousness, of something previously observed, in some other thing. (Thibaut 1994, Part I, 4); smṛti-rūpaḥ paratra pūrva-dṛṣṭāvabhāsaḥ. (Bhatt 1978, 350)

I am quoting Śaṅkara's definition of adhyāsa for two reasons. First, to substantiate my claim that adhyāsa is the mechanism behind every act of cognition. Whenever we "meet" the world, we "pull out" from memory a readymade "tag" and "fit" it to that "something" that we perceive. And second, to underscore the continuity from Śaṅkara to DK. Yes, a continuity from "the voice of the tradition," at least the Advaita tradition, to a contemporary heretic; heretic in the sense that DK refuses "to follow suit," and reads classical texts through his own caśmā, his unique magnifying-glass, which is hardly committed to any traditional reading. DK uses the concept of adhyāsa rhetorically, as a sharp closing-line for his paper ("the propounders of the theory of Adhyāsa have themselves imposed one"), but he thought and wrote on adhyāsa, separately, in his paper "Adhyāsa: A Non-Advaitic Beginning in Śaṅkara's Vedānta" (1965). Here, as always, he is a visitor in the text, reading it with fresh eyes and requesting the traditionalists, whom the text "belongs" to, to respond to his "different reading." DK reads the first, famous sentence of Śaṅkara's *Adhyāsa-Bhāṣya*, and comes up with a surprising observation. In this opening sentence, as every student of classical Indian philosophy knows, Śaṅkara writes:

> The object (viṣaya) and the subject (viṣayin), manifested respectively in the ideas of "you" (yuṣmat) and "I" (asmat-pratyaya), are different from one another like darkness and light, and should not be identified with one another. (I work with the Sanskrit text as in Bhatt 1978, 349)

DK is surprised by Śaṅkara's definition of adhyāsa as the mistaken identification of "you" and "I." From an Advaitic, non-dualistic perspective, DK thinks out loud, the error should be the other way around. For the Advaitin, and Śaṅkara is supposed to be the champion of Advaita, anything that diverts from the equation "I am Thou"—as DK's contemporary Ramchandra Gandhi titled his magnum opus (1984)—is an error. Why and how, then, DK wonders, does Śaṅkara choose to open the introduction of his commentary with a formulation of adhyāsa that is compatible with the position of his rivals from the Sāṃkhya school of thought? Traditionalists would make an attempt to justify the great Ācārya at any cost. They would claim (and in fact claimed) that this is not a Sāṃkhyan beginning to the *Brahmasūtra-bhāṣya* as implied by DK, but a pre-Advaitic position, submitted by Śaṅkara before readers who are rooted in the commonsense perspective that distinguishes between object and subject, and are not yet acquainted with his Advaitic framework. Some went as far as speculating that Śaṅkara's move reflects his personal transition from Yoga (which adopts the dualistic metaphysics of Sāṃkhya) to Advaita. This speculation was raised by those who were willing to accept that Śaṅkara, this Śaṅkara, the Advaitin, is the composer of a commentary of the *Yogasūtra* titled *Yogasūtra-bhāṣya-vivaraṇa*. I cannot delve here into the question about the authorship of this yoga commentary and, more broadly, which texts were "in fact" written by Śaṅkara.[6] It is DK's unique capacity to raise the unasked questions, hence to stir up a lively discussion, which I am concerned with at present.

Before I turn to DK's interlocutors in our Saṃvād, I wish to discuss an insider's critique of DK's earlier paper "A Non-Advaitic Beginning." This critique, by G. R. Malkani, anticipates the response of those who participated in the Saṃvād on Vedānta in the first millennium. It illustrates the deep abyss between insider and outsider. It is not easy for the insider to accept, and certainly to appreciate the perspective of the outsider. The insider is not just defensive about the traditional narrative that he is rooted in but often simply cannot understand the questions of the outsider, articulated in a non-traditional language and challenging the solidity of the very ground on which he stands.

In his paper "A Discussion of Daya Krishna's Views on Advaitic Adhyāsa" (1996), Malkani writes:

> Adhyāsa means the superimposition of one thing upon another, or more generally, it means taking one thing to be what it is not. There must therefore be two different things in any adhyāsa. These two things are somehow confused with each other, or in some sense identified. So far,

> all schools of thought may be said to be in agreement. There is no such thing as Sāṃkhyan adhyāsa as distinct from Advaitic adhyāsa. (1996, 81)

My immediate response to Malkani is that Śaṅkara's definition of adhyāsa in his *Adhyāsa-Bhāṣya* is different from the definitions of other schools. Śaṅkara in fact quotes definitions of other schools (Nyāya, Yogācāra, Mīmāṃsā, and Mādhyamika) to highlight this difference. His own definition ("the apparent presentation in the form of remembrance") highlights the fact that for him—as I suggested earlier—adhyāsa is an error merely from the metaphysical perspective, but otherwise, it is the a priori mechanism that enables consciousness to function in its phenomenal (vyāvahārika) mode. Moreover, adhyāsa in Śaṅkara as I read him, is the principle that explains the endurance and unity of consciousness, including the cognitive operation of memory. The human person can remember his past merely owing to the fact that an a priori pattern connects his present perception with his past experiences. Consciousness, according to Śaṅkara, always works according to the same pattern, and the gaze of whomever is rooted in avidyā, unfreedom, or worldliness, or phenomenal existence is determined by this pattern that Śaṅkara refers to as adhyāsa.

After a short analysis of the opening section of Śaṅkara's *Adhyāsa-Bhāṣya* as he reads it, Malkani further writes:

> There is really no paradox here, but Daya Krishna maintains there is. [. . .] Daya Krishna makes no valid or interesting point in his paper. He does not support the standpoint of Advaita Vedānta. He does not find fault with it, either. He merely misinterprets a very important distinction which Śaṅkara makes at the very beginning of his Bhāṣya. He fails to grasp the force of Śaṅkara's logic in radically distinguishing the objects of the intuition of "I" and the intuition of "this." No one can presume to have understood Advaita Vedānta who does not appreciate the absolute opposition of the respective objects of these two intuitions. It is difficult under the circumstances to believe that Daya Krishna has entered into the spirit of Advaita Vedānta, or that he is competent to find fault with the father of the system. (1996, 424–5)

Malkani opens this paragraph by rejecting DK's discovery ("a non-Advaitic beginning"). Not refuting, but rejecting. "There is no paradox," he asserts with full authority (and Malkani was certainly an authority in the field of Vedānta). Malkani then suggests that "Daya Krishna makes no valid or interesting point. He does not support or find fault with the standpoint of Advaita Vedānta." This statement, for me, shows that Malkani does not know how to digest DK's critique. Indeed, DK's aim is not to refute the Advaitic position. He is not a classical opponent, belonging to a competing school of thought. His attempt is altogether different. He reads the *Adhyāsa-Bhāṣya* with "new eyes," and raises a pertinent query about a notion—adhyāsa—at the heart of Śaṅkara's philosophy. But this query is dismissed by Malkani as "misinterpretation." Finally, Malkani feels that as an outsider, DK fails to grasp "the spirit of Advaita Vedānta" and is therefore incompetent to criticize Śaṅkara, "the father of the system." But DK never claimed to have captured this spirit and, moreover, his aim is not to become an insider. An outsider by choice, he reads Śaṅkara in the same way that he reads any other philosophical text, Indian or Western, classical or contemporary. He treats him as a philosopher, leaving aside other dimensions—traditional or religious—of the famous Ācārya. A self-conscious outsider, DK does not see Śaṅkara as a father, but as a fellow-thinker, an interlocutor, even if more than a thousand years separate between them. It is a dialogue across eras, and since Śaṅkara cannot respond to his queries, DK appeals to the Śaṅkarites, the insiders of Vedānta, for their response and thoughts.

Now back to our Saṃvād. Among the "insiders," Suresh Chandra suggests—in response to DK's discovery that Vedānta hardly had textual impact in the first millennium—that Vedānta existed, during this period, in the hearts of the believers and in their religious practice. "A common practitioner," he writes, "knows Vedānta not through its intricate philosophical arguments" (2004, 107). DK, in "The Shock-Proof," has nothing to say about such a response. If it is a matter of the heart, then it is a different discourse, hardly philosophical or textual. And hearts are difficult to read, especially "historical hearts" that ceased to beat more than a thousand years ago. The next respondent, Godavarish Mishra, suggests that there must have been Vedānta texts unrecorded by Potter, Thangaswami, and earlier sources that they rely on. "Are we to suppose that there never existed such texts, just because some of the manuscript collectors did not come across them, and consequently did not record them in their bibliographies?" he asks. Here again, DK has nothing much to say in response. A different data would certainly require different analysis. But as long as the present data is available—and Mishra hardly provides names of unknown texts and authors, his argument is almost hypothetical—DK's conclusion remains unshaken. I wrote "almost," since Mishra does quote a statement from the *Śrībhāṣyaprakāśikā* of Śrīnivāsācārya (sixteenth century), a commentary on Rāmānuja's *Śrībhāṣya* (eleventh century), according to which "there existed ninety-six *bhāṣyas* [commentaries] on the *Brahmasūtra* before Rāmānuja, who refuted all those views in composing his *Śrībhāṣya*" (2004, 133). "If the statement of the author of *Śrībhāṣyaprakāśikā* is correct,"

DK writes in "The Shock-Proof," "then obviously my main contention stands refuted. But," he adds,

> there remain many questions still to be answered by Prof. G. Mishra and others who accept the truth of this statement. [. . . Since] mere refutation of a position does not entail that the view so refuted belongs to a separate independent text, unless the name of the author is specifically mentioned by the person who is refuting this view. Many a time the views which are being refuted are imagined as pūrvapakṣa by the author himself. (2004, 141)

More details are needed to ascertain that the allegedly refuted texts in fact existed. Otherwise, one cannot brush aside the possibility that we are dealing with a pūrva-pakṣa, that is, objections raised by Rāmānuja himself, by refuting which he constructs his own position. Moreover, the round and impressive number of refuted commentaries, ninety-six, could be brought about to eulogize Rāmānuja and to celebrate his philosophical work, whether these texts really existed or not.

Here I wish to suggest that since more than two decades passed since DK's debate with the pandits, it is time to count the texts again. It is not implausible that new texts have been found, and the question is: How such texts, if indeed found, change the situation? Is it really, still, the Buddhist millennium, as suggested by DK?

DK is further challenged by R. Balasubramanian. First, it is interesting to notice that Balasubramanian uses the terms Vedānta and Advaita Vedānta (or simply Advaita) interchangeably. For him, Vedānta is primarily Advaita Vedānta. Second, his critique of DK focuses on the concept of adhyāsa. He accuses DK of using this term too loosely. If the framework is broken, he argues, and anyone can use a term, here adhyāsa, in his own way, a meaningful dialogue cannot take place. If the exchange between DK and the "insiders" is about historical hegemony, then Balasubramanian takes this hegemony debate in a new direction, concentrating on hegemony and language. The question is: What is legitimate, or illegitimate in language, or what amount of "freedom" is allowed when using a classical concept such as adhyāsa? It is a question about context and framework, fidelity and transgression.

"The theory of adhyāsa as formulated in Advaita," Balasubramanian writes,

> is well known. Adhyāsa is perceptual error, which is different from errors in reasoning as well as errors in interpretation. [. . .] Since there is no scope for adhyāsa in the context of historiography of Indian philosophy,

> it is wrong to say that the Advaitin has imposed his theory of adhyāsa on the history of philosophy. [. . .] It seems to me that Daya Krishna wants to beat the Advaitin with his own stick, but he does not succeed, since he has chosen an instrument which has no use in the present case. (2004, 81)

The concept of adhyāsa, Balasubramanian explains, is a matter of perceptual error and has nothing to do with historiography. Hence DK's remark ("an adhyāsa imposed on the history of philosophy") has no meaning. He implies that unless context and framework are kept, there is no common ground for mutual understanding. DK's present concern is Vedānta in the first millennium, but he will come back to adhyāsa in and out of context, and to the philosophical implications of this pivotal concept in a separate article, a sort of appendix to the present Saṃvād, titled "Can the Analysis of Adhyāsa ever lead to an Advaitic Conclusion" (2001).

Balasubramanian continues to attack DK severely, and refers to him as "idol worshiper." "Of the various idols," he writes,

> which Daya Krishna seems to worship, that of the number is very conspicuous. We know that in politics the strength of a view is dependent on the number of persons who support it. A particular view becomes dominant and prevails over others if its supporters are numerically in a majority. However, the politics of number has no place in philosophy. (2004, 81).

This is a wonderful paragraph. First, since Śaṅkara—whose notion of adhyāsa became the bone of contention between Balasubramanian and DK—prefers the abstract, nirguṇa Brahman over the palpable, saguṇa deities, hence devalues idol worship; to call DK an "idol worshiper" is again to imply that he is an outsider to Śaṅkara's philosophical framework. But DK is not just an idol worshiper. He is an idol worshiper of the worst kind. His idol, according to Balasubramanian, is the number. A master of rhetoric, Balasubramanian accuses DK of defiling the "pure" realm of philosophy (and moreover, spirituality) with politics. The number belongs to politics, he writes, not to philosophy. "Ouch!," was my first response. But the whole discussion here is about the politics of ideas. DK hints that owing to modern agendas, neo-Vedānta imposes a picture of Indian philosophy that projects Vedānta as dominant from the very beginning, namely, from the Upaniṣads onward. Balasubramanian, a master of Vedānta, quotes from Śaṅkara's commentary on the *Taittirīya-Upaniṣad*, where he claims that "a philosophical position cannot be considered to be sound just because the number of its votaries is legion," as

Balasubramanian puts it (2004, 82). Moreover, metaphysically, Śaṅkara anyway prefers the one over the many. But is it a convincing objection to DK's counting experiment, and to his conclusion that the majority of texts in the historical period under discussion are non-Vedāntic? "The prejudice for number is deep-rooted in human nature," Balasubramanian continues to twist his knife, "and Daya Krishna's argument in this case shows that he is a victim of the IDOLA TRIBUS" (2004, 82). Balasubramanian, we discover, is not just a first-class Sanskritist but a frequent visitor in another classical language, Latin. The phrase IDOLA TRIBUS (the capital letters are Balasubramanian's) refers to "the idols of the tribe." DK is lucky, I thought to myself as I read Balasubramanian, that he was not accused by his knowledgeable opponent of falling victim to the IDOLA FORI, "the idols of the market place." It is said of Moshe Sneh, an Israeli politician and member of the first Knesset (the Israeli parliament), that he wrote on the draft of one of his famous speeches, "weak argument, raise voice." My feeling is that the Latin phrase in capital letters works in the same way as raising one's voice. Balasubramanian opens the final paragraph of his response with the claim that "The Vedāntic thought of the Upaniṣads constitutes the *philosophia perennis* which has endured through the ages," and closes this paragraph and his whole paper with this complementing claim:

> The Vedānta philosophy of the Upaniṣads is, indeed, the Rock of Ages, which one has to encounter and reckon with in doing philosophy. (2004, 104)

The phrases "philosophia perennis" and "Rock of the Ages"—again Latin and capital letters—surely convey the conviction of Balasubramanian and the other "insiders" who participated in the Saṃvād about the significance of Vedānta philosophy and its essential texts. Balasubramanian strives to place a firewall between "the trusted insiders" and the "intruding questions" of the "outsider." No wonder, then, that DK titled his reply to Balasubramanian and the others "The Shock-Proof, Evidence-Proof, Argument-Proof World of Sāmpradāyika Scholarship of Indian Philosophy," sāmpradāyika standing for uncompromising identification with the credo of one's sampradāya, that is, school, or thinking tradition.

10 Daya the Rebel

DK usually thought and wrote as a pūrva-pakṣin, a "philosophical opponent" who raises questions, objections, and counter-perspectives. Moreover, as I hinted earlier, he often played the role of the child in *The Emperor's New*

Clothes who points out (against authority, against majority, and against thinking-habits) that the emperor is naked. But one rainy morning (the Jaipur version, or monsoon version, of "one sunny morning"), DK decided to write a textbook of his own, an introduction of his own to Indian philosophy, *Indian Philosophy: A New Approach*. Like many of DK's other writings, this subversive, daring book, remained under the radar, and hardly received the attention it deserves. Here he offers an alternative to the conventional picture that as a pūrva-pakṣin he attacks, and as the child from *The Emperor's New Clothes*, he exposes as vastu-śūnya, that is, naked, empty of any convincing reference or evidence, fueled by the power of repetition, and driven by agendas that he does not hesitate to reveal. In this textbook, DK seeks to show that one can do without the usual, worn-out picture of "Six plus three, what else?" and the inevitable duo of duḥkha and mokṣa ("suffering" and "final release"). If duḥkha and mokṣa are the alpha and omega of Indian philosophy, then it is philosophy in the service of the spiritual quest, a common view that DK challenges again and again.

A short diversion from the main road—in his paper "Of Gambling" (2014), Sibaji Bandyopadhyay suggests that,

> the number four is of immense significance in the textual imagination of India. Used for centuries to configure a variety of discursive units, the number has a special force accrued to it. [. . .] Who can navigate the ocean of Indian texts without the guidance of lighthouses such as: the corpus of hallowed texts collectively called the Four Vedas; the amalgam of rank and prestige signified by the Four varṇas ["castes"]; the stipulated stages of life or the Four āśramas; the endowments of dharma-artha-kāma-mokṣa ("customary as well as customized propriety, material gain, pleasures of love and lust, and deliverance"), holistically termed as the Four vargas [and Bandyopadhyay continues to list significant foursomes, from the four faces of Brahmā to the four yugas, or Ages with a capital A, as he renders this notion]. (2014, 3)

Four, and not six, is the winning number, or the winning throw (kṛta) in the classical Indian game of dice. Bandyopadhyay shows us that number four is to be found "everywhere" in the Indian textual world. By visiting not just the famous dice game in the Sabhāparvan of the *Mahābhārata* but even Dostoevsky's novella *The Gambler* (1866, set in the imaginary town of Roulettenberg, and written by Dostoevsky under a strict deadline to pay off his own gambling debts), Bandyopadhyay implies that gambling is an integral part of the business called "life." Like Yudhiṣṭhira of the *Mahābhārata*, who astonishingly gambles on "everything," including his brothers, his wife, and even himself, we are all gamblers, taking a bet and rolling the dice of our life, consequently effecting the lives of others around us, playing according to the rules, or breaking them, winning, losing, and always striving for "just one more round." The soundtrack of the great game of dice between Yudhiṣṭhira and Śakuni, the shake of the dice, the moment of silence in which they are suspended midair before they fall, and the declaration "I win" (or alas, vice versa) when they show their verdict, is the soundtrack of human life if one is willing to listen to the epic overtones of one's seemingly mundane existence.

But what is the connection to DK?

First, DK, as much as Bandyopadhyay, is interested in chance and probability. His concept of "KWC," to be discussed in Chapter 3, shows that like Bandyopadhyay, he evaluates probability and chance—not unrelated to the notion of gambling—as integral to who we are and to the ways we operate.

And second, in the present context of DK's attempt to refute and dismiss alleged axioms within and about Indian philosophy, it is interesting to notice that many of these axioms, or myths, are formatted and conserved, as Bandyopadhyay points out, in quadruple paradigms. DK aims his philosophical arrows at each of these paradigms. Four Vedas? See DK's paper "The Yajurveda Text—The Heart of the Veda Yajña: One, Two, or Too Many?" (2007), or the introduction to his final project "The Jaipur Edition of the Ṛgveda" (2007), where he touches on the significance of the Vedic śākhās, which he sees as a sign of plurality and pluralism at the heart of the Vedic tradition.[7] Four varṇas and four Āśramas? See DK's paper "The Varṇāśrama Syndrome of Indian Sociology" (1992). "The issue in the case of Indian social reality," he writes here, "is why it tends to articulate itself primarily in terms of "caste," and sees itself predominantly in its terms alone" (I quote from the author's original manuscript). DK further wonders about the politics behind the classification and hierarchy in the complementary schemes of Varṇa and Āśrama ("caste" and "stages of life"), and he pleads for thinking in new terms about "man, society and polity" in India. But DK's plea for transformation, and profound change is not confined to theory. As Chapter 4 will illustrate, DK's strives for social change in practice, in life, in the world.

The next quadruple paradigm in Bandyopadhyay's list is the paradigm of the four Puruṣārthas ("human goals"), also known as the Caturvarga ("the four elements"). DK challenges this paradigm in his paper "The Myth of the Puruṣārthas" (1986). With a sharp philosophical screwdriver, he unscrews the rusty screws that hold together the four constituents of this old scheme. He highlights the "essential ambivalence," as he puts it, between mokṣa ("deliverance" in Bandyopadhyay) and the other human goals listed here, especially dharma (which is the framework of life and living in the world), and parallelly between gṛhastha and saṃnyāsa (householdership and world renunciation) in the Āśrama scheme. DK challenges the authority and the axiomatic status of the Puruṣārtha scheme, and grieves the reduction of Indian ethics to these four elements alone. Why only four? What about other significant goals or human strivings? "What about philosophy as a puruṣārtha?," Mukund Lath asks apropos DK's appeal to broaden the scope of thinking about human goals and strivings (personal communication, September 2019). To de-schematize and broaden the scope, DK visits the *Mahābhārata*, the mahā-text of Indian ethics, where values clash and where maxims and principles are revealed as inherently ambiguous. Furthermore, he looks into the notion of kāma as a puruṣārtha (desire, or pleasure, as a human goal) vis-à-vis Bhojarāja's treatment of the related notion of śṛṇgāra, the rasa (aesthetic emotion) of erotic love. Through Bhojarāja, the eleventh-century philosopher-king, author of the *Śṛṇgāraprakāśa* (Light on Śṛṇgāra), DK opens a vista for aesthet(h)ics, interlacing the aesthetic and the ethical.

But DK does not just challenge quadruple schemes. He is always willing to challenge any scheme that monopolizes "all thinking" in a certain field or discipline. As another example of DK's attempt to de-schematize and demystify conventional formulas in Indian philosophy, take his reading of the fivefold vṛtti-scheme in chapter 1 of Patañjali's *Yogasūtra*. Here Patañjali classifies the vṛttis, the "movements of the mind," which the procedure of yoga aims to extinguish, into five rubrics: valid knowledge (pramāṇa), invalid knowledge (viparyaya), verbal construction (vikalpa), sleep (nidrā), and memory (smṛti). DK will ask why *these* five, and whether anything is "missing" in this famous scheme, but he opens his critical reading of the *Yogasūtra* by questioning the fundamentals: "What exactly is a vṛtti, and 'how' does it 'arise' and 'cease,' and 'why' does it happen to be so?" (2012, 92). This quote is from his paper "The Undeciphered Text: Anomalies, Problems and Paradoxes in the Yogasūtra" (2006/2012). So much has been written on the *Yogasūtra*, both traditionally and contemporarily, and yet DK sees the text as "undeciphered." The title conveys his working method. It is the "undecipherability" of the text—any text, from Patañjali to Kant—which invites philosophical reflection.

Before I turn to DK's textbook, questioning as any of his other writings, I would like to quickly visit one of DK's most famous essays, "Three Myths about Indian Philosophy," originally published in 1966 and later republished as the opening chapter and the hallmark of his *Indian Philosophy: A Counter Perspective* (1991, 1996, and 2006). Here his philosophical arrows are aimed at three "myths" that "are treated," he writes, "as indubitable facts about Indian philosophy. They seem so self-evident to enthusiasts and detractors alike, that to question them is to question the very concept of Indian philosophy" (1991, 3). The first of these "myths" is the "myth" about Indian philosophy as rooted and soaked in spirituality. "Who does not know," DK writes here sarcastically, "that Indian philosophy is spiritual? Who has not been told that this is what specifically distinguishes it from Western philosophy, and makes it something unique and apart from all the other philosophical traditions of the world?" (1991, 3). The second myth, which DK aims to refute in "Three Myths," is the myth about the authority of the Veda as the watershed that distinguishes between the "six" and the "three," that is, between the so-called "orthodox" and "unorthodox" schools of Indian philosophy. The third myth is the myth of the schools, allegedly fixed and homogenous. "Without the myth of the schools," DK writes here, "no book on Indian philosophy has yet been written" (1991, 12). No book, until his own textbook, which is an experiment in thinking through new frames.

DK's "Three Myths" received several responses. I will mention just two, by two significant voices of contemporary Indian philosophy, Karl Potter and J. N. Mohanty. The former responds not to "Three Myths," but to another variation of the same critique in DK's paper "Indian Philosophy and Mokṣa: Revisiting an Old Controversy" (1984, which became chapter 3 of *Indian Philosophy: A Counter Perspective*). In his paper "Are all Indian Philosophers Indian Philosophers?" (1985), Potter suggests that Indian philosophy and mokṣa are inseparable, and that since DK refuses to accept this "fact," he is not an "Indian philosopher." You are Indian, Potter tells DK, and of course a philosopher, but not "Indian philosopher," in the same way that I (Potter) am American and a philosopher but not an "American philosopher," since my (Potter's) work has nothing to do to with pragmatism and transcendentalism that define American philosophy. The colonial trap is always around the corner, waiting for every Western scholar working on/with Indian materials. In attempt to defend the centrality of mokṣa in Indian philosophy, Potter enters the minefield of "identity" and excludes DK from Indian philosophy. "Can't Daya be happy being an Indian philosopher who is not an Indian philosopher?," he asks (1985, 147), implying that mokṣa is the "entry ticket" to the arena of Indian philosophy. Potter further implies that "Indian philosophy" and "philosophy in India" are two different things. In a recent paper, "Philosophy in India or Indian Philosophy? Some Post-Colonial Questions" (2018), Bhagat Oinam deals with this question, and the underlying theme of identity, in a different way, taking into account, apropos the "Indianness" of Indian philosophy, what he refers to as "the minor traditions of India." "There are several indigenous philosophical narratives," Oinam suggests, "among ethnic communities inhabiting the northeastern and central parts of India. Several rich narratives found in the orature of these indigenous communities are equally important, and must be mapped and shown as part of the Indian philosophical tradition" (2018,

467). Oinam's suggestion ("must be mapped") is effective, since he broadens the scope of Indian philosophy, and of Indianness at large, as to include new areas, both geographical and philosophical. Oinam implies that colonialism is not confined to European, or Western "intrusions." One can think of internal colonialism, of which India's Northeast, for example, finds itself at the receiving end.

Another response to DK's crusade against "myths masqueraded as facts" in Indian philosophy is J. N. Mohanty's paper "Some Thoughts on Daya Krishna's Three Myths" (1996). Mohanty agrees with DK that a one-sided reading of Indian philosophy as spiritual "is shallow and after all a myth" (1996, 68). This does not mean, both for DK and Mohanty, that mokṣa is not a central theme of Indian philosophy. It does mean, according to DK, that Indian philosophy is multicentered, and includes significant players uninterested in mokṣa. Mohanty, more cautious and rooted in the tradition than DK, suggests that,

> not all the concerns of a darśana [school] appear to have a conceivable relevance for the founding project of being instrumental to, or at least exhibiting the possibility of achieving mokṣa. (1996, 73)

According to Mohanty, the ideal of mokṣa does reverberate in each and every darśana, or school, whether strongly or subtly; but nevertheless, he agrees with DK that the institution of darśana and the concept of mokṣa need to be rethought in a more flexible, less schematic way. "I am convinced," Mohanty writes, that

> a darśana is not a closely-knit, organic unity, as the historical development of a system shows. Many old doctrines are reinterpreted, modified, rejected, and new ones added. [. . .] We need to notice that the cliché of "six systems" does not and cannot claim antiquity (did it all begin with Max Muller?). Mādhavācārya's *Sarvadarśanasaṃgraha* [the famous fourteenth-century Compendium of Darśanas] lists many more, including the Grammarians and the Paśupatas. [. . . But] there is no doubt that from very ancient times the location of "schools" did figure out prominently in philosophical interchange. Even the best of philosophers thought from within a "school." (1996, 73, 74, 75)

The fact that even the best philosophers do not claim originality but are committed to the darśana framework, results, Mohanty further writes, in "a certain blindness, in the culture, to the thoughts of an individual qua that individual, to the innovative and interpretive originality of the thinker." But there are exceptions, he suggests, namely, rare cases in which an individual thinker "proclaimed his defiance of the school's tradition and insisted on his own innovation." Raghunātha Śiromaṇi, Mohanty writes, is "a striking example of this individualism." "We only wish," he adds on a personal note, "there were many more like him, so that the appearance of rigidity of the systems could have received the severe jolt it needed" (1996, 76).

Raghunātha Śiromaṇi takes me to *Indian Philosophy: A New Approach*, DK's alternative textbook. But is a textbook of Indian philosophy without mokṣa and the schools on its very first page, and moreover without the "myths" and "syndromes" that DK devoted a lifetime to refute, imaginable? DK aims at the allegedly unimaginable. First, he emphasizes philosophy of language, which crosses boundaries, rigid or loose, of schools, systems, and traditions of thinking. Second, he highlights debates, disputes, and disagreements. In DK's narrative, Indian philosophy develops and expands from one debate to another. Third, DK replaces old exclamation marks with new question marks. He invites his readers to think with him, to sketch this alternative picture together with him. And since he does not merely write about the history of philosophy in India, but "does" philosophy (yes, even when he writes a textbook he is thinking in the present tense), his reflection applies both to the texts, thinkers and ideas that he writes about, and to his own reflection, to his own lens. Fourth, DK elevates the social and political to center-stage. He does not write a "sterile" history of Indian philosophy. Colonialism and casteism are not below or besides his frame. The ugly and the uncomfortable are as much part of his discussion as the beautiful and the spectacular. And fifth, DK emphasizes what he sees as newness and creativity, for instance in a chapter dedicated to Raghunātha Śiromaṇi, or "Raghunātha the rebel," as DK calls him.

"The philosophical traditions of India," DK opens his chapter on Raghunātha,

> have seldom seen a person like Raghunātha, the great Nyāya thinker of the 16th century, who openly and deliberately flouted and criticized the well-known accepted positions of his own traditional school of thought. (1997, 174).

And Jonardon Ganeri opens a chapter of his own on Raghunātha (in his abovementioned *The Lost Age of Reason*), suggesting that,

> Raghunātha Śiromaṇi (1460–1540) is the first modern philosopher, his ideas single-handedly responsible for the emergence of a new form

> of Navya-Nyāya, the "new reason," in the sixteenth and seventeenth centuries. (2011, 39).

DK spotlights Raghunātha's critique of the padārtha system of "categories," as formulated in the *Vaiśeṣika-sūtra*. In a previous chapter of his textbook, "The Crystallization: Jaimini and Bādarāyaṇa, Gautama and Kaṇāda," DK touches on the ambiguity of the concept of padārtha, often rendered as "category," that intermixes ontology and epistemology (1997, 38). The title of this chapter is interesting. DK does not speak of the schools of Mīmāṃsā, Vedānta, Nyāya, and Vaiśeṣika, but of the authors or compilers of the sūtras, the root-texts that these schools worked with and from. DK rectifies that "certain blindness to the thoughts of the individual," that Mohanty spoke of. He engages in a dialogue with these compilers or authors, agrees, takes issue with, and raises questions. He shifts aside their legendary status as "forefathers" and thinks with them, through them. DK is bowled over by the fact that Raghunātha "challenge[d] the whole theory of padārtha and show[ed] that the theory was both incomplete and inadequate." This challenge, DK adds, "marks a radical break in the tradition of philosophizing in India, as it is the doctrine of categories which is at the heart of the understanding of both knowledge and reality in any philosophical tradition" (1997, 175). DK enumerates the six categories of the padārtha system, as also the later addition of abhāva, "absence" or "non-existence," as a supplementary category.[8] He further discusses the addition of new categories, or padārthas, by Raghunātha himself. I cannot delve here into the details, but I would like to suggest that like Raghunātha, whenever DK looked into a classical scheme, or theory, he questioned its completeness and adequacy. We saw earlier that such is the case with the quadruple theory of the puruṣārthas ("human goals"). In his textbook, DK discusses a fifth puruṣārtha, "Bhakti, the New Puruṣārtha: The Tidal Wave from the South," as the title of chapter 12 suggests. Still in his chapter on Raghunātha, DK confesses that he lacks source materials that will enable him to write the chapter in a more comprehensive way. He therefore relies on the work of Karl Potter and Wilhelm Halbfass. His confession about lack of accessibility is significant. DK used to write to friends, colleagues, and libraries, in search for materials. Back in the 1990s, when the textbook was written, archive digitization and the internet, that many of us now take for granted, were not where they are today. But even today, in numerous places on this planet, there are ardent scholars and students of philosophy with lesser degrees of accessibility. DK inspiringly shows that thinking is not and should not be fully dependent on accessibility. He used the materials available to him at the time, reached the conclusions they enabled him to reach, and invited/encouraged further research into the contribution of Raghunātha. Such research can be found in Ganeri's *The Lost Age of Reason*, that DK did not live to read. Raghunātha Śiromaṇi is one of Ganeri's protagonists, alongside other intriguing protagonists such as Dārā Shikoh (eldest son of Mughal emperor Shāh Jahāṇ) and Yaśovijaya Gaṇi, "one of Jainism's great intellectuals," as Ganeri introduces him (2011, 32). If the protagonists are new, both in DK and in Ganeri, then the story is new. A new story of Indian philosophy—this is what Daya the Rebel was striving for.

2

Thinking Creatively About the Creative Act

A Dialogue with Daya Krishna

This chapter enacts a "grafting" of two texts: DK's paper "Thinking Creatively About the Creative Act" and my own "commentary," interwoven between the lines and the paragraphs of his text. Grafting is also the crux of DK's paper. He suggests that it is through one's meeting with the arts that a grafting of being and becoming occurs. Becoming in DK, is the never-ending creative process bubbling under the surface of every work of art, including the human person as a work of art, which each of us makes, or can make, of ourselves.

"Thinking Creatively" is in fact a lecture delivered by DK at the University of Punjab, Chandigarh, sometime in the late 1990s, later transcribed and published in the *Punjab University Research Bulletin*. It is a paper in aesthetics, but interestingly, DK's paradigmatic example for the creative act, as he puts it, that a work of art, any work of art is the product of, is philosophizing, or "the act of philosophy." If Bharata, author of the *Nāṭya-śāstra*, the root-text of art and aesthetics in India, dated "somewhere" in the first centuries CE, focuses on theatre, and his great commentator, Abhinavagupta (tenth century, Kashmir), writes on art and thinks primarily of poetry, then DK's model of fascination, the art-form closest to his heart, is the philosophical text and the thinking-thread that binds it together, what he refers to as "the art of the conceptual." He therefore speaks here about the meeting, interaction, or dialogue with a philosophical text, as the emblematic example for any meeting with a work of art. "I understand a text better," DK says, "when I ask myself what this person [the author] is trying to do. I make that text my own [. . .] I get into his work, into his thought process [. . .] and carry it in a direction where it was not taken." This is exactly what I intend to do in the following paragraphs with DK's own text. I will get into his work, into his thought process. I will write this chapter together with him. The procedure is this: after every few lines or paragraphs by DK, I will "interfere" and respond, explain, contextualize, decontextualize, raise a question, criticize, or emphasize a point or argument of his. “One cannot understand any work,” DK says, “unless one ceases to see it as a finished product.” Moreover, he suggests that a text is always an invitation for a dialogue. I accept the invitation, and work simultaneously as guest and host: a guest in DK’s text, and a host of his text and ideas on my own canvas. His paper is reproduced here in `Courier New`, my response in Times New Roman.

> Friends,
> I have nothing to show you on the screen, rather I would like you to recall things on the screen of your memory. After all, art is not such an isolated separate thing from life that each of us, at least to some extent, has not had an experience of it.

DK is interested, as the title of his paper indicates, in the creative act. Since the products of creativity are not his focus, there is “nothing” to show on the screen. But at the very beginning of his talk, DK makes a significant move: he expropriates the theme under discussion from the hands of the specialists. As usual, his usual, DK refuses to accept any authority. To think about the creative act, it is implied here, one need not be an insider, whether an accomplished artist, gallerist, collector, or pandit of the Alaṅkāra-Śāstra. The screen of one’s memory and a questioning approach are enough.

> In fact, the first thing I would like to consider is whether the usual way of thinking about the arts is the way it ought to be done.

The “usual way of thinking” about the arts and the aesthetic experience, that DK is about to criticize, is thinking along the lines of the Theory of Rasa. This is not the time or place to expand on this theory or to try to capture the meaning of the notion of “rasa.”[1] In a nutshell, I propose that this theory, from Bharata to Abhinavagupta, is essentially subjectivist. This is to say that that it “measures” a work of art according to the “taste” (rasa) or the emotional effect that it leaves on the viewer, listener, reader, or more broadly, the appreciator. The emphasis is on the subject. But the word “subject” is tricky, since the arts—according to this framework—have the capacity to reveal an ideal appreciator in each of us, a perceptive selfhood so to say, hidden deep under (or beyond or between the lines of) personal circumstances and predicaments. This is the sahṛdaya, rendered by KCB in his classical essay “The Concept of Rasa” as the Heart Universal (2008, 354). He explains:

> Artistic enjoyment [rasa] is not a feeling of the enjoyer on his own account; it involves the dropping of self-consciousness, while the feeling that is enjoyed is freed from its reference to an individual subject and eternalized in the Heart Universal. (2008, 354)

It is the distance from the object, and moreover from the subject, as long as the subject is "colored" by "objectivity," which makes this theory subjectivist; subjectivist in the (almost) ātmanic sense of the Heart Universal. But the object, namely, the work of art, is not insignificant. Its significance lies in the fact that it has to be crafted or executed in a way that will ignite a certain "taste" or aesthetic emotion. The emotive trace, which is the heart of the matter, depends on and results from one's meeting with a work of art. Hence for the Theory of Rasa, by and large, the artwork is instrumental, and subordinated to the effect at the subtle layer of consciousness, or even meta-consciousness, which the notion of sahṛdaya refers to. DK's critique is not against the Theory of Rasa, but against its authority and monopoly. He criticizes the reduction of art to emotion alone. This critique finds its sharpest expression in his paper "Rasa: The Bane of Indian Aesthetics" (2004). For DK, Rasa is a bane in the sense that it prevents thinking about the arts in other ways, not necessarily through the prism of emotion, and moreover since it marginalizes the object, the material, the work of art. According to DK, art and aesthetics cannot and should not be reduced to a single element or dimension, whatever this dimension or element is. Aesthetics and art, he emphasizes, should not be analyzed and evaluated always with the same tools, with the same measuring stick.

What would be an alternative way of thinking? For instance, to focus on the social and political aspects of a work of art. This is what Gopal Guru aims to do in his paper "Aesthetic of Touch and Skin: An Essay in Contemporary Indian Political Phenomenology" (2016), in which he speaks of cricket, of sports, as aesthetic experience. The handmade leather cricket ball is the center of focus on the TV frame. It is extracted and abstracted away from its maker, the Dalit worker. The ball is considered beautiful, the worker ugly; the leather of the ball appealing, the skin of the "untouchable" worker repulsive. Guru mockingly describes the "purity ritual" in which the upper-caste cricketer spits on the ball and "cleans" it (from its history, Guru implies) with his saliva, before bowling. Guru's conclusion is that "the aesthetic life of the cricketer and cricket lover is unreflective. It is also without any moral responsibility" (2016, 304). He lets the cat out of the bag, and suggests that "Dalit aesthetics hints at the language of justice and morality" (2016, 310). "Aesthetics without ethics," he finally writes, "is breath-less" (2016, 314). It is without breath, without life. It is dead.

But is Rasa aesthetics blind to the social realm? Not if you ask Sheldon Pollock. In his paper "The Social Aesthetic and Sanskrit Literary Theory" (2001), Pollock argues that even though Rasa deals with the emotive aspect of consciousness, and hence seems distant from the world and the society, in truth this is not the case. As a matter of fact, he writes, "the social impinges on Sanskrit literature and literary theory at every possible level" (2001, 223). Drawing on Jagannātha Paṇḍitarāja's mid-seventeenth-century *Rasagaṅgādhara*, Pollock suggests that Rasa is rooted in ethics. "The aesthetic sentiment," he writes, "has transmogrified [in Jagannātha] into something like aesthetic moralism" (2001, 214). Pollock works with the intriguing notion of rasābhāsa, pertaining to "false feelings," as he puts it.[2] "There is no uncertainty," he writes, "as to the fact that rasābhāsa results from some transgression of the social order measured against a set of moral norms" (2001, 213). According to Jagannātha, desire for "inappropriate objects," for instance for someone beyond one's station (the queen or a teacher's wife), violates the social order and hardly produces the erotic rasa (śṛṇgāra) "in its pure or authentic form." The stock example for rasābhāsa, DK suggests in "Rasa: The Bane of Aesthetics," is "Rāvaṇa and the way he feels for Sītā" in the *Rāmāyaṇa*. "Why should this not be an example of śṛṅgāra, but only of rasābhāsa, or pseudo-śṛṅgāra," he writes, "remains the unanswered question for the theory [of Rasa]" (2004, 126). Pollock would answer that this is the case since it is an unethical desire (Rāvaṇa's) for another man's wife (for Sītā, Rāma's wife). In reply to this claim of "moral appropriateness," DK wonders if the emotion of erotic love, śṛṅgāra in the Theory of Rasa, is not always intermixed with a sense of transgression. Pollock admits that "the entire question of rasābhāsa becomes intelligible only against the background of a broader normative discourse" (2001, 211). In this respect, he mentions the sahṛdaya, the abovementioned ideal appreciator of art. "When one learns to be a good reader, a rasika or a sahṛdaya," Pollock writes, "one is learning what is normative in the everyday world" (2001, 215). But what if this so-called normative social structure needs to be shaken and transformed? Gopal Guru is interested not in the indulgences of kings such as Rāma and Rāvaṇa, but in the hardships of the weakened and the marginalized. Aesthetics interlaced with moral responsibility, Guru maintains, cannot be rooted in a social order that allows exclusion, marginalization, ghettoization, and bracketing (these painful concepts are from his paper "Dalits from margin to margin," 2000). Rather, it should aim to subvert, rearrange, and challenge every unethical social order. Art, for Guru and DK, is not just about "purifying" or "elevating" the emotive dimension of the rasika, the ideal appreciator. It has a transformative social role to play, which for both of them is one of its most significant prayojanas, or goals.

Back in "Thinking Creatively," still in the opening paragraph, DK writes:

Art is certainly close to us all in some form or another. We all remember poems, or songs, or Urdu couplets, or some paintings, a piece of architecture or a song that we have heard which has taken us out of ourselves. It takes us out of our daily round of living when we recall it. And when we have recalled it, it comes with a freshness to us again, and makes life worth living. What exactly is this experience? How shall we think about it? Shall the thinking about the arts be confined to the view of the specialists who consider themselves to be the connoisseurs? I suggest that this is a wrong approach. There may be many sampradāyas, as we call them, or schools which attempt to understand art. But, basically, what is the understanding of a work of art? The whole problem of demarcation has already failed to even distinguish between science and non-science. The problem of demarcation is the problem of criterion and classification; and whatever criteria or classification one adopts, it is bound to have ambiguous instances where the decision to apply it or not to apply it is a purely arbitrary one. And yet, we do make classifications. We do point out differences that seem to be important to us. And thus, the notion of art connotes and denotes something which is considered to be important enough to be differentiated. But, what is the criterion of differentiation? Art is a paradigmatic example of the creative act. Can art be conceived without thinking that someone created it? Not only this, can we conceive art without reference to the senses that we have? We, of course, talk about the visual and the aural arts. We, of course, talk of tactile qualities but not of an art built on tactuality alone. But, what about the senses of smell and taste? There is the art of perfumery and the art of cooking, for example. But they never achieve the status of either an art or craft. Why not? One should reflect on this question as to why only the eyes and the ears are supposed to give rise to art.

Why only (or mostly) eyes and ears? DK would have enjoyed Salman Rushdie's novel *The Enchantress of Florence* (2008). Here, the art of perfumery has a significant role, at least when a mysterious yellow-haired man attempts to make his way into Emperor Akbar's court in Fatehpur Sikri of the sixteenth century and meet the Shahenshah ("king of kings") himself. A prostitute called Mattress "turns his body into a symphony for the nose," as Rushdie puts it, the symphony metaphor "elevating" the art of perfumery to the level of music. The depiction of the artist (Mattress) at work is fabulous ("anointing him with civet and violet, magnolia and lily, narcissus and calembic, as well as drops of other occult fluids whose names he did not even like to ask, fluids extracted from the sap of Turkish, Cypriot, and Chinese trees, as well as a wax from the intestines of a whale"). "Before you reach the emperor's presence," she explains the logic behind her artistry to her client who now carries her art on him, "you will have to satisfy many other men. So the perfume for the emperor will lie hidden at first beneath the fragrances that will please lesser personages, which will fade away when you reach the imperial presence." And it works. These perfumes take him all the way to the Diwan-e-Khas , the House of Private Audience, but here he has to face Abul Fazl, the grand vizier of the Mughal emperor. "Excellency," Abul Fazl turns to him sardonically,

> I perceive that you have perfumed yourself with the fragrance devised for the seduction of kings, and I deduce that you are not entirely innocent of our ways—in fact, not innocent at all. I did not trust you when I first heard about you some moments ago, and now that I have smelled you I trust you even less.

The visitor, Rushdie tells us, "understood that he was like a man stripped naked beneath the all-seeing gaze of the king's favorite, and that only the truth, or something as convincing as the truth, would save him now."[3] The art of perfumery casts a spell on the royal guards all the way up to the vizier. Now another art is needed to prolong the spell, an art closer to Rushdie's heart, the art of storytelling.

In his introduction to *The Bloomsbury Handbook of Indian Aesthetics and the Philosophy of Art* (2018), Arindam Chakrabarti visits chapter 3 of Vātsyāyana's *Kāmasūtra*, which enumerates the sixty-four kalās, including—he tells us (and selects a few examples from the long list)—"singing, playing musical instruments, dancing, etiquette, culinary arts, the arts of weaponry and war, gymnastics, knowing how to compose and scan verses, arithmetic, clay-image making, knowing how to guess human character from conduct and gestures, cosmetics, bed-making, wine-preparation, making artificial flowers, and the art of painting and well-decoration" (2018, 4). He does not mention perfumery (or the art of making perfumes, gandhayukti), which is also included in this list. But what is kalā? Art? Craft? Both together? "The concept of kalā," Chakrabarti suggests, "may extend far beyond the European notion of art. But that should not lead us to jump to the conclusion that the sixty-four arts are mostly crafts. Like the notions of justice, or rationality, the notion of art has also got to be trans-culturally available" (2018, 4). Chakrabarti later repeats the same plea and writes that the components of the kalā list "should not be sniffed as mere crafts" (2018, 5). His articulation ("sniffed") is reminiscent of the art of perfumery, and he rightly warns against the imposition of Western categories on classical Indian formulations. It is not implausible that DK thinks through the concept of kalā, and keeps in mind the *Kāmasūtra* list, or a parallel list, when he asks, "why only the eyes and the ears?"

Back in "Thinking Creatively," DK continues to question:

> What is this attempt to understand the arts? We try to understand nature, but can art be understood in the same way as we understand nature? Can we use the same methodology, the same categories with which we try to understand an object which we consider to be given to us by nature? Even within what man creates there is a diversity. Man creates for all sorts of purposes and sometimes he creates only for the joy of it, for the playfulness of it, or just for the adventure of exploration. What is this that he does? In the understanding of this, shall we use categories and concepts that are totally different from that of understanding a work of inanimate nature?
>
> I would like to share with you an attempt at understanding the phenomena of creation itself which, as far as I know, has not generally been attempted. What attracts our attention is the product of creativity and not the process of which it is the end result. We are taken in by the products of an activity.

DK calls attention to the act, the action, the process, the forces in operation instead of the products of art. The picture of world and self (the arts are located somewhere between world and self, working with and within both) as stable, or fixed, is for him both illusory and a matter of habit. We have been taught, almost programmed, to think in terms of "things." It is no wonder that DK's very last paper, which he never completed, is titled "Thinking without Things, Without Identity, without Non-Contradiction and Yet Thinking Still."

> When one sees a painting, one sees a frame; something is framed there. I was just saying to someone in the tea-break, one of the participants, that the space in the painting is different from the physical space in which the painting is located on the wall; yet in a certain sense, the space of the painting is far more real than the space of the canvas. But it is the "unreal" that one values, which is not the "real," i.e., the space of the canvas on which the "unreal" space of the painting is created.
>
> Just a few minutes ago, a problem had arisen in the conversation. What about the "space" that architecture makes visible? It seems difficult to answer this question, as unlike painting, the contrast between the two "spaces" is not visible itself. Is it the same type of unreal space that is created in painting, or does it raise new problems? There is the flatness of the space in the canvas contrasted with the depth of the space that is created in the painting, or that which appears there, or that has been made to "appear." In architecture, the space is made visible by enclosing it through walls or by any other structure. But what is the relation of the space that is made to appear in architecture to the space in which architecture itself is built? In architecture, it is very difficult to say, because there is no contrast. There is no contrast between space and the space that appears. There is the space, and that space itself is made visible. How is it made visible? By setting up boundaries. Let the boundaries collapse and that which was made visible by drawing the boundaries also collapses into nothingness. The infinity of space cannot be seen, cannot be made visible. It is made visible by drawing finite boundaries around it. I was referring to this conversation because I think it points to a factor which I would like to emphasize today and to share with you, a point that I have been thinking about for some time and have tried to apply to the understanding of the arts.

DK suggests that a work of art "exists" in a space and time of its own that unstitch the ordinary, day-to-day time and space and enable us to go beyond them. Cinema is a wonderful example. Whenever I watch *Mughal-e-Azam* (1960, directed by K. Asif, a film that deserves to be watched again and again), I find myself in Emperor Akbar's court in sixteenth-century Fatehpur Sikri (the same royal court that Rushdie brings to life in *The Enchantress of Florence*). A good movie takes me away from my own life, with its spatial-temporal frame, into another realm. I am sure that the readers would share the shock of "falling back" into one's life when the movie is over, finding oneself suddenly in the streets of Tel Aviv or Jaipur, catching a bus or a rickshaw back home. But DK realizes that art does not merely cross borders but also works with them, uses them, plays with them. DK speaks in praise of borders (in architecture), and at the same time illustrates the effectivity of blurring borderlines, intermixing a tea-break conversation with his lecture. The intimacy of this conversation, where he is not "the speaker" but an interlocutor, is brought into the formal lecture, and changes the relationship between speaker and listeners. The listeners are now participants, equal partners who think with DK on the creative act.

> The title I had suggested for this lecture is "Thinking Creatively about the Creative Act." Of the two sets of creativity here, one is the creative act of which the paradigmatic example is exhibited in the arts. On the other hand, we "think" about it. Thinking is the second level of creative activity, and when it is done about the art, it assumes a first level of exercise of that creative activity which resulted in the production of what we call the "art object." We want to understand it. But what is this "thinking" about the arts? Is this thinking itself a "creative" activity? Or does it merely reflect on the nature of the art object, or upon the creative activity whose end result is the work of art, or both? What does it do? Because unless we understand "thinking" itself, we cannot understand it. Why do we not talk about creativity in the realm of thinking? It is because we are taken in by the illusions of the creations of thought. If you take a book, or, for example, the papers that have been presented and will be presented to you [here today, in this conference], they have a beginning and an end, and you can read them from start to finish. But what is

> the process that has gone into their production? Is that just a logical process, or a mechanical process, or something else?
>
> I want to shift your attention from the products to the process, and from the process to that which lies beyond them. For example, one cannot understand any work unless one ceases to see it as a finished product. The same person who has written an article will go back and write on the same subject again, unless he has become intellectually dead. Also, he is not the only person who is thinking; others are also thinking, and not just as the result of the activity of one "single" person alone. But if we take this aspect seriously, then the work that is produced would not be seen as something "finished" and "final." Instead, it will be seen as a temporary halting place for thought, which at that point of time the author who had been merely an "instrument" of thought, felt that there was something worth saying, even though he "knew" that what he was saying was incomplete and had some objections to it for which at least at that time, he had no answer. But still he thought that in spite of the incompleteness and the unanswered objections, it was worth saying. The reader, on the other hand, has the illusion that it is something complete, something final. The tentativeness of the work, which is so obvious to the author is hidden from the reader, and he is taken in by the format in which the thought is presented.

For DK, thinking is a form of art. Therefore, thinking about the arts is a matter of dialogue between two art forms—thinking and whatever art-form or artwork one thinks about, with, and from. Moreover, creativity, according to DK, is a collective endeavor, both in thinking and in any other medium of art. DK sees the products of creativity as tentative, as a moment in the never-ending flow of creativity. Therefore, more than being interested in a certain painting, poem, or philosophical argument, DK is interested in the collective, perennial process that they are an instant of. He criticizes the "distance" of the Theory of Rasa from the work of art, that is, the fact that it sees the artwork as secondary and instrumental. But his "process, not products" approach bears a similar flaw. If it is primarily the process that deserves our attention, the subterranean stream of creativity, bubbling under the surface of every work of art, then the artwork itself (the painting, this specific painting on the wall of the gallery), just like in Rasa, takes a backseat.

DK's insistence on the primacy of the process sits well with the way classical narratives are seen and worked with in India. Take, for example, the continuous retelling of the great epics, from medieval India to Bollywood. Or as A. K. Ramanujan puts it in his seminal paper "Three Hundred *Rāmāyaṇas*," "the story has no closure, although it may be enclosed in a text" (1991, 46). But again, I see a tension between the "process first" approach and DK's persistent plea, paper after paper and book after book—a plea to all those interested and involved in Indian philosophy—not to forget the objective world, the material aspects of life, for the sake of "subjectivity" of any kind, from the arts to metaphysics or the spiritual quest.

> But, in the realm of thought, it was something "cognitive" that troubled the author. It may have been a question to which he wanted to seek an answer, or it may have been a problem to which he wanted to seek a solution. These questions and these problems might have arisen accidentally in his mind, or for any reason whatsoever. But because the question became his question, because the problem became his problem, he tried to answer it. But we who read the book do not see the question or the problem to which the author was finding an answer or seeking a solution. We do not ask ourselves what the question was to which the thinker was seeking an answer, or what the problem was to which he was seeking a solution. However, the question that he asked is in a sense, perennial, because he may again write another book as he may find the earlier answer unsatisfactory. The thinkers who come after him either take up from where he left off or raise some new questions. Thus the story goes on, and we have in this country at least three thousand years of recorded history where such thinking has been documented.
>
> The impression that the present thinking is the only thinking that goes on in one's culture or in one's language is an illusion. Just as there is the illusion of finality about the book, there is the illusion of finality about the present. We all seem to believe that the present is the only reality, but at the end of the biological journey, or

> the journey of thinking, or the journey of creativity, one is almost where one was at the beginning. Have you ever met a person with a great reputation, whose books you have read and then gone to meet him and talked to him? You might have been surprised to find that he feels himself to be even more unsure than he was when he began his career.

DK emphasizes again the perennial "journey of thinking, or journey of creativity." Interestingly, he asks his listeners if they ever met an author whose work they have read. Such a meeting has the capacity of revealing to the reader the "living" process of creativity, hence to release him from "the illusion of finality." Like in Roland Barthes ("The Death of the Author," 1967), DK hardly believes that the text "belongs" to its author (or in India, when the author is often anonymous, to a certain tradition). For DK, we have seen, the text is an invitation to take part in the thinking process that produced this text among other texts, already written and that are about to be written. For DK, like Barthes, the question is not what the author meant, and the task of the reader is not to decipher this "original" meaning. The crux of the matter for him is to think with and through the text. In Barthes, the death of the author is a matter of challenging authorial authority. The death of the author corresponds with the death of God (Nietzsche) and the death of the father (or the fantasy about his death, as in Freud's Oedipus Complex). Likewise, DK refuses to accept the authority that comes along with the text. This refusal is transparent when he reads classical texts—the Veda, the Upaniṣads, the Sūtras—and treats their authors (known or unknown) exactly in the same way that he treats contemporary interlocutors. In traditional circles, this approach was not always accepted with great tolerance. In Chapter 1, I quoted G. R. Malkani, who writes on DK's critique of Śaṅkara that "It is difficult to believe that Daya Krishna is competent to find fault with the father of the system." Malkani's choice of the word "father" aptly fits my present discussion.

Back in "Thinking Creatively," DK continues to explain his "text as a process" approach:

> I understand a text better when I ask myself what this person [the author] is trying to do. I make that text my own and then see what question arises in my own mind about what he does, about what he is saying. And then, I try to see whether his thoughts moved in the same way as mine or not. And thus, I get into his work, into his thought process, and then I see that he has been making choices all the

> time among paths that he did not take, but which he could have taken. In fact, the interesting thing about the work is not what has been done, but what has been left undone. And then I take up the same thing, and carry it in a direction where it was not taken. By "I," I mean anybody who approaches the text in this way and thus joins the perennially ongoing process of thinking, whose beginning no one knows and whose end no one can foretell.

To say "whose" on the process of thinking is an interesting choice. It implies that this process has its own persona and agency. In his abovementioned paper, "Identity through Necessary Change," Mukund Lath portrays the rāga, a non-translatable notion pertaining to the basic "unit," "entity," or aesthetic form at the heart of classical Indian music as a "living" and "felt" entity. Moreover, he suggests that in the ālāpa, the overture of any execution of a rāga (whether it is sung or played), the musician invites or evokes the rāga to introduce itself to him and his listeners. Along similar lines, in his commentary of *Yogasūtra* 3.6—in reply to the question when should the yoga-practitioner proceed from one yogic stage (bhūmi) to the next—Vyāsa (Patañjali's foremost commentator) states (or possibly quotes from another source) that "yoga is the teacher" (yoga eva upādhyāyaḥ). This is to say that the practitioner of yoga should ask no one but yoga itself (depicted as a "living" and "felt" entity, like the rāga in Lath's formulation) if and when to take the next step. Along similar lines again, I would suggest that according to DK, the thinker often feels the "independence" or the "autonomic power" of thinking—thinking that takes him in a certain route, which he did not necessarily foresee or planned to take.

DK's present paragraph ("I understand a text better," "I make the text my own") is interesting also in the sense that DK invites his listeners into his philosophical laboratory, or philosophical kitchen, and shares his working method. His whole project of reading classical materials anew is folded in this short paragraph.

> But, how do we apply this to the understanding of the arts? In my view, thinkers are conceptual artists. They deal with concepts, create new worlds of concepts by giving prominence to one concept rather than another. They bring concepts into being, or change old concepts by bringing them into relationship with other concepts in the context of which they had never occurred before.

This in a nutshell is DK's understanding of "newness" in the realm of ideas, in thinking; newness that he constantly, ceaselessly, pleads for.

> How can we apply what we call "the art of conceptual creativity" to the understanding of the creative act which is embodied in a work of art? I suggest that the understanding of an artist will be totally mistaken if it is not seen in terms of its own creativity. Most attempts at understanding are attempts to deny the creativity aspects of the creative act itself. They try to think about it in causal terms.

Here, DK's distinction between "creativity" and "causality" is to be noted. In his terminology, "creativity" is the antonym of "causality." In truth, this paper ("Thinking Creatively") should be read together with its twin-paper "Thinking with Causality about Causality: Reflections on a Concept Determining All Thought about Action and Knowledge" (2005). The twinhood of these papers is a demonstration of DK's argument about the continuity of thinking from one "product" (here, paper) to another. The title ("Thinking with Causality") personifies the concept of causality. In the same way that the musician is in dialogue with the rāga (as we saw earlier), the conceptual artist listens carefully to the concepts with "whom" he works. Causality is not transparent for DK. He notices it, works with it, and mainly, refuses to be determined by it. In the following lines, he continues to explain the distinction between causality and creativity:

> We may have a psychoanalytic approach, but how does it help? Why should I be interested in somebody's subconscious drive? In fact, the causal understanding at any level, whether it is sociological, philosophical, or historical, at whatever level it may operate, does not help. It is totally irrelevant to the understanding of the creative novelty of the act. To the extent that such approaches to the understanding of art are successful, they merely show the failure of the artist to achieve what he was trying to achieve. I can argue for this position at least to some extent in the field of which I know a little better, "the history of thought." I can take a great thinker and show that such attempts to understand him are wrong because they do not illuminate what he was trying to do.

> Therefore, the next point that I would like to share with you is that any understanding of the arts which sees them in terms of causality, at whatever level, is mistaken, though most people will continue to do so because they do not know what else to do. It is so easy to find or to suggest the causal factors, without even caring or worrying as to what would validate their contention. A causal hypothesis can only be validated if one can reproduce the conditions and see if the effect will be reproduced or not; even if we have a probability hypothesis, the effect will be reproduced most of the time. Would you like the work of art to be "reproduced" in this manner? Certainly, I hope, not.

DK's critique evokes the question of context. Creativity, for him, is not and cannot be bound by context. Here Mukund Lath's portrayal of the ālāpa, the locus of creativity in Rāga music, comes to mind again. "The rāga pattern," he writes,

> is given and forms the basis of a free and open ālāpa, or improvised elaboration according to a set of rules which assume the pattern, but allow room for imagination. [. . .] Identity in a rāga cannot be restricted to a given pattern or even rules, since a good ālāpa reweaves them in its own way, and a great ālāpa can even transform them. (2018, 7–8)

Lath touches on the subtle position of the musician between nāda-rūpa and bhāva-rūpa, the structural and the creative aspects of the rāga, respectively. The interplay between these two is what makes the rāga. However, it is the non-causal (to use DK's terminology) bhāva-rūpa that is the crux of the matter. "The question of the identity of a rāga," Lath clearly suggests, "can be seen as: what is rāga-bhāva?" (2018, 10), or what is creativity, or the creative power that reweaves and transforms structure, pattern and rules?

The question of reproduction in the field of art, or of "the work of art in the age of mechanical reproduction" (apropos Walter Benjamin's famous 1935 essay), is beyond my present discussion, but it cannot be dismissed with "certainly, I hope, not," as DK has done here.

> Therefore, causal understanding, though tempting, is always irrelevant to the situation. However, one shall always be tempted to use it, as this

> "model of understanding" is built on our understanding of nature in respect to which we want to reproduce the events by having knowledge of the causes. As we are interested in power, we are interested in reproducibility; we are interested in controlling the cause so that we may control the effects. In fact, if one has causal knowledge but no possibility of control over the phenomenon, the knowledge becomes totally irrelevant. It is only when one can control the causes that causal knowledge is worthwhile.
>
> Most frameworks of understanding rest on the assumptions of a causal understanding in some form or other. Causal understanding sometimes may be contextual understanding by nature. But unless one can free it of the context in which it arises, or to which it is bound, the understanding does not have much significance. When I think, I think in a particular language; I think in a particular tradition. I am situated somewhere in space and time and culture; I have friends and I have a biography. But to the extent that I am bound by these, I am determined by them in my act of creativity.

The last few lines, written in the first person, resonate DK's claim and belief that thinking, perennial and collective, is necessarily broader than one's circumstances ("I am situated," "I have," "I am determined").

> Every great master used a language that he has learnt, but he is not bound by it. Similarly, one may situate a person's thought in the matrix of previous thinking, but if it could be totally explained by it, it would be a total failure. One would not be interested in it. I suggest that any attempt at understanding any work of art in which there is any element of creativity, in terms that have little to do with creativity, or that have only a partial relationship with it, in terms of either materials or conditions, will not help one to understand it. If what I am saying is even partially true, then I would like to suggest some new dimensions in which we might try to understand a work of art in a non-causal creative perspective.

Firstly, there is a radical division between the arts, that is, the literary and the non-literary. Language, to which the literary arts owe their being, is one of the strangest entities in the world. It has no being-for-itself. It has a being which is completely outside itself. But even when something is undeciphered, that is, we do not know what exactly is "outside" of it, we still call it a language. But until it is deciphered, it does not "exist" for us. Even the greatest piece of literature in a language one does not know is a "closed," "dead" thing for that person. What then, exactly, is the reality of language, which completely exists outside of itself? Language is not always transparent, though it is always presupposed that it ought to be so. One has to first understand its meaning, but what is "meaning"? The whole realm of literary arts presents one with a very strange situation. New words certainly arise, but how few they are. The new vocabulary that is added to language by a succession of writers even across centuries is negligible. Rather, it is with new combinations of the same words that new worlds of meaning are created. But what is this creation of new worlds of meaning? What is meant by the novelty of meaning? This "meaning" is not exactly cognitive in the sense that it has no "reference" which could possibly make it true or false. It is not a scientific fact to be tested to find whether it really is, as it has been stated in the language. In fact, the question of truth or validation does not operate in this context. Why does it not operate? Let me give you a simple example. Two drinks, if taken separately, will not have much effect on one. Gin and Dry Vermouth are the obvious examples. But if one mixes them in a certain proportion, one gets a very strong drink called Dry Martini. The same happens to be the case with language; single, isolated words may not have much effect, but a master brings them together and there is a sudden explosion of new meaning. This happens in the conceptual realm also. Two concepts are brought together, and suddenly a new thought emerges. But the world of meanings that one builds

> is a strange phenomenon that needs a long exploration of its own. However, I would not like to discuss this issue further, as I wish to return to the issue of the non-literary arts and the problem regarding their understanding.

Regarding "the reality of language, which exists outside of itself," the idea is that "ordinary" words can create something extraordinary, in a poem for example. There is an evocative dimension to language besides and beyond its denotative aspect. Or, to use two classical Sanskrit notions, language is made not just of abhidhā but also—and this is the heart of the matter when it comes to what DK refers to as the "literary arts"—of vyañjanā. "Abhidhā," Mukund Lath explains,

> is denotative, indicative meaning, and vyañjanā may be characterized as evocative [. . .] the significance of vyañjanā lies in a meaning which is addressed not to our intellect but to our emotive, felt consciousness. (2013, 94)

The point is that in our daily life, abhidhā is always at the foreground. We tend to forget, or to hardly notice the vyañjanā aspect of language. Practicality demands accurate (or as accurate as possible) denotation. In art, it is vyañjanā that is at the center. Art reminds us of this aspect of language, and in this respect—this is one of DK's main points in this paper, as the following paragraphs will further reveal—art can (and should, DK insists) transform our daily, mundane life, by revealing a poetic dimension that is here all the time but seldom noticed. In another paper, "Art and the Mystic Consciousness" (2007), DK speaks of vyañjanā and poetry. "A poem," he writes,

> "frees" the word from the "world" to which it was "bound," so that it may create a "world" of its own. The "hidden" power of language is revealed through poetry, which to all "rational," "objective" thinking seems doubly illusory, as it not only "mocks" it but also misleads one into thinking, at least for a moment, that what one has considered as "real" is not real at all, or at least far less real than one thought before. (Author's original manuscript).

But the paragraph from "Thinking Creatively" that I am engaging with here raises another central issue, that is, the abovementioned question of newness in the realm of ideas. Newness and creativity are interlaced. Is there, or can there be anything "new" in philosophy? There is nothing new in philosophy, a classical scholar, Hari Shankar Prasad, argued passionately in a conference on DK's philosophy held at the University of Delhi in 2016. "Ālū Gobhī," he enunciated, "is Ālū Gobhī. Even if you change the masālās [the spices], it remains potatoes with cauliflower. Nothing more, nothing less." His culinary illustration remained with me. I am sure that no chef would agree with him, but the question about newness in philosophy is a pertinent one. DK believed in the possibility of newness. The illustration used by him is from another department of the culinary field, the department of alcoholic beverages. Dry Martini is the result of a mixture ("in a certain proportion," DK specifies), a potent mixture that creates "a very strong drink," as he explains for the sake of the uninitiated from among his listeners. Consequently, DK speaks of "a sudden explosion of new meaning" that a mixture of concepts can bring about. It is implied here that a good philosophical argument, which for DK necessarily involves a measure of newness, is as intoxicating as the best of cocktails.

> What is the artist trying to do through the creation of a work of art? We started by pointing out that most of the non-literary arts build on the visual and the auditory worlds that our ordinary senses naturally create for us. The artist tries to create new worlds out of these, which have only a deceptive, illusory relation to them. The ordinary act of "understanding" these arts is taken in by this deceptive illusion and, combined with the natural tendency of the intellect to understand in causal terms, tries to understand them as if they were "worlds" on a par with the "normal," actual world which we see or hear with our senses. But what is this world created for? This is a world which we would like to enter and live in, leaving the world which we inhabit most of the time. It is a world where the possible becomes the actual, and the constraints of the biological world no longer operate. It is also the world where causality ceases to function in the way we find it in the inert world of nature. A work of art, then, is an invitation to enter and live in, at least for some time, a world that is more meaningful than the world we ordinarily find ourselves in. What exactly is the nature of this world or worlds that art creates and invites us to enter? It is

> a world more profound, more meaningful and more significant, where "freedom" obtains in a deeper sense than we are ever able to find in the so-called "normal" world we live in. The ordinary realm in which we live, in which our senses function, is the realm of necessities. This is a world where causality reigns, and causal knowledge is used by us to achieve wealth and power and control over others. But such a knowledge does not give enlightenment or freedom in the sense that it is not essentially an exercise of power over others, but the achievement of a state of consciousness which is not only permanent in a deeper sense than the world we live in, but where what we aspire for is actualized to a greater extent than it can ever be in the day to day world to which we are bound by the necessity of existence itself. There is, thus, a feeling of "release" when we enter the world of art, along with the feeling that we can return to it again and again whenever the ordinary world allows us some time to do so.

DK depicts the aesthetic experience as permeated with a sense of freedom from "the realm of necessities," namely, "the ordinary realm in which we live." First among these necessities, he soberly writes, is "the necessity of existence itself." DK further speaks of recurrent "visits" to the realm of aesthetic experience. This is also how he sees the mystic, spiritual, or metaphysic experience, namely, as a recurrent experience that one "enters" and "exits," participates in and returns to the so-called mundane sphere. In both cases, that is, in the aesthetic and mystical experiences, there is a return, which for DK is crucial. These visits to other realms, freer realms, are significant, he believes, if and only if they transform and enrich the world one returns to—if one can "import" a measure of freedom from the arts, or the art of meditation, and work with it at the mundane level. In this respect, Jay Garfield (in his paper "Love, Law and Language: Continuing to think with Daya-ji," 2018) rightly suggests that DK "insists on fusing the secular and the transcendent, by rendering it [the secular] symbolic, or meaningful." But this is not all. Freedom for DK is a matter of free travel between worlds, realms, standpoints. For him, the return from the aesthetic or the mystic realm is as much a free act as the "withdrawal" from the here and now for the sake of these realms. For him, freedom includes, must include, the return. For him, freedom is embedded in this "back and forth." But what about the possibility of not returning, of living in the arts, or in the realm of samādhi, of "spiritual ecstasy," without return? DK is skeptical about the possibility, surmising that the gravity of the mundane eventually "brings back" those who dive deep into the aesthetic or mystic experience; at the same time, he believes that total absorption in any realm beyond, if at all possible, is unethical. For him, freedom cannot be divorced from one's duty to the other, to others in the plural, to the world, and must be "exercised" through action that is loka-saṃgrahārtha, "for the sake of the whole world," or "for the sake of humankind," if I may borrow this phrase from Śaṅkara's commentary on *Bhagavadgītā* 3.20.

DK continues to write on "the return":

> However, this world of freedom is itself a strange world. There are those who create and those who appreciate. Art is an invitation from one person to another to enter into a world where necessity is minimized and freedom is maximized. But this freedom can be of different sorts, and the differences between the arts and the works within the same art form may be seen in terms of the "freedom" they embody and the possibilities they seek to actualize. Yet, whatever the freedom that is embodied or the possibility that is actualized, one has necessarily to come out of it, even though there was the freedom to enter it or to return to it. Thus there is continuously a dialectical interplay between the freedom to enter the worlds that art creates, and the necessity to leave them and return to the ordinary world. What happens to one when one returns to this ordinary world after a visit to that other world which art had created, and in which one lived for a certain while? What survives is only a memory of what was "lived" in that world and "experienced" more intensely than it can ever be in our lives. Besides this, it sometimes affects our sensibility, or alters our way of looking at things, and even the way we feel about them.
>
> The sensibility, however, that is cultivated and developed through our resort to the world of one particular form of art, which is generally centered in our senses, does not normally affect our sensibilities in other fields. The greatest artists

have shown that they only have sensibility in one domain. A great painter may appreciate music that is third rate. A great musician may appreciate bad paintings, and great artists, in their own life, may not be very good human beings, that is, sensitive to what other human beings feel or do. Similarly, those who are connoisseurs of art are not always connoisseurs of human relations.

Thus the creativity that is revealed in works of art and the sensitivity they display and infuse, to some extent, in one who beholds and appreciates them, is fragmented and partial. It therefore needs to be supplemented by a deeper and more comprehensive vision that relates them to the roots of creativity that lie in the self-consciousness of man, which continuously challenges him to transform everything that he apprehends in the light of some vague, immanent ideal which demands to be actualized both in himself and in his relation to everything else in terms of knowing, feeling and action.

The understanding of a work of art, therefore, has to ultimately be in terms of the creativity that lies behind it, and which sees it as a tentative product in the pursuit of the realization of a vision that informs the created work with the possibility of a different world that is freer, more sensitive, and more significant. In consequence, our encounter with it, however brief, may change and modify our ordinary living with a subtler, deeper sensitivity to nature, human beings, and above all, the transcendent which surrounds us all the time. The understanding of art, then, can only be successfully attempted in terms of the apprehension of both the actualized and unactualized possibilities that are there in the created work, and that open directions which the immanent vision embodied in it suggests for its further realization and actualization. It is also to be done in terms of the types of the possible worlds that have been created and suggested in the work of art, and thus invite a critical evaluation of it in terms of all that man seeks to realize and actualize in all the diverse domains of his being.

DK's depiction of the world or worlds, actual or potential, which the arts open as "world[s] where necessity is minimized and freedom is maximized," is a potent depiction. On the necessary return to the world of necessities, DK writes that one's visit to the "freer" worlds that art creates can "alter our way of looking." This is to say that one returns to the "ordinary world" with "new eyes" that enable him not just to see, but to design with his sight a "new world." "Those who are connoisseurs of art are not always connoisseurs of human relations," DK adds. Hence for him, "human relations" are art in itself. Moreover, he implies that there is a common ground to the arts and "the art of living" (that human relations are part of), a source of creativity and sensitivity, as he puts it, which gives rise to both.

Back in "Thinking Creatively," DK reaches his final paragraph:

> The arts then, are ultimately rooted in what may be called "the art of living," and unless life is seen in terms of an artistic creation, we cannot understand the creation which is embodied in a work of art. It is, of course, true that we all are, most of the time, bad artists as far as the art of living is concerned. But then, how few are the works of art that are really good? Most of them are inferior and very few attain a greatness that endures in time. A Gandhi is as rare as, say, a Shakespeare or a Michelangelo. To link creativity in the field of arts with the creativity that lies at the foundations of life itself is to see the world and ourselves with a transformed vision that challenges each one of us to look at ourselves and the world anew, and face the challenging task of creating ourselves and the world we live in, in a better, more beautiful way. The "grafting" of being through the act of becoming is the secret of both ourselves and the world, and it is through art that we learn this truth most easily. Let us try to understand the arts in this perspective, and perhaps our lives will become a little more akin to art than they have been until now.

DK's portrayal of Gandhi, Mohandas Karamchand Gandhi, as an artist on par with Michelangelo and Shakespeare is a strong move. We all know what the latter two created. But what did Gandhi as an artist create? On which type of canvas did he paint? Gandhi represents here what DK refers to as "the art of living." And since this is the case, I would suggest that Gandhi is the creator of two different, but not unrelated, artworks. The first is Gandhi himself, the man, the Mahatma if you wish. This is to say that Gandhi is artist and artwork in one. Gandhi's self-crafting is described in detail in his famous autobiography, *An Autobiography or The Story of My Experiments with Truth* (originally written in weekly instalments and published in his journal *Navjivan* between 1925 and 1929). He speaks in all honesty of his transformation from a young law student in London with rebellious hair ("my hair was by no means soft, and every day it meant a regular struggle with the brush to keep it in position"), striving to master the violin ("I thought I should learn to play the violin in order to cultivate an ear for Western music, so I invested £3 in a violin and something more in fees"), and ballroom dancing ("I must have taken about six lessons in three weeks, but it was beyond me to achieve anything like rhythmic motion, I could not follow the piano"),[4] into something totally different: a world-changer. This takes me to Gandhi's other work of art, namely, India. I do not wish to delve into the question: in what sense, if at all, modern India, from independence to the present day, was created in the image and the likeness of Gandhi. For many, Gandhi is certainly a model of fascination, and through his numerous writings, through the numerous Gandhi statues scattered literally everywhere in India, through every Khādī Ghar and every MG Road in every city and town in the country, he is still present, and the tall ideals of ahiṃsā and satyāgraha, nonviolence, and truthfulness-in-action are still written large on his canvas, open for interpretation, both in theory and in practice.

DK closes with grafting. This is his main point: grafting of being and becoming. Becoming is the process, the creative act that stands at the center of his whole talk-turned-paper. He calls attention to the becoming and urges his listeners-readers to see the inseparability of becoming and being. He insists on "opening" the text, the artwork, to expose its creative vein, to shatter the illusion of finality, which the frame of the painting, or the walls of the gallery, or the cover of the book create.

3

Freedoms

Freedom is not there once and for all, something which one is born with, that is intrinsic and innate to one, or something irretrievable that one can never lose. [. . .] Rather, it is as empirical as anything could be, limited, constrained, conditioned and even, to some extent, determined.

Daya Krishna, "The Cosmic, Biological and Cultural Conditionings, and the Seeking for Freedom," 159–60

1 Prologue

In this chapter, I will discuss DK's conception of freedom. The crux of his argument is presented in the epigraph given here. In the forthcoming segments, I work primarily with the paper from which this quote is taken, "The Cosmic, Biological and Cultural Conditionings, and the Seeking for Freedom" (2006, henceforth "The Cosmic"). In this paper, one of his very last, summarizing a lifelong engagement with the question of freedom, DK aims his sharp philosophical arrows at two notions of freedom: freedom as disengagement and freedom as omnipotence. I will discuss these two notions as we move on. At this point, I will only say that despite the difference between these notions, which DK extracts from Patañjali's *Yogasūtra* (kaivalya and siddhi, respectively), there is a common denominator between them. Both notions pertain to "ultimate freedom," freedom without any constraint whatsoever. But DK hardly aspires for freedom in the ultimate sense. He rather pleads, in "The Cosmic" and elsewhere, for sobering up from what he sees as the illusion of ultimate freedom.

What is surprising about "The Cosmic" is that freedom of choice, the first conception, or at least one of the first conceptions that come to mind when thinking about freedom, is not the focus here. DK does think about and dedicates a thorough discussion to freedom and choice in one of his earliest papers, "An Attempted Analysis of the Concept of Freedom" (1952, henceforth "Attempted Analysis"). "Man," he writes here (and please note that DK's "man" includes women),

> is the only Being who can choose not to BE. Therein lies his greatest freedom: the freedom from ends, from Life, from Conscious Being. He is the only animal who can commit suicide—a self-conscious annihilation of itself. Still, the self-conscious annihilation does not present itself as a "must." It merely presents itself as a choice—a choice that is the ultimate foundation of freedom in man. [. . .] If death is merely seen as external or internal necessity, man can only submit to it—whether with a protest or not, it does not matter. It is only when Death is seen as choice, as the self-conscious annihilation of one's own Dasein, that it appears as Foundational Freedom. (1952, 553, the capital letters are DK's).

DK distinguishes here between two types of suicide. The first type is what we usually call suicide. It takes place when life fails to fulfill one's expectations, and one drowns in suffering and frustration. It is not a matter of free choice but of "a choice that one has been constrained to make," owing to unbearable pain. In such a situation, it is life that triumphs, not freedom. In the second type of suicide, which is the core of DK's present discussion, "one chooses Death, if one really decides to choose it, not because life has failed him, but because, well, one chooses it." And DK adds that "face to face with one's inmost freedom to choose not to be, one can choose otherwise" (1952, 553). Hence it is all about the capacity to choose death, whether this choice is finally made or not. At this moment of existential resolution, the moment of choice, if one CAN really choose death (DK's use of capital letters is contagious), "what one chooses in the face of this ultimate possibility," DK writes, "is not our concern." His only concern here is freedom born of choice, whether to be or not to be. In both cases, the "given" (death and life) is transformed into "voluntary," voluntariness which, according to him, entails freedom.

It is the irreversibility of the choice not to be that instigates Foundational Freedom (again in capital letters). DK's articulation here is very cautious. "It is only when death is seen as a choice [. . .] that it appears as Foundational Freedom." Death is death. But the human gaze ("seen," "appears") can transform its inevitability into a choice and can metamorphose the death sentence with which each of us is born into an expression of utmost freedom. For DK, any claim about "not dying" or "release from death," uttered by those whom he refers to as "spiritualists," is mere delusion. In this respect, he soberly writes many years later that,

> the body decays, gets old and is subject to illness, disease and disability, and finally dies. [. . .] No one is spared, not even a Buddha. [. . .] Neither the Noble Truths nor the Path could save him or anybody else. [. . .] Tall claims about release from death seem vacuous and vain. (This

> quote is from DK's paper "Bondages of Birth and Death: Emerging Technologies of Freedom on the Horizon and the Hope of Final Release from the Foundational Bondage of Mankind," henceforth "Bondages," 2006, 509–10).

The next line of this paper says, "Death, however, can at least be a matter of choice." Hence according to DK, there is no "release from death," but a different type of release, release embedded in the choice of death or life. If one chooses not to die, not to commit suicide, despite the possibility, not the hypothetical but the actual-existential possibility, one's life is no longer "given" but is a matter of choice.

Ramchandra Gandhi, DK's contemporary, dedicates a long discussion (in his essay "On Meriting Death," his books *I am Thou* and *Svarāj*, and in one of his final talks, "Mokṣa and Martyrdom," 1981, 1984, 2002, and 2006, respectively) to the question of freedom and death, or freedom with death. For DK, it is death as a choice, as an "ultimate possibility," which injects life into life. Along similar lines, Ramchandra Gandhi finds a sense of freedom in what he refers to as "life in the face of death." In his inquiry, he travels between the *Kaṭha-Upaniṣad* and the assassination of his grandfather the Mahatma on January 30, 1948, blurring the borderline between the mythological and the historic. In both cases, in Naciketā's fearless conversation with Death, and at the crucial moment, when the Mahatma received the assassin's bullets in his chest, "emptied of all but love," as Tridip Suhrud beautifully depicts Gandhi's death (2013, 3), Ramchandra sees rare clarity, or śraddhā, awakened by the presence of death. In the light of this clarity, he suggests, a common human denominator, which he refers to as Advaita or Ananyatva—non-duality and non-difference, respectively—is disclosed. In the face of death, a level of interconnectedness or non-apartness, which Ramchandra calls "deathlessness," is unveiled. Deathlessness not in the sense of life devoid of death, but as an experience of inseparability, which death does not interrupt but rather reveals. Since death is inevitable, Yudhiṣṭhira—one of Ramchandra's protagonists—rightly describes the human longing for perpetuity (sthāvara) as "astonishing" (āścarya). "What can be more astonishing than that?" he asks in the Yakṣa-praśna ("the riddles of the Yakṣa, the pond deity") episode of the *Mahābhārata*. In Ramchandra, this perpetuity, or again deathlessness, makes sense not in terms of not dying, since there is no escape of death. Like in DK, it is the human gaze that allows a measure of freedom. If life and death are not seen as "my life" and "my death," if one can connect to a broader network, death is no longer a threat. Ramchandra's position is in accord with classical verses such as "nirmamo nirahaṃkāraḥ, sa śāntim adhigacchati," "without mine and me, he [the seeker] reaches the sublime" (*Bhagavadgītā* 2.71). Or, with the Upaniṣadic narrative, which implies (in *Bṛhadāraṇyaka-Upaniṣad* 1.4.10) that whoever knows that he is Brahman, "the whole," becomes this very "whole" (sarvam abhavat). The author of the Upaniṣad goes as far as suggesting that even the gods cannot stop a human being—whom they consider as their property, and benefit from him in the same way that he benefits from his livestock—from this release born of realization. It is release from a viewpoint that is both fragmented and fragmenting. If someone thinks of the other, even if this "other" is god, that "he is different [from me] and I am different [from him]" (anyo'sāv anyo'ham asmīti), it is a sign that "he [who holds such view] does not understand" (na sa veda), the author of this ancient text tells us. In Ramchandra Gandhi, this is true not just between man and god but also, primarily, between one human person and another. Like DK, Ramchandra wanders at ease between and within classical texts. But if DK reads the *Gītā* or the Upaniṣad in the same way that he reads any other philosophical text, suspending his reverence and engaging, as usual, in a steamy philosophical debate, Ramchandra's tone and incentive are altogether different. He is (or has become over the years) one of those referred to by DK as "spiritualists." He is rooted in tradition-texts. Yudhiṣṭhira and Naciketā are his intimate interlocutors. He aims to make sense of classical notions and ideals, and primarily the ideal and notion of advaita, now and here, in life, in practice. But despite their different philosophical temperaments, both Ramchandra Gandhi and DK are interested in release, or freedom, not from or despite, but with and through death.

For DK of the "Attempted Analysis"—young and existentialist—death as a choice evokes Foundational Freedom. But what is the difference between DK's Capital-F Freedom and the spiritualist's "ultimate freedom" that he so harshly criticizes? In the abovementioned Upaniṣadic narrative (*Bṛhadāraṇyaka-Upaniṣad* 1.4.10, which I visited in correspondence with Ramchandra Gandhi), a salient distinction is made between humans, rishis ("seers"), and gods (manuṣya, ṛṣi, and devatā respectively, and the distinction between the rishi and the ordinary human being is especially interesting). Whatever category one belongs to, one can and should strive "to be the whole," hence, to transcend this worldly hierarchy. I return to this narrative in order to suggest that DK's Fundamental Freedom is the freedom of the manuṣya *qua* manuṣya, of the human being as human being, his freedom to stand naked before himself, with all his vulnerability. A human being is not endowed with the rishi's broad vista, derived from his "distance" (like a photographer stepping back to accomplish full sight), which is a matter of withdrawal, the fruit of his unworldliness. Moreover, a human being is hardly omniscient, omnipotent, or omni-anything-else as the gods might be. He rather embraces his mortality, or again, his vulnerability, an embrace that alone puts him at Prince Hamlet's crossroad. The choice made here, if one dares to make this choice, gives rise not to "ultimate freedom" but to that which is "ultimate freedom for a human being." It is freedom with and within all the boundaries and the limitations that being human entails. It is "fundamental" in the sense that life and death are at stake. But evaluating DK's writings as a whole, from "Attempted Analysis" onwards, way onwards, my conclusion is that for him, "empirical freedoms" in the world, in the social and political domains, are not only as significant as his early Capital-F Freedom but are even more significant, applying as they are to the collective sphere, to "us," not just "me." These freedoms, at every level of life in the world, apply to "the whole," not in the metaphysical sense of the Upaniṣadic Brahman, but in the sense that the world in which we live is a jigsaw puzzle made of numerous interconnected pieces, of which I am just one piece. Such a realization, which breaks the walls of "the prison house of I-centricity," as DK puts it, is therefore more fundamental than the Fundamental Freedom of his "Attempted Analysis."

2 "The Cosmic"

In the following paragraphs, I aim to travel through "The Cosmic." The paper will not be reproduced here fully, as I did with "Thinking Creatively" in Chapter 2, but I will quote extensively from DK, as to create, yet again, a dialogue with him, and to allow the readers to listen to him directly, not just in paraphrase. The paper is titled "The Cosmic, Biological and Cultural Conditionings, and the Seeking for Freedom." DK's choice of words is interesting. First, consider the word "conditionings" that hints at the psychological dimension. Second, consider the phrase "cosmic conditionings." One can imagine what biological and social conditionings are, but what are "cosmic conditionings"? And finally, still in the title, DK, the conceptual artist, the hardcore philosopher, does not speak of the concept of freedom, but of "the seeking for freedom." Again, it is implied that he has something to say about the "psychology of freedom."

"The fact of dependence and inter-dependence," DK opens his paper,

> is so large, that even the blindest eye cannot escape it, and yet man "feels" free and believes that he can have more of it, if he so wills and endeavors and makes the effort. (I work with DK's original version, hence I will not provide page numbers).[1]

This is a striking opening: we, humans, earthlings, are so "dependent and interdependent," as DK puts it, that the very thought of freedom, if freedom amounts to independence, sounds like a misnomer. And yet we are enchanted by freedom as ideal and experience.

"A hurricane," DK continues,

> can blow off everything, an earthquake can occur, destroy or damage the earth itself. At the mercy of it all is the helpless creature called man who, like all living beings, is pre-programmed by his genetic make-up to repeat the life of his species and follow the journey to old age and death, unless "accident" intervenes and something happens to him.

Here the meaning of "cosmic conditionings" begins to be revealed. We are at "the mercy" of hurricanes on one hand and genetic inheritance on the other, restricted both externally and internally. How can we strive for freedom, then?

"But whatever the restrictions or compulsions are," DK further writes,

> there is always the possibility of a change, and this defines the difference between "nature" and "culture," both of which constitute the "determining" and the "conditioning" circumstances of man as a biological species, as also a socio-cultural being which he alone is, and which differentiates him from all the other species.

The quotation marks, as usual, are crucial. Nature and culture are different. It makes sense to strive for a change under the rubric of "culture," and DK—I implied earlier, and will further emphasize in the next chapter—was an active contributor in the direction of social change. But "nature" too is hardly fixed or unchangeable, and moreover, we live in an era—and DK was attentive to every scientific breakthrough—in which the borderline between the notions of culture and nature becomes more and more blurred. Yes, even genetics is no longer beyond the capacity of human intervention. And since such is the case, the words "determining" and "conditioning" are written with quotation marks. Between the lines of determination and conditioning that define the human situation, hides a promise of freedom. One can change the world and himself.

DK moves on to shoot a philosophical arrow at both Śaṅkara and Descartes. He criticizes what he sees as "the indubitable self-certainty of the I-consciousness, whether in the cogito of Descartes or the aham-pratyaya of Śaṅkara." "Freed from the contingent bondage of all objectivity," DK writes,

> the "I-consciousness" feels itself to be the centre of certitude and freedom, and thus also of the suffering caused by that which is "other" than itself and thus need not necessarily be.

DK suggests that there is a sense of delusion in the act of introspection, as it magnifies and prioritizes the "I-consciousness" over everything else. Moreover, DK dares to speculate (or is it me who speculates as I read him?) that the Advaitic and parallelly the Cartesian projects were conceived as a remedy for one's fear of the other. In both formulations, the other is subsided, if not totally annihilated. In the Advaitic formulation, the other is "swallowed up" by the all-encompassing self. The precedence of the self over the other is lucidly reflected, I would add, in two creation-myths that occur in chapter 1 of the *Bṛhadāraṇyaka-Upaniṣad* (BU 1.4.1-8 and 1.4.17). Both myths open with the phrase "ātmaivedam agra āsīt," "In the beginning there was the self" (or "In the beginning there was the ātman"). This is an astonishing beginning. Compare it with the Biblical myth (in *Genesis*, chapter 1), which opens with the words "In the beginning God created the heavens and the earth." Man was created last, on the sixth day of creation, when God completed the creation of the whole world, sky and earth, sun and moon, plants and animals. The Jewish commentators refer to man as "nezer habri'a," "the crown of the creation." Everything was created for him, but unlike the Upaniṣad, he is hardly located "in the beginning," and he is "man" or "the first human" (Adam), not a "self." Nevertheless, as the pinnacle of God's creation, he is still at the center. DK's critique of I-, or self-centricity is the heart of the matter here (and for the sake of the present discussion, the difference between "I" and "self" is not essential). This critique applies, then, both to the Upaniṣadic and to the Biblical narratives, despite the dramatic differences between them. DK would rather rewrite the Upaniṣad. The first verse of the Daya-Upaniṣad would be: "In the beginning there were Many."

2.1 Against Disengagement as Freedom

The aloneness of the self, according to DK, is a problematic move. "There could not be an emptier freedom than this," he writes in "The Cosmic,"

> as there is nothing to be changed or affected, and hence the very exercise of freedom is made impossible in principle. The dream of a "freedom" unconditional by anything else has turned into the actualization of an absurdity, as there is nothing left to be conditioned by it.

Without the other, and without the world, DK suggests here, the notion of freedom is empty. Freedom is "something" that needs to be exercised and actualized. Therefore, abandonment of the world and the worldly, other subjects and everything objective, seems to DK as a step away from freedom. "Both the Sāṃkhya and the Advaita Vedānta traditions," DK continues to formulate his argument elsewhere,

> face the very same dilemma, as their analysis lands them in the paradoxical situation where the attainment of "freedom" results in the total loss of freedom, as one becomes intrinsically incapable of exercising any freedom at all. One has voluntarily given up the "freedom to return," and one is left with one's own "aloneness," with no possibility of relating to anything whatsoever. ("The Undeciphered," 2012, 93–4)

For DK, withdrawal from the world is both useless and unethical, unless it is followed by a return, return that has an effect in the world. It is useless since freedom, we saw, needs to be effective. It is unethical owing to one's responsibility to the world. "The suffering humanity has been at the center of the spiritual consciousness," DK writes,

> and the masters have always "returned" from the "withdrawal," as the Buddha is said to have done long ago, and also so many others in the history of humanity. (2012, 100)

Patañjali's ideal of kaivalya, literally "aloneness" or "apartness," as expounded in the *Yogasūtra*, is perhaps the most extreme version of "disengagement as freedom." Despite its popular reputation among yoga practitioners today, grounded in "photoshopped" translations of this classical text (like Indian food in Tel Aviv, cooked with just a friendly amount of mirch-masālā), the *Yogasūtra* is a manifesto of world renunciation, of withdrawal without return. Its author envisions "freedom" as a yogic stage in which consciousness has emptied itself of any content, mental and psychological, and remains "locked" in this emptiness, resistant to any external influence whatsoever. This reading of the *Yogasūtra* takes its cue from the notions of vairāgya, pratyāhāra, and kaivalya (withdrawal, withdrawal, and withdrawal) as the central coordinates of Patañjali's yoga-map. Vairāgya (YS 1.12, 1.15 and 1.16), literally "dispassion," stands for "thirstlessness toward objects seen and heard" (1.15), and "ultimately toward the guṇas" (1.16). The guṇas are the "activating forces" behind the objective world, according to metaphysics of the Sāṃkhya, that Patañjali adopts. Hence vairāgya stands for dispassion toward the world, both on and under the surface. Pratyāhāra (YS 2.29 and

2.54), the fifth "limb" of the aṣṭāṅga, that is, "eight limbs of yoga" scheme, refers to "withdrawal of the senses from their objects." And Kaivalya (YS 2.25, 3.51, 3.56, 4.26, 4.34), if I may focus on the very final lines of the *Yogasūtra*, is a yogic stage in which "the power of empty-consciousness (citi-śakti) abides in itself (svarūpa-pratiṣṭhā)" (4.34), once time stands still (4.33) and everything worldly (prakṛti, including the human consciousness) recedes to a state of mere potentiality (4.34 again). Krishnachandra Bhattacharyya (KCB), a contemporary commentator of Patañjali (and much more), suggests that "Yoga," that is, yoga as explicated in the *Yogasūtra* and its commentarial body,

> is essentially the will to nivṛtti and not to pravṛtti, the will to mukti, to freedom as the power to stand distinct of power to create objective values indefinitely. (2008, 305)

For KCB, pravṛtti and nivṛtti, outward-facing and inward-facing consciousness, respectively, or "intentional consciousness" and "disengaged consciousness," are forms of what he refers to as "willing." Yoga, in his reading, is willing toward sheer disengagement from the world and the worldly, from objects and objectification, and even from will itself. It is willing not to will. Correspondingly, the utmost yogic power, conveyed by the phrase citi-śakti (in YS 4.34), is what KCB refers to as "the power to stand distinct of power." But DK refuses to accept this narrative. "Why the outgoing movement of consciousness [pravṛtti]," he writes,

> should be regarded as something undesirable in itself, or the inward movement intrinsically desirable, has remained the unasked question of the Indian tradition. ("The Undeciphered," 2012, 92)

DK prefers free travel between withdrawal and return, between the "flight mode" of consciousness so to say, and full connectivity. For him, these two modes of consciousness, conveyed by the notions of nivṛtti and pravṛtti, together, cover the full human scope. "Freedom," he writes in "The Cosmic,"

> lies in this double capacity of consciousness at the human level to move outward or return inward as it pleases, bound neither by the one or the other, and hence at another level, feeling itself "free" from both. Neither of these can define it exclusively, or exhaust its reality as it "appears" to itself as transcending both, no matter if this is "judged" to be illusory by the consciousness itself when it "sees" the situation "objectively" and tries to understand it. Both the "outward" and the "inward" movement seem to have in-built limitations not exactly known to man, and perhaps,

> "unknowable" in principle, as the former encounters the "givenness" of the body and the physical world on the one hand, and the socio-cultural and politico-economic "worlds" on the other; while the latter seem to result from the very nature of consciousness and self-consciousness, and the interactive inter-relationship between them.

DK does not merely argue that nivṛtti and pravṛtti complement one another, but further implies that free travel between them allows freedom from both. Yes, according to DK, one needs to become free not just from his worldly mode of existence but even from the "freedom from the worldly." Moreover, DK refuses to comply to the verdict given by consciousness itself, when it retreats inwards, that everything worldly is marginal or secondary. This takes us back to DK's critique of self-centricity, from Śaṅkara to Descartes. The "feeling" of I-amness, as these two thinkers show, each in his distinct way, is powerful, and yet, DK suggests, misleading. The inbuilt limitations on one's freedom, he writes here, and for me this is a crucial point, occur both at the pravṛtti and nivṛtti modes of consciousness. We usually consider merely the former as limited and think of the obvious constraints at the outer level, namely, the "givenness" of body and physicality, and numerous restrictions related to our social and political life. But consciousness in itself, DK suggests, is also limited. It depends on its own structure. This returns to the "illusion" of "In the beginning there was the self" (or "in the beginning I am," as Descartes puts it). Both modes of consciousness, then, the detached and the engaged, the detached as much as the engaged, have their own limitations.

But DK's dispute with "the spiritualists" who prefer nivṛtti, that is, detached consciousness, over pravṛtti, namely, engaged consciousness, does not mean that he cannot understand the "why and how" of their position. "Illusion" and "reality," he writes in "The Cosmic,"

> are both rooted in "self-consciousness," which simultaneously "feels" itself transcending all that is an "object" to it, and yet feels restricted and constrained by it. Its "relation" to any "object," whatever be its ontological status or nature, is always ambivalent and ambiguous as it can neither accept it nor reject it completely.

This paragraph is written in response to KCB's influential essay "The Subject as Freedom" (1930), a pioneering work of philosophy without borders. At the level of self-consciousness, DK agrees with KCB—a "spiritualist" in his own way—one "feels" a sense of apartness from everything objective. Objectivity is "seen" here as a limitation, and one is inclined to become absorbed in "pure subjectivity," subjectivity that in KCB borrows from the Advaitic notion of the ātman. This inherent ambivalence, or knotty relationship between subject and object, can lead to the conclusion—and this is indeed the spiritualist's conclusion—that final separation, or divorce if you wish, is preferable. But DK, we saw, refuses to accept this conclusion. We also saw that for him, each of us has a responsibility toward the other, toward the world. And yet, again, we saw that according to him, nivṛtti, or consciousness in-itself, has its own limitations, parallel to the more noticeable constraints of the pravṛtti-worldly mode of consciousness. DK continues to write that,

> the feeling of "unrelatedness" is founded on the illusion created by the fact of withdrawal, which if reflected upon sufficiently, would itself show its illusoriness. "Withdrawal," obviously, is a withdrawal from "something," and makes sense only in relation to it.

DK puts the word "withdrawal" in quotation marks to convey its paradoxicality. Withdrawal makes sense only in relation to that from which one withdraws. Hence, withdrawal from the objective world, in fact, confirms and validates the very world that one claims to withdraw from owing to its illusory-ness.

DK returns to the crux of his critique of "disengagement as freedom": "The delusion," he writes, "is structurally inbuilt in the nature of self-consciousness, as it cannot but see itself as the centre of the world." When I suffer from eye-infection and see two moons up in the sky instead of one (if I may borrow a popular Advaitic illustration), I know that my eyes deceive me and I dismiss what I see as "error," even if I continue to see two moons. In the same way, the eye of self-consciousness projects an erroneous picture of the self as the center. This picture, DK claims, is the only conclusion that self-consciousness can come up with, owing to its "operating system." This is how self-consciousness works. DK elaborates on this point in his work *Towards a Theory of Structural and Transcendental Illusions* (completed in 1998, published posthumously in 2012, henceforth "Illusions").[2] Just like the case of seeing two moons, when the self-consciousness eye projects this picture, one must dismiss it as "illusion." By using the term "illusion," not "error," DK turns the tables on the Advaitic position. If the Advaitin, the proponent of Advaita, sees the world as "illusion," then DK implies that it is the projection of the world as illusory, which is the outcome of an illusion, the illusion that merely "I," the self, or the ātman—all three notions pointing at the same direction, inwards—is indubitably "real."

In his paper "Freeing Philosophy from the Prison House of I-Centricity" (2003), DK further writes:

> There can be no privileged subjectivity. [. . .] it is only an illusion superimposed on oneself by self-consciousness, and elevated to the status of the most indubitable fundamental certainty by the rope-trick of the philosopher, be his name Descartes, Fichte, Śaṅkara, or anyone else. (2003, 137–8).

Here, Fichte is added to DK's intricate network of "philosophical correspondence." But I quoted this paragraph because of the phrase "privileged subjectivity." DK refers to the marginalization, or peripheralization, of the worldly, for the sake of a so-called privileged subjectivity as "the rope-trick of the philosopher." The trick is this: a rope rises up into the air. Someone climbs up and disappears. The metaphor, as used by DK, conveys not just the deceptiveness of the "feeling" that "I am the sun around which the planets revolve," as he puts it in *Illusions*, but also the fantasy of ascending to skies above and beyond everything worldly. However, the worldly includes not just the objective realm but also the other, you. Hence any notion of "privileged subjectivity" is always at the expense of the other. "The acknowledgement and admission of other beings like oneself," DK writes in "The Cosmic,"

> would limit my "freedom" in a more fundamental and radical sense than the acceptance of all the other "types" of being put together. The neglect and the denial of the importance of society, economy and polity in the thinking of most philosophers who have thought about these problems is an evidence of this, just as the "mystical," the "spiritual" and the "aesthetic" consciousness has almost inevitably tended to do all the time.

We are back with "In the beginning there were Many." DK suspects that it is the "inconvenience" posed by the other, by the many, by their very existence, that gave rise to the ideal of the self-in-itself, away from everything and everyone else. The other is a threat on my freedom, hence one is quick to deny, or to marginalize his existence. But for DK, the price of this move is intolerable. In the name of spirituality, mysticism, or even aesthetics, the now and here, the world in which we live, is too easily forgotten and neglected. "Freedom," DK competes his critique,

> is not in "aloneness" alone, or "aloneness" all the time, but also intrinsically and inevitably with the other, or rather others. They can be the source of enhancement, enjoyment and deepening of one's freedom,

> or of its negation, constriction, lessening, and even turning into its opposite, or feeling of bondage, of being imprisoned with nowhere to go, and being able to do nothing, just Nothing. "Hell is other people," said Sartre, but so is heaven also.

Hell is other people, but likewise is heaven. This is a strong closure, and a forceful response to Sartre's famous claim (in his 1943 play *No Exit*).

2.2 Against Omnipotence as Freedom

We saw that freedom, according to DK, needs to be exercised, otherwise it is empty and futile. To exercise freedom one needs power, and we also saw that DK does not buy the narrative of the power to give up power. This narrative leads to "aloneness alone," kaivalya in Patañjali's formulation. However, Patañjali highlights yet another notion of power, besides citi-śakti (the abovementioned power-as-mere-potentiality of "empty consciousness" which defines kaivalya), namely, the notion of siddhi. The fact is that Patañjali dedicates almost an entire chapter of his treatise (chapter 3 of the *Yogasūtra*) to a long list of siddhis (powers, special capacities, or yogic attainments) to be acquired by the yogin, the practitioner of yoga, through meditation (the term used here for meditation is saṃyama). The object of meditation varies in Patañjali's long list of meditations (delineated from YS 3.16 onwards) on the scale between the gross (for instance, the sun or the "sun gate" in the navel region, the moon, the pole star, the navel wheel, and the heart) and the subtle. At the subtle or abstract end of this scale, Patañjali prescribes for example meditation on the distinction between the different components of language (the word, its reference, and the idea that comes to mind when one hears this word), or on the distinction between short-term and long-term karma, or on the distinction between moment and sequence, the components of time. Distinction occupies a central place in the *Yogasūtra*, leading eventually to the final distinction (kaivalya) between the self (puruṣa) and everything else (prakṛti). The twist is that the category of "everything else" covers not just the world but even consciousness. Yes, Descartes's "I think" belongs to the category that according to Patañjali has to be peeled off for the selfhood beyond to be carved out. Each of the meditations prescribed in chapter 3 of the *Yogasūtra* results in a certain siddhi, power, or attainment. Many of these siddhis, are in fact different types of knowledge (jñāna is the word used here). They include knowledge of the universe, knowledge of the arrangement of the stars, knowledge of the movement of the stars, knowledge of the arrangement of the body, knowledge of the sounds of every creature, knowledge of the content of other minds, knowledge of the subtle, hidden and remote, foreknowledge of death, knowledge of previous births, knowledge of past and future, knowledge of puruṣa (the self), knowledge of the distinction between puruṣa and prakṛti (the self and everything else), and, finally, awareness (pratipatti) of the distinction between similar things, which cannot be distinguished by origin, characteristics, or location (namely sattva-buddhi, human consciousness in its most transparent form, and puruṣa, the self beyond). It is implied here that for Patañjali, knowledge and power are interconnected. Other siddhis depicted in this chapter of the *Yogasūtra* pertain to special capacities that the yogin develops. These include the capacity of becoming invisible; the capacity of miniaturizing one's body; the capacity of moving freely in space; the capacity to overcome hunger and thirst; the awakening of extraordinary senses of hearing, feeling, seeing, tasting, and smelling; the capacity of the mind (citta) to enter another body; the capacity of determining the time of one's death at will; mastery over the senses; mastery over the elements; and finally, mastery over the pradhāna (which according to Sāṃkhya philosophy is the hidden from the eye foundation of the objective world).

I mention the different objects of meditation and the different siddhis born of these meditations in such detail, since this dimension of Pātañjala-yoga is rarely discussed. So much is written on the *Yogasūtra* today, both academically and popularly, but hardly anyone takes the siddhis seriously. At the popular level, it is astonishing to see that the two notions at the center of DK's discussion, kaivalya and siddhi, which convey the "goals of yoga" according to Patañjali, are rarely introduced to āsana-practitioners, the yoga-posture enthusiasts worldwide, who are the target clients, or buyers, of the flourishing yoga-market. The *Yogasūtra* is projected in this bazaar as the Bible of Yoga, but a quick browse at the numerous publications that this popular market produces shows that the focus is merely on the first two chapters of the text, and mainly on chapter 2, the aṣṭāṅga chapter (even if only the first five "yoga limbs" are presented here, the final three, dealing with meditation, are explicated in chapter 3). The notions of siddhi and kaivalya, each conveying a different sense of freedom, are developed (mostly) in the next two chapters of the *Yogasūtra* (chapters 3 and 4), which DK closely investigates. He wonders (in "The Undeciphered") about the relation between these two types of freedom: freedom as disengagement and freedom as omnipotence. Amid a long list of meditations and the powers, or capacities that they give rise to, Patañjali suddenly remarks that,

> these (siddhis) are obstacles to samādhi (to "yogic introversion"), but are nevertheless siddhis (attainments, powers) when the consciousness

> is directed outwards (to the world; te samādhāv upasargā vyutthāne siddhayaḥ). (YS 3.38)

This remark sits well with KCB's abovementioned reading of Patañjali as exponent of "the power to stand distinct of power." On the siddhis, KCB writes that,

> there is general skepticism at the present day not only about any mental activity actually yielding the capacity of producing magical effects in nature, but even about the possibility of willing in the mistaken faith in such magic, skepticism not only about the yoga-vibhūtis [supernatural powers] but about the psychological possibility of yoga itself. [. . .] Whoever admits free willing, in a sense, admits magic in some form or other. (2008, 290)

KCB depicts the siddhis (or in his formulation, vibhūtis) as "magical effects in nature" produced by "mental activity" (that is, by meditation). And he rightly suggests that "at the present day" there is "general skepticism" about them, and more broadly about the estimation that the yoga adept can obtain "mastery which extends from the minutest particle to the largest entity," as Patañjali puts it (parama-aṇu-parama-mahattva-anto 'sya vaśīkāraḥ, YS 1.40). The striving for supernatural powers might look fantastical, imaginary, and almost childish, compared with the ideal of kaivalya, of "aloneness alone," or "aloneness beyond." Therefore, KCB writes that striving for powers, such as those explicated in chapter 3 of the *Yogasūtra*, can be perceived as "willing in the mistaken faith in such magic." But his own vision is altogether different. He rather believes that,

> some preliminary experience of the magical efficiency of yoga is necessary for an aspirant, in order to have a motive for the practice of yoga proper. (2008, 315)

The classic commentators, from Vyāsa onwards, imply that the siddhis, or yogic powers, are side-effects or byproducts, which dawn on the yoga-practitioner spontaneously, uncalled for, as he walks along "the path." As such, they can be seen as "road marks" indicating that one has not lost the way and is moving in the right direction to kaivalya. Or they can work as "the last temptation of the yogin" on his way, again, to kaivalya (see YS 3.52), the "final destination of yoga," which is reachable only if these powers are given up. But KCB suggests that a certain amount of "magic," as he puts it, is needed to establish faith (śraddhā) in the practitioner of yoga, to provide a preliminary "proof" that "willing" works; a proof that "reality" as conventionally perceived can be played with, manipulated, transformed, even annulled through the power of consciousness. This, according to KCB, would be "yoga proper." This would be the "real magic." KCB therefore concludes that,

> to doubt yoga-vibhūti [the siddhis, the powers] is to doubt yoga itself, and to doubt yoga is to doubt the freedom of free will. (2008, 291).

The only common denominator between KCB and DK as far as the siddhis in Patañjali are concerned is that both take them seriously, and include them in their discussion of freedom. KCB, rooted in classical commentaries of the *Yogasūtra*, sees kaivalya, apartness, aloneness, the willing not to will, and to stand distinct as the crux of the matter, and the siddhis, the powers, as supporting and fitting with this final goal of yoga. DK's reading is altogether different. His aim is not to establish coherency between different aspects of the *Yogasūtra*. His aim is not to present us with a lucid as possible picture of Patañjali but, instead, to think with and through Patañjali. I wish to remind the readers that the title of DK's paper on Patañjali is "The Undeciphered Text: Anomalies, Problems and Paradoxes in the Yogasūtra." The very title conveys a sense of freedom—freedom from authority, freedom to touch the original text with one's bare hands, not with gloves of reverence. DK sees an ambivalence between the concepts of siddhi and kaivalya; he sees them as conveying conflicting ideals of freedom, the former with and within (and DK would wish, for) the world, the latter rooted in a state of "aloneness alone," oblivious to anything worldly. For DK, this conflict or ambivalence is what makes the *Yogasūtra* an interesting text to work-think with. We saw earlier that for DK, freedom is not freedom without power. "Freedom without power," he writes in "The Cosmic," "seems an empty thing, and one does not know what to do with it." But this power, without which freedom is an empty shell, has nothing to do with the omnipotence that DK sees in Patañjali's list of siddhis. "The idea that the ideal of omnipotence is involved in the notion of freedom," he further writes,

> is as much mistaken as the complementary idea that freedom involves the possibility and the necessity of being free of everything else, including one's own desires, seekings, aspirations, in short all the vṛttis [the workings of consciousness] as Patañjali's *Yogasūtra* puts it, and, of course, all the saṃskāras [the genetic inheritance, both literally and metaphorically] which the whole past history of the universe, at all its levels, has left in one, as it has had to, because one is its child, its creation, just as everything else is.

DK's articulation is always interesting. He depicts kaivalya as "freedom from everything," and primarily from everything that one usually considers as "me" and "myself." The world and the worldly are not merely "out there." They are in me; they are part of who I am. Hence Patañjali prescribes total "emptification" of consciousness by consciousness itself; emptification, or purification of anything worldly that has been internalized. For DK, this is unacceptable. We saw that for him, withdrawal without return hardly amounts to freedom. And moreover, desires, seekings, and aspirations are necessary for worldmaking and world-changing upon return. Therefore, DK rejects Patañjali's dismissal of these vital human ingredients.

DK makes an intriguing connection between "the illusion of omnipotence," as he puts it, mistakenly taken as a sign of freedom, and the huge leap of science and technology in the second half of the twentieth century and the beginning of the third millennium. "It is not dharma [the ethical life], or the socio-cultural realities [of our lives]," he writes in "The Cosmic,"

> that give meaning and identity to a people. It is rather "development" in all fields and all directions that is seen as its defining function.

DK is not foreign to the notion of development. He spent decades of his thinking-life (as the next chapter will show) to theorizing at the social, political, and economic domains for India as a developing nation-state. His present critique pertains to our fascination with "development," often regardless of its ethical and social consequences. In this respect, he speaks of

> the advances in knowledge and the resulting technologies that had been cumulatively accumulating since the time of Galileo and Newton, and whose pace has increased dramatically since the middle of the twentieth century, when man achieved the first nuclear chain reaction in Chicago under Enrico Fermi and later, when the voyage to the moon was successfully planned and executed under the orders of the late President Kennedy in the USA.

The example given by DK for "development," which implies a sense of omnipotence mistaken for freedom, is the atomic bomb. Here the "feeling" (in DK, the illusion) of freedom comes from one's capacity "to play God," in this case a destroying God. Sibaji Bandyopadhyay writes of J. Robert Oppenheimer, "father of the Atom Bomb" and colleague of Enrico Fermi, that,

> Watching with his naked eyes the first atomic explosion on the desert-field of New Mexico's Los Alamos—a spectacular and deafening burst [. . .]—Oppenheimer felt that the awesome scene was only a replay of sorts. [. . .] He was reminded of chapter XI of the *Gītā*. Of the two verses from the *Gītā*'s "The Lord's Transfiguration" (Viśvarūpadarśana Yoga) chapter that flashed in the mind of the nuclear scientist then, one was XI.32: "Time am I, world-destroying, grown mature, engaged here in subduing the world." (2014, 5-6)

I did not know, before reading Bandyopadhyay, that in 1933, already an established physicist, Oppenheimer started to study Sanskrit at Berkeley with Professor Arthur W. Ryder, a famous linguist and translator. His enthusiasm about the *Bhagavadgītā* (the *Gītā*) finds expression in letters that he wrote to his brother, and astonishingly, at the crucial moment at Los Alamos, he was reminded of the verse in *Gītā* where god Krishna reveals his "real face" as Time (with a Capital-T, but Kāla, Time, is also Death)—Time that devours every creature, each of us, instant after instant. This verse (quoted by Bandyopadhyay in Swami Prabhupada's translation), and this fierce vision flashed in Oppenheimer's mind, astounded and terrified of the possible destructive consequences of his own creation. The "freedom" to destroy?

However, DK thinks of the illusion of omnipotence as freedom not just vis-à-vis the atom bomb, but also with reference to advanced technology that has become not merely part of our lives but also part of who we are. Take, for example, the yoga-siddhi, or power, of travelling freely in space (ākāśa-gamanam). "Through meditation (saṃyama) on the relation of body and space, and contemplation (samāpatti) on the lightness of cotton," Patañjali writes in YS 3.43, "one achieves the ability to travel freely in space." Nowadays we travel freely in space in airplanes and space shuttles. Does it grant us more freedom? At a certain level, of course. I can reach the other side of the globe within a day, which is undoubtedly a miracle. But did our ancestors, who could not travel very far, saw it as a crucial limitation on their freedom? "Freedom," DK writes in "Attempted Analysis,"

> is only within a framework. Nobody feels unfree because he cannot reach the moon. It would be a wrong conclusion, therefore, to think that people were not free when there were no airplanes, or when there was no interplanetary travel. In the ages when there were no motor cars, radios, televisions, printing presses, and a thousand other amenities of modern life, people felt not less free, for they did not feel at all the lack of these things. The existence of these things today does not make us feel more free, for they are accepted within the framework of modern life. (1952, 551).

I agree and disagree. Freedom is indeed a matter of framework and expectation, and the fact that I cannot travel into space hardly bothers me or makes me feel unfree. But our forefathers certainly felt "the lack of these things," a lack that triggered the development of cars, radios, etc. And the fantasy of reaching the moon, of literally—not just literarily—touching the moon with the tip of one's finger, made this impossible achievement possible. Besides obvious political agendas, reaching the moon (just a few days ago, on July 22, 2019, India launched Chandrayaan 2, a "lunar orbiter, lander, rover," the papers explain, scheduled to reach the moon in less than a month) is also a matter of making the impossible a reality, conveying a measure of freedom not just in the "omnipotent" sense but also in the creative sense of invention and innovation across previous limits.

Technology flies forward. In his Shimla Lectures (2005) and, in fact, on every occasion, DK shared his astonishment over every new technological advancement that he read about, for instance, cloning. Since cloning hides around the corner, it is not implausible or, in fact, it is very likely that sooner or later humans will be industrially manufactured rather than (or besides) given birth to in the "natural" way. This will have a dramatic effect on the institution of the family as we know it. Will the Oedipus complex disappear, DK wonders half-jokingly in his abovementioned paper "Bondages of Birth and Death: Emerging Technologies of Freedom on the Horizon and the Hope of Final Release from the Foundational Bondage of Mankind"? The title (as usual) is intriguing. It tells a whole story—the story of hope, through the ages, throughout history, for a "final release" from the "fundamental bondage," or bondages, of the human being, namely, birth and death. It takes us back to DK's early paper "Attempted Analysis" with its Shakespearean dilemma. But unlike the early paper, written in the 1950s, in "Bondages," the technological factor is taken seriously into account. Will cloning outdate the Oedipus complex, then, or just intensify the problem by creating, say, a "phantom Oedipus complex"? And moreover, what type of children will we manufacture for ourselves? It could be like entering an American supermarket. The choices will be numerous, but how will we choose? What, for instance, will be the color of the eyes of the industrially manufactured child that one buys for oneself (or orders in Amazon.com)? Blue (the pain of Toni Morrison's *The Bluest Eye* comes to mind)? Or the manufactured child's overall complexion? These questions, which I am hardly the first to raise, are not necessarily fantastical, imaginary, impossible. Technology is full of pros and cons, advantages and risks. But with all its risks, and the ethical questions involved, technology cannot be stopped. The speed of technology, according to DK, just sharpens the need for new thinking about the notion of freedom. He relentlessly reminds his readers that technology is not freedom. Whether it contributes to freedom, or not, and how, and freedom in what sense—all these are worthy questions for reflection.

Apropos omnipotence and freedom, I am reminded of the superhero movie-wave coming these days from Hollywood. As I write these lines, "Spider-Man: Far from Home" has just been released. Perhaps Spider-Man's omnipotence (or at least special powers) compensates for our limited capacities despite technology. The movie offers a concentrated dose of what DK refers to as "the illusion of omnipotence," and at the same time 129 minutes without gravity, providing the lovers of the genre a sense of freedom from the numerous necessities that we live with and within. And one more thought about the "omnipotence" that technology allows: the beauty here is that it is not "my" omnipotence. The fact that I can fly from one place to another is the outcome of a collective effort. It is power, capacity, or siddhi, born of collaboration and available not just to advanced yogīs but to many of us, almost everywhere. In Patañjali, each practitioner of yoga is "alone" in the pursuit and achievement of freedom, whether outward-facing freedom (through the siddhis) or inward-facing freedom (in the apartness of kaivalya). The fruits of technology, despite agenda and greed of governments and private-owned mega-industries, are still available more globally.

2.3 "As Empirical as Anything Could Be"

Toward the end of "The Cosmic," DK returns to what he referred to earlier as "the fact of dependence and inter-dependence that even the blindest eye cannot escape." Here he writes that,

> freedom can be cultivated and enhanced, just as it can be lessened, or destroyed by oneself, or others, or by events over which one has no control, as in paralysis, or coma, or Parkinson's disease, or other of such kind. Amnesia, or forgetfulness, or loss of memory, can make one practically helpless, as one may hardly recognize things, or even where one is, and where the pathways in different directions lead to.

I read this passage, written when DK was in his eighties, as born of personal observation. He looks around and notices that old age has taken away many of the freedoms of friends and acquaintances. Therefore, he further speaks of "the unbelievable fragility and dependence of freedom."

Here I am reminded of Prince Siddhārtha, the Buddha to be, who naïvely asks his charioteer when he sees an old man for the first time in his life, "will this evil affect me too?" (kim eṣa doṣo bhavitā mamāpi? I quote from Aśvaghoṣa's *Buddhacarita* in Patrick Olivelle's translation, 2008, 70–1).

The young prince is shocked to discover that old age, sickness, and death await him on the path called "life." This shock triggers him to seek release, "ultimate release," from these three doṣas, as Aśvaghoṣa puts it, "evils" in Olivelle's translation. For DK, these "evils" are inescapable, besides illness that can perhaps be avoided if one is lucky (lucky genes?). Here medicine and medical technology can play a crucial role and provide a measure of freedom from disease and pain. DK is not in search of "ultimate release," but of a sense of soberness about life with its "good," "evil," and "beyond," and numerous freedoms that can be achieved with all the internal and external limitations that are part of who we are. But freedom, for DK, is not just about me. Social and political freedoms, which he fought for throughout his life, are for the many, and go beyond "my" old age, illness, and death. In the Introduction, I quoted from a letter sent by DK to his old friend Ramesh Chandra Shah, when the latter was worried about DK's illness. In this letter, we saw, DK is more interested in illness as such, than in his own medical condition. Can rust, or the black hole, or even philosophy, he wonders, be seen as "illnesses" of matter and language respectively? If one can shift "I" and "mine" from center to periphery, even for an instant, as DK does here, a quantum of freedom is achievable, even in severe illness, as in his case. This is, if you wish, DK's re-interpretation of the Buddhist notion of anātman, which he would render as selflessness, but not in the iconic sense of Buddhahood for the sake of all sentient beings, but as a daily, mundane habit of seeing and being.

DK closes "The Cosmic" with this plea:

> Thinking about freedom has to be freed from the illusion of its being there as something "given," as something ontological, or transcendental, or non-natural, something God-given to man alone, "given" as fixed and final, rooted as it is in the nature of human reality itself; forgetting that there is no pre-given, unchanging nature of man, or of anything else, and that the dream of power associated with it, leading to the idea of even the possibility of omnipotence, will turn it into a nightmare for others, if not for oneself, and create a "hell" instead of that which one has hoped for and dreamt. At a level still deeper, the illusion about freedom will lead to a greater unfreedom and bondage for oneself and others, a bondage from which one would find it increasingly difficult to extricate oneself.

DK pleads for freedom from the illusion of a "given" freedom. Since the human being and the human situation are constantly changing, why postulate an unchangeable notion of freedom? DK shoots a final arrow at the idea of omnipotence as freedom, and reminds his readers that freedom is "something" that has to be negotiated between different members of the society, to make sure that my freedom is not achieved at the expense of your freedom, and vice versa. The idea of omnipotence, or unlimited power of one person, DK realistically suggests, can become a nightmare for others. "The illusion of omnipotence has gripped mankind," he further writes, "which seems to have learnt nothing from the disaster created by this mentality in the Soviet Union and Nazi Germany in the previous century." But we can also think of smaller-scale cases of exploitation resulting from power imbalance. DK finally warns that the striving for a "fixed and final freedom" can become a source of "unfreedom and bondage for oneself and others." This is to say, yet again, that in the name of "ultimate freedom," the here and now is as usual forgotten, including the numerous freedoms, "as empirical as anything could be," which are available to us now and here, and which for DK are far more significant than anything "ultimate."

In the next segment I will discuss a new model of knowledge, "KWC," that DK developed in a series of papers (written from 2005 onwards). I touched in the Introduction on the interface between freedom and knowledge in DK. The next segment mirrors our discussion of freedom so far (in the Introduction, I also depicted DK's oeuvre as a conceptual Hall of Mirrors). It reinforces and amplifies DK's critical approach to the notion of freedom. The following lines will show that DK attempts to demystify knowledge by bringing it, like freedom, down to earth. In both cases, interlinked to one another, he adds to the metaphysical (if not fully replaces it with) a vital empirical foundation. In both cases, DK refutes givenness and unchangeability, highlighting knowledge and freedom as processes and perennial strivings. Moreover, he hints at the politics that underlie and the psychological habits that determine our thinking about freedom and knowledge. Finally, in his discussion of knowledge, as much as in his discussion of freedom, DK is not blind to the growing role of technology. Like freedom, he argues, knowledge is not "out there" waiting to be discovered, or "hidden deep within" waiting to be recovered or retrieved. It is constructed, and even manufactured, according to needs and agendas that have nothing to do with old, romantic, but long-expired notions, such as "truth" and "certainty." Finally, I would like to suggest that DK's notion of KWC is an exercise of freedom. DK takes the freedom to rethink knowledge, the most central concept of philosophy.

3 KWC: Knowledge without Certainty

In a letter to his friend and colleague D. P. Chattopadhyaya, dated August 2006, DK writes:

> Philosophy as it has developed up till now has become irrelevant to the emerging situation where "engineered transformation" of all reality, including man himself, life in general, along with the exploration in space are questioning everything. The earth-centricity and bio-centricity of man have determined his thinking. In the realm of nuclear physics, new forms of matter are being created, with properties which question the old notions of matter, space, time and causality. In the field of economics, and to some extent of politics, the situation is even more alarming. The basic parameters on which the sciences of economics and sociology were based are in jeopardy, as the notions of land, labour and capital have gone a sea-change, as they are not there as something "given," or as a constraint, but instead as something which can be overcome by human ingenuity and effort. This is the challenge to philosophers, as I see it. Whether we can come to terms with it in any meaningful way is difficult to say, but we must become aware of it, and try to deal with it, so that our thinking may be relevant to the incoming generation which increasingly finds all past knowledge irrelevant to their "living" concerns.[3]

This paragraph captures the background behind DK's attempt, in the last years of his life, to sculpture a new concept of knowledge, applicable to a new world, in which the giant leap that science has taken changed and continuously changes everything, from matter, to the concepts of land and labor. DK is neither afraid of change nor nostalgic about old concepts that determined our life and thinking, and that are now sent to the museum of ideas. He is curious about the "replacements," about new concepts that will shape our life in new ways, and bring about new forms of freedom and bondage. Here I think of the fact that we are hooked today, everywhere, to our "screens," a phenomenon that DK could hardly foresee. I use the word "hooked," further thinking of Nir Eyal's book *Hooked: How to Build Habit-Forming Products* (2014). "A 2011 university study," Eyal writes in his introduction,

> suggested people check their phones thirsty-four times per day. However, industry insiders believe that number is closer to an astounding 150 daily sessions. Face it: We're hooked. The technologies we use have turned into compulsions, if not full-fledged addictions. It's the impulse to check a message notification. It's the pull to visit YouTube, Facebook, or Twitter for just a few minutes, only to find yourself still tapping and scrolling an hour later. [. . .] The products and services we use habitually alter our everyday behavior, just as their designers intended. Our actions have been engineered.[4]

"My goal," he further writes,

> is to provide you with a deeper understanding of how certain products change what we do and, by extension, who we are.

Eyal's book works in two opposing directions. On one hand, he teaches his readers, potential hi-tech designers, how to build a habit-forming product. On the other hand, it is implied that if the reader, any of us, will come to know "how it works," if a window is opened to the backstage of our screens, this will enable us to be less depended, addicted, and unfree. Or, as Eyal puts it, it will enable us not to become Zombies. But is there a way back from the "Zombie-ness" described here ("still tapping and scrolling an hour later")? Eyal's book reinforces DK's hunch, conveyed in the letter quoted earlier, that philosophy should move on to work in new spheres, such as the internet, "the screens," technology. Here, knowledge should be rethought to remain meaningful, rather than becoming a historical relic, alongside other dinosaur notions. And moreover, the question of self-identity needs also be addressed anew ("certain products change who we are," Eyal bluntly writes), as also numerous ethical questions pertaining to our "cyber existence."

Back to DK's KWC: How can we even begin to think about a concept of knowledge that embraces, rather than rejects uncertainty, ambiguity, probability, and chance? Yes, these are the new companions that DK assigns to knowledge instead of truth and certainty. Such a concept of knowledge stands in sheer contrast to everything we connote with knowledge. In his paper "Knowledge: Whose is It? What is It? and Why Has It to Be True?" (2005), DK writes:

> Knowledge does not belong to anybody, even though one may say "I know" [. . .] knowledge is a collective, cumulative affair of mankind, and if it had to be regarded as "belonging" to anybody, it would be to mankind as such, and not to this or that "I." But mankind includes not only those who lived in the past, but those who will live in the future also. [. . .] knowledge is an ongoing human enterprise, a collective puruṣārtha. [. . .] A puruṣārtha is a matter of seeking, perennial seeking, as perennial as time itself, and hence not something that can be possessed, or meant to be possessed. (2005, 185)

Knowledge "does not belong to anybody," both at the individual level and at the level of caste, or class. For DK, any attempt to exclude anyone from knowledge and knowing is a crime, nothing less. Knowledge, according to him, should be open for all. Often in his writings, he fights against the notion of adhikāra, "entitlement," the Sanskrit version of the notice "The Management Reserves the Right of Admission" that one finds today in restaurants or hotels. In his Shimla Lectures (2005), DK refers to the exclusion of śūdras, the "low-castes," or "outcastes," not just from the Vedic ritual but even from the Upaniṣadic striving for Brahman/mokṣa, namely, from the right to learn, to know, and to acquire a sense of beyondness and a measure of freedom, as "the original guilt of the Indian civilization." He sees knowledge as a collective puruṣārtha, or "human seeking." As such, it necessitates a dialogue between the members of "the interrelated and interacting community, both visible and invisible," as DK puts it (in "Conversation, Dialogue, Discussion, Debate and the Problem of Knowledge," 2007, 9). The phrase "invisible community" refers not just to the "invisible" (in the eye of whom?) "outcastes" or "low-castes" (Ralph Ellison's *Invisible Man* comes to mind, even if it was written in a different context and culture), but moreover, to the thinkers of the future. For DK, one's thinking is in constant correspondence not just with the thinkers of the past, and of the now, but even of the future. But what does it mean to correspond with thinkers who are not yet born, and with thoughts that are not yet conceived? For DK, a questioning approach, which conveys the understanding that nothing about my thinking is "final," since thinking is a continuous, open-ended process, is a good start.

DK's KWC is the "antonym" of Śaṅkara's Brahmavidyā, "Brahman knowledge," or "knowledge pertaining to the Brahman alone," as the paradigm of any "religious knowledge." DK is worried that the "theological hangover," as he puts it (in "Thinking vs. Thought," 1988, 48), namely, blind acceptance of authority—in Śaṅkara, the authority of the scriptures, the Upaniṣads—is not a matter of the past but is a continuous approach even today. "The tribes of Marxians, Freudians, Fregeans, Wittgensteinians, Husserlians and Chomskians are legion," DK writes, "and one may easily extend the list if one is inclined to do so. The disciples proudly proclaim the final findings of the master, little realizing that each of them has been rejected as untenable by followers of the other group" (1988, 52). For Śaṅkara, "real knowledge," or "true knowledge" (as against avidyā, which amounts to the shadows of the Platonic cave) pertains merely to the Brahman, an "eternal beyondness" that is supposed to be the crux of each of us; a sense of selfhood, or ātmanhood, which transcends the everyday "I." Śaṅkara depicts Brahmavidyā as trikālābādhita, "unrefuted and irrefutable in any of the three times," namely, past, present, and future. For him, "knowledge" (and his grand project was to "knowledgify" the Advaitic, non-dualistic, metaphysical experience) is unchangeable by definition. The future, absolutely irrelevant for Śaṅkara's Brahmavidyā, which falls out of time and temporality, is at the heart of DK's KWC as inherent uncertainty. "What is known," DK writes,

> is not only incomplete, but full of inaccuracies, inadequacies and errors, about which one knows nothing, except that they must be there, if the enterprise of knowledge has to go on, as it must. ("Definition, Deception and the Enterprise of Knowledge," 2005, 88)

The future will "fill the gaps" of knowledge as we know it today, and it will have its own new "gaps" to be again filled in the future's future. The future will not bring about the certainty that DK's concept of knowledge sobered up from. It is knowledge aware of its own limitations and unavoidable lacunas. Contrary to Śaṅkara's unchangeable Brahmavidyā, DK's KWC anticipates and invites change. In a paraphrase on Leibniz's famous maxim, KWC is "pregnant with the future."

But what is new about DK's KWC? Does he not take the same path, for instance, as Karl Popper, who famously suggests (in his essay "Science: Conjectures and Refutations," 1963), that a scientific theory is a theory that is open for refutation, hence knowledge (if I may apply Popper for our discussion) is rooted in theories that have not been refuted yet? Like Popper (even if in a different context and framework), DK emphasizes refutability over proofability. But moreover, he challenges the synonymity between knowledge, truth, and certainty. DK's argument is that despite the changing world of scientific breakthroughs (only yesterday I read that at Tel Aviv University, researchers "printed" the world's first 3D vascularized engineered heart, using the patient's own cells); despite new logics (non-classical, or non-Aristotelian) and new geometries (non-Euclidean), which we all know about and can easily read about and delve into the details of—we remain entrenched in old notions and models of knowledge. We live in the present but think in the past. It is this imbalance that DK calls attention to. As in other domains, DK highlights changeability, plurality and the unknown, over the alleged unchanging, singular and familiarly known. DK invites us to calibrate our thinking to the world in which we live.

As he was working on KWC, two texts were lying on DK's desk: John Horgan's essay "The Death of Proof" (1993) and Jacques Derrida's collected essays *Eyes of the University: Right to Philosophy 2* (2004). In his paper "Reading Derrida with Daya Krishna: Postmodern Trends in Contemporary Indian Philosophy" (2018), Dor Miller underscores DK's ambivalence toward Derrida and "postmodern thinking." On one hand, a modernist through and through, DK is threatened by the postmodern project. "The story of a civilization," he tells his listeners at Shimla (2005),

> closes at the point where the notions of reason, rationality and argumentation are being shattered. Postmodernism is the classic word

> for it, and Derrida and Rorty are perhaps the best examples. For them, there is no such thing as reason, and logocentrism is at a discount. [. . .] Postmodernism has destroyed everything. These people have destroyed their own house, their own foundations. And now they are looking around, complaining at the debris which is around them. It is the strangest situation, where man has self-consciously, gradually committed suicide, and then he asks "What is happening to me?"

But according to Miller, DK is much closer to Derrida than he is willing to admit, or even aware of. I agree with him that there is a "deconstructive" dimension to DK's work. In an interview with Steve Paulson, Gayatri Chakravorty Spivak, speaks of

> that part of deconstruction which said that you do not accuse what you are deconstructing. You enter it. Remember that critical intimacy? And you locate a moment where the text teaches you how to turn it around and use it.[5]

Spivak's articulation, especially the part of "entering" a text and "locating a moment where the text teaches you how to turn it around" is for me, an accurate description of DK's project of reading classical Indian sources anew, raising the "unasked questions." But there is also the process of "opening the text," in which one needs to confront authority, be it the authority of the text, the author, or the tradition that claims possession of the text. Or as Spivak puts it:

> Deconstruction simply questions the privileging of identity so that someone is believed to have the truth. [. . .] It is constantly and persistently looking into how truths are produced. (*The Spivak Reader*, 1996, 27)

Spivak's articulation again captures DK's working method. Both in the sense of questioning the belief that "someone" is the holder, or the owner of truth, and when she speaks of a persistent look into the politics of "truth-making."

Miller focuses on Derrida's abovementioned *Eyes of the University: Right to Philosophy 2*, which he reads with DK, namely, vis-à-vis DK's writings. He notices a mutual concern shared by these two contemporary thinkers. In Derrida, it is concern about the "right to philosophy," as implied by the title of the anthology, which according to him is under threat, and consequently, about what he refers to as "the future of the unconditional university." This articulation is from his essay "The future of the profession or the unconditional university (thanks to the "humanities," what could take place tomorrow," 2005). Derrida is concerned with conditions and conditionings that affect the "unconditional" status of the university, seen by him as the crux of the academic endeavor. In other words, the French thinker is worried about the future (which is perhaps already here) of academic freedom, yet another freedom for our discussion of freedoms. DK shares this concern. In his case, it is articulated in terms of "the future of knowledge." The problem, DK argues, is that knowledge has become sponsored and dependent on its sponsors. It is like searching for the coin under the lamppost. Knowledge is becoming more and more determined and less free. It is losing its open-endedness, which for DK is a crucial aspect of what knowledge is all about.

In his Shimla Lectures, DK tells his listeners (who might be still romantically associating knowledge with truth, even Capital-T Truth) that,

> the attitude to knowledge is nowadays determined by governments, large companies, industrialists. They determine what will be done with it, and how it is to be produced. Knowledge is no longer independent of the purposes which we want to derive from it. And the purposes are only two: economic profit and military. Knowledge today is funded and controlled. It is controlled by big corporations, big business centers, or funded for military purpose. Power or profit! This is, to my mind, a very dangerous game. (2012, 85–6)

Miller reads DK's appeal for "independent knowledge" through Derrida's pertinent distinction (in his essay "The Principle of Reason: The University in the Eyes of its Pupils," 1983) between "fundamental" and "end-oriented" research. Derrida depicts the former as "disinterested research with aims that would not be pledged in advance to some utilitarian purpose" (1983, 12). The latter, which becomes increasingly dominant, he portrays as "research [that] may 'pay off,' be usable." What is mutual in DK and Derrida is not just the concern, but their belief that it is the responsibility of the intellectual, the academic, to protect academic freedom, namely, to encourage research that is not "oriented," or "usable," as Derrida (or more precisely Catherine Porter and Edward P. Morris, his English translators) put(s) it. Interestingly, with reference to the responsibility of the academia to protect itself, Derrida mentions—and rightly so—the academic presses. It is in their hand to support, namely, to publish, "fundamental research." Both thinkers, DK as much as Derrida, believe that it is the responsibility of the intellectual to make sure that "the eyes of the university" remain wide open, and fight against "forces that are apparently external to the university," as Derrida puts it again, which aim to blinker the academic horse and make sure that he runs in "the right direction," namely, the direction that serves them best.

On this backdrop, DK appeals to his listeners at Shimla and says:

> Friends! We are suffering from nostalgia. We are thinking of the past, of the golden age of India, when the ṛṣis [the seers] walked around and meditated; when the ātman [the self beyond] was sought and the ātman-Brahman identity [the identity of self and Whole] was taught; when the Bhaktas [devotees] were singing their songs and engaged in kīrtan [devotional chanting]; when people were talking of sāmarasya [harmony] between Śiva and Śakti [the ultimate masculine and feminine principles]. We live in a private world; we live in a nostalgic world. We live in a world which is very strange. When I talk to people, they seem to be unaware of what is going on. They know something of what economics is doing; they know something of what politics is doing; but they do not believe in the reality of politics and economics. For them these realms are unreal or belong merely to the vyāvahārika [worldly] realm. (2012, 114–15)

DK speaks to classicists, in love with "the wonder that was." He feels that his listeners, or at least many of them, do not wish "to get their hands dirty" with politics, budgets, interests, and agenda. They prefer to hold onto the innocent idea of "pure knowledge." But were Plato's academy, or King Janaka's court, free from politics and agenda? According to DK of the Shimla Lectures, every intellectual must become aware of "what is going on" and must wake up into the now, if the academic enterprise is dear to his heart. Miller finally shows that for DK, the weapon of the intellectual against any threat on his/our academic freedom, against the end-oriented approach and the demand for usability at all cost, is a questioning approach. "To ask a new question," Miller quotes DK, "is to disrupt the closed circle of accepted knowledge, and to open a new vista for thought. Asking a new question is an invitation to look at things anew" ("Thinking vs. Thought," 1988, 49). Questions are powerful. They open new routes of thinking, not necessarily in accord with the tune called by the paymaster.

In the next chapter I will continue to discuss, in dialogue with DK, bondages and freedoms in the social and political domains.

4

Concepts and Actions

Daya Krishna and Social Philosophy

But Friends, the vyavahāra [the here and now, everyday life] matters!

Daya Krishna, Shimla Lectures, 2005

The arrogance of knowledge is as much an arrogance as the arrogance of power, and both lead to essential asymmetries. [. . .] A questioning attitude may prick the pretentions of both, as neither is as certain or secure as it usually proclaims itself to be.

Daya Krishna, "Thinking vs. Thought: Strategies for Conceptual Creativity," 1988, 48

1 Prologue

In the preface of his magnum opus *The Art of the Conceptual*, a collection of articles composed over three decades—"a long time in the life-span of an individual," as DK soberly remarks, "scarcely noticeable in the history of thought" (1989, xi)—he summarizes the main themes that occupied his thought over the years:

> The relation of logic to reality and its relevance to philosophy or philosophizing, the multifariousness of values and their essential conflict with one another, the essential irreducibility of diverse realms and the concepts and categories through which we demarcate them, the centrality of consciousness and the strange fact that beliefs tend to bring corresponding realities into being through the actions they influence, and the strange and paradoxical nature of social reality as the continuing creation of a plurality of free beings, each simultaneously a subject and an object, an agent and a recipient, all rolled into one. (1989, xi)

This list is interesting as it reveals DK's broad spectrum of thinking. His deep commitment to the worldly (he uses the word "reality" three times) is evident, as much as his interest in the interconnected social and ethical domains. But moreover, DK insists that the conceptual realm, abstract and theoretical as it is, must not remain isolated from "reality," from the world. We saw that for him, the spiritual quest and the metaphysical aspiration remain "empty" unless they effect the now and here. His vision of philosophy and philosophizing is not different. The philosopher, according to DK, has a responsibility toward the world, this world, our world, and philosophy can and should contribute in the social and political spheres. Or as D. P. Chattopadhyaya—philosopher and statesman, a modern avatar of the classical rājarṣi, rāja (king) and ṛṣi ("seer") in one—puts it,

> Actions, Daya Krishna maintains, imply a direct reference to the effectivity of consciousness, for actions and concepts, according to him, are not causally unrelated. (1996, 162–3)

DK once spoke to me about three types of "world-changers": the scientist, the philosopher, and the yogin. The scientist changes the world through his scientific discoveries that modify our worldview, and are often translated into technology that becomes part of our life; the philosopher, by opening a reflective space and daring to ask the difficult questions; and the yogin, the yoga adept, by transforming oneself, disclosing the subtle reciprocity between self and world (personal communication, January 2006). Inclusive as ever, DK did not see this threefold formulation as excluding other "world-changers." In effect, everyone can and should contribute to the shaping of the world that we all share. Belonging to the second category, DK took the task of "changing the world" very seriously. He was both a theorist and an activist: an activist through his writings and academic presence. As a theorist, he aimed at setting up a new social theory for India, first by "calibrating," or "bending" (I borrow both terms from A. Raghuramaraju), or adapting Western theory for what he saw as the needs of India as a newly born nation-state, and consequently by looking into classical Indian sources, from the epics to Kauṭilya's *Arthaśāstra*, a project that resulted in his work *The Problematic and Conceptual Structure of Classical Indian Thought about Man, Society and Polity* (henceforth *Man, Society and Polity*). It is a groundbreaking book in the sense that it shifts the social, political, and even legal to center-stage, hence reviving and revising the notion of vyavahāra, pertaining to our phenomenal existence, a notion often used and presented by mokṣa-authors derogatorily.

DK's early writings in social philosophy ("Social Change: An Attempt at a Study in Conflicting Patterns of Social Action," *Planning, Power and Welfare*, *Considerations Towards a Theory of Social Change*, *Social Philosophy Past and Future*, and *Political Development: A Critical Perspective*—1954, 1959, 1965,

1969, and 1979, respectively) were written in the first three decades after India's independence as his contribution to the newly born state. DK worked with notions such as "welfare" and "development" conceptually, theoretically, toward their practical application. I wish to add that the word "toward" that I use here is a prevalent phrase in the titles of DK writings. His "towards" titles include the abovementioned *Considerations Towards a Theory of Social Change*, and his papers "An Attempt Towards a Theory of Ethics" (1957), "Towards a Saner view of Development: A Comment of Fred W. Riggs' Comment" (1976), and "Towards a Field Theory of Indian Philosophy: Suggestions for a New Way of Looking at Indian Philosophy" (1998). His monograph *Towards a Theory of Structural and Transcendental Illusions* (1998/2012) is another "towards" work, which still awaits a comprehensive exploration. I would like to suggest that DK is a "towards thinker." This is to say that he never submits (or believes in the possibility of submitting) a "complete" work before his readers. Instead, he invites them to join him in his thinking process, to become his interlocutors, to raise questions, and to travel with him "towards." But toward what? "The art of philosophical thinking," Arindam Chakrabarti suggests,

> is a journey towards clarification [. . .] Daya's preferred method of clarification of a basic concept consisted in teasing out all possible oppositions to and misunderstandings of that concept, and then rejecting or correcting those objections and mistakes. (2011, 20)

Chakrabarti draws on DK's own assertion, in his first work, *The Nature of Philosophy*, that "philosophy lives in the clarification of its own confusions, a clarification that is its own death" (1955, 230). The depiction of philosophy as "always living on the verge of death" is interesting. First, since there is a sense of clarity in the face of death, as numerous thinkers, from the author of the *Kaṭha-Upaniṣad*, through Albert Camus (I think of the last few lines of *The Stranger*), to Ramchandra Gandhi (as we saw in Chapter 3) imply. And second, since it projects DK's "towards" as a perpetual process. He invites his readers to embark with him on a never-ending journey of clarification, "a journey with many departures, but no final arrival," as Chakrabarti beautifully puts it (2011, 3).

I wrote in detail (in Chapter 1) on DK's Saṃvād Project, his dialogic meetings with the pandits, the Sanskrit classicists, for the sake of establishing "something new" in Indian philosophy. But in fact, DK's first Saṃvād took place much before the interactions with the pandits. It was a dialogic brainstorming of thinkers from Asian countries, each rooted in his own cultural framework, in the endeavor of establishing "something new" in the social and economic domains post-independence, after the British. It was an attempt for an early Brexit if you wish, an inverted Brexit. Not of the British from the European Union, but of the former colonies from British economy and, more broadly, from British intervention in every aspect of their life. Simultaneously, it was an attempt at departing—or at least taking first steps in this direction—from "soulless thinking and shadow mind," as KCB puts it in "Svarāj in Ideas." This Saṃvād occurs on the pages of DK's early work *Planning, Power and Welfare* (1959). It is a dialogue between DK, then at the department of philosophy, Sagar University, and economists Vu Quoc Thuc of the University of Saigon, Vietnam, and Nurul Islam of the University of Dhaka, Bangladesh. It is an intra-Asian dialogue between three scholars from the non-West, attempting to decolonize the concept of welfare. DK's later motto, "when people gather together, something new emerges" (1988, 54), captures the incentive behind this dialogue. But a dialogue is no easy task, especially when the participants belong not just to different countries and cultures but also to different disciplines. DK, the publisher of this early Saṃvād notes, "is not a professional economist. That may perhaps be the reason why he is able to approach the subject from a fresh angle" (1959, 4). But what appealed to the publisher as "fresh" was not necessarily seen as such by the economists. Many years later, DK would look back at his work in different areas of philosophy and remark that "the questions that we asked them [specialists of different disciplines, here the economists] appeared both new and inconvenient" (2001, 8). The advantage of the "outsider," he further explains—and for him the philosopher is always, necessarily, an outsider—is that his "inconvenient" questions can work in the direction of "disrupting" old frames, hence opening new horizons for thinking. In his Saṃvād with the economists, DK enquires about the human person, the individual. He wants to know how the particular villager or urbanite, man and woman, participates, fits in, or enjoys the fruits of the master-game called "economic development." He is further interested, and works toward the clarification of the connection between welfare and concepts such as power and freedom.

Another saṃvād in social philosophy occurs on the pages of *Development Debate* (1987). Here DK is in conversation with Fred W. Riggs, a scholar of public administration. As I write these lines, I googled Riggs to discover that besides his affiliation to the University of Hawaii at Manoa, known for its intercultural spirit, he was born and lived the first eighteen years of his life in China. These biographical details might explain his willingness to engage in a dialogue with DK, unlike other Western scholars who were not always enthusiastic despite the best of DK's efforts. As Bryan Van Norden shows in *Taking Back Philosophy: A Multicultural Manifesto* (2017), too many Western philosophers, famous names included, believe even today that the sun of philosophy, or even rationality, rises in Western Europe and sets in North America. Riggs is famous for his "fused-prismatic-diffracted model," which covers "economic life, social structures, political symbols, and the allocation of power" (Wen-Shien Peng, 2008, 529). In conversation with DK, Riggs explains that this model aims "to establish a general framework in which all societies can be compared, and a better understanding reached about their developmental status and prospects" (1987, 57). There is something old-fashioned in a debate on a universal model that is meant to cover "all societies." DK, at least in retrospect, is not unaware of the fact that this "All"—reminiscent of pre-Socratic philosophers, or the Buddha's "sabbaṃ dukkhaṃ" (All is suffering), or Hegel, or Sri Aurobindo—is fast becoming an exhibit at the museum of ideas. With reference to his book *Prolegomena to Any Future Historiography of Cultures and Civilizations* (1997), which also belongs to the "All" genre, DK admits that "it has become unfashionable to think large." "No one wants to be caught speculating about things in general," he writes sarcastically, "this is just not scientific" (I quote from a letter, dated August 2004). His own take is altogether different. He sees merit both in the wide-lens of "thinking large"—globally, universally, and comparatively—and in the zoom-lens, or even nano-lens approach, predominant in the academia today. As always, DK prefers free travel between alternatives, or extreme poles—in this case two modes of thinking, sarvārthatā and ekāgratā—panoramic and one-pointed, or focused.

I cannot delve into the details of the dialogue between DK and Riggs, but here is just a taste of it. At a crucial moment of the discussion, the post-colonialist in DK suggests that according to the development model of his interlocutor, one can reach the conclusion that "subjected, exploited and enslaved societies," crushed under the colonizer's boot, have actually "developed" during their colonized phase or at least achieved "cultural and political base for development." This is hardly in accord, DK further suggests, with Riggs's own assertion that development is "a process whereby human societies become less determined by environmental constraints, and more able to shape their own destiny" (1987, 72). DK sees Riggs's latter contention as "a move in the right direction," except for the vague phrase "environmental constraints." "The environment of a society, or a nation-state," DK remarks, "consists primarily of other societies and nation-states, and only secondarily of what may be considered as the natural environment" (1987, 73). Development, according to DK, should not be measured merely by economic and technological parameters. Development in his formulation is not just an external display. Therefore, the colonizer cannot be seen as truly "developed." Release from the claws of colonialism, on the other hand, is certainly a sign of development. Freedom and development are closely related.

In the next segment I will discuss DK's essay "Socio-Political Thought in Classical India" (1997, henceforth "Socio-Political"). This essay was published as chapter 16 of Eliot Deutsch and Ron Bontekoe's edited volume *A Companion to World Philosophies* (1997). Another chapter of the book, "A History of Indian Philosophy" by J. N. Mohanty, is dedicated to the "duḥkha to mokṣa" narrative, which is usually seen as defining Indian philosophy. "From the very beginning," Mohanty writes here,

> philosophy in India had a practical orientation. Since it was generally held by the religions and philosophies that human existence is characterized by suffering, and that the goal of the reflective life was to be free from suffering, philosophical knowledge of whatever is real, especially of one's true self, was regarded as a means to that goal. (1997, 42)

"Even you Brutus?" DK would ask his old friend Mohanty. To correct the situation, and to offer an alternative to the standard narrative that depicts Indian philosophy as no more than a remedy for "human existence as suffering," DK writes on social and political philosophy. "The historical development of the socio-political thought of India," DK writes here,

> has not been paid much attention by those who have written on Indian philosophy. [. . .] It is in the social, political and legal thought of India, that one may find a counter-picture to the still prevalent one that has been developed around the centrality of the renouncer tradition. (1997, 246–7)

If human existence is indeed a matter of suffering (and even pleasure is seen in this narrative as long-term suffering, since whatever it is that we enjoy is necessarily transient and time-bound), then the aspiration for that which is more than human, trans-worldly, and supramundane makes sense. In this respect, DK speaks of "the centrality of the renouncer tradition," which aims to renounce and transcend everything worldly. He himself, we already know, utterly rejects the diagnosis of human life as suffering, and is far more interested in the now and here than in world renunciation, beyondness, and so on.

2 A World of Relations

Sociopolitical thought in India, DK writes in the very first lines of "Socio-Political," had to deal with the abovementioned renouncer tradition, namely, with Buddhist and Jaina thinkers, who portrayed the daily and the mundane as inferior compared with "the ultimate pursuit of man," namely, beyondness, or transcendence, or out-of-the-world-ness. But the evaluation of the worldly as inferior, DK continues to write, raises a "basic dilemma," since "both these religions [Buddhism and Jainism] spread with the active support of kings and wealthy merchants" (1997, 137). Power and wealth, DK knows all too well, "constitute the very basis and foundation of every worthwhile pursuit of man, including spiritual pursuits." However, it is not just wealth and power that enable and facilitate the spiritual quest, but also nature, the elements, matter in the most essential sense of the word. "Just as the living body is there, very much there," DK writes,

> helping one to be in a state of meditation, so is the air one breathes, the earth on which one sits and all the rest which supports the earth and the air in the universe. ("The Undeciphered," 2012, 98)

Denial of the world, of matter, and of one's responsibility toward the world (these lines are written as Brazil's Amazon rainforest is in flames) is for DK a sign of ungratefulness on behalf of the yogin, the aspirant of beyondness. Withdrawal and return, with emphasis on the return, DK endorses wholeheartedly; denial and repudiation, he totally rejects. Śaṅkara—master of the "beyondness beyond" and a lucid voice of world renunciation—suggests (in his commentary on *Chāndogya-Upaniṣad* 2.23.1) that under conditions of "hunger etc." (bubhukṣādi), the bhikṣu, or renouncer (which in his present discussion is a synonym of brahma-saṃstha, "one who is deeply rooted in Brahman"), might be distracted from his "conviction of unity" (ekatva-pratyaya, *Ten Principal Upaniṣads with Śāṅkarabhāṣya*, 2007, 407). Food is essential, even for the "enlightened" or the "awakened." In a paraphrase on Rabbi Elazar ben Azariah's famous maxim (in Pirkei Avot of the Jewish *Mishnah*), "if there is no flour, there is no Brahman," or at least one might forget his Brahman nature. Therefore, DK appeals (still in "The Undeciphered") to the *Taittirīya Upaniṣad*, which says "annaṃ na nindyāt" ("Do not speak ill of food," TU 3.7.1) and "annaṃ na paricakṣīta" ("'Do not despise food," TU 3.8.1). The spiritual and the worldly are closely related.

I suggested in the Introduction that contemporary Indian philosophy is a unique genre of philosophy, corresponding both with classical Indian sources and with Western materials, classical and modern. DK's appeal to the Upaniṣad is just an illustration. An alleged heretic or non-traditionalist, a modernist, and perhaps even postmodernist, he is nevertheless rooted in the Upaniṣads and pulls out the relevant verse at the right moment. To read and to engage in a dialogue with DK, one needs to have at least a certain amount of acquaintance with a broad spectrum of sources between which he wanders with ease. If one is versed in the Upaniṣads and Śaṅkara, it is a good start, but Kant, Hegel, KCB, and numerous other thinkers and texts, Indian and Western, are as essential, if one wishes to join DK on his philosophical journeys.

In "Socio-Political," in fact a summary of DK's abovementioned *Man, Society and Polity*, he visits the *Dharmasāstra*, the *Vyavahāraśāstra*, and the *Rājanītiśāstra*. "The term śāstra denotes systematic body of knowledge," he explains to the uninitiated, and the terms dharma, vyavahāra, and rājanīti "denote what is generally conveyed in English by morality, law and polity" (1997, 137). Society, DK suggests, is the realm where each individual has an obligation to the other. The notion of dharma covers this self-with-others constellation. The term "vyavahāra," DK further suggests, namely, law, is far more concrete than the often evasive notion of dharma. And then there is rājanīti, the political domain. The relation between these three interfacing realms is complicated, DK writes, by a number of factors, and primarily by the fact that thinking about society in India has always been in terms of varṇa, that is, caste or class. We saw that he makes a similar argument in "The Varṇāśrama Syndrome." In "Socio-Political," DK returns to the Puruṣa-Sūkta (The Hymn of Man) of the *Ṛgveda*, the Vedic hymn that is supposed to have provided the blueprint for thinking in terms of caste. However, this hymn is not just about the varṇas, the castes, but about the creation of the whole cosmos. Why and how, then, has Indian social thinking become fixated with these four classes, DK wonders out loud, and continues to be haunted by the hierarchy that places the Brahmins on top and the śūdras at the low bottom. He further visits other texts (the *Śukla Yajurveda*, the *Upaniṣads* and the *Mahābhārata*), which mention other social rubrics and sectors besides the four varṇas, thus opening a window to a broader social web. DK works with the interlinked notions of varṇa and jāti (caste and sub-caste, or the fourfold scheme versus the manifold caste-divisions), and continues to wonder about the equivalence, if any, between theory and practice, theory and life, as far the caste system is concerned. DK's critique is hardly new; however, he adds his voice, and the full weight of his intellectual stature, to those who wish to abolish casteism, both out there, in the world, and at the level of consciousness. Castes of the mind need to be eliminated as much as castes at the external, empirical level. In his journey, DK visits the *Nāṭyaśāstra*, the source-text of Indian art and aesthetics, which introduces itself as sārvavarṇika, namely, as open to every varṇa or caste. For him, this is a protest against the exclusion of the so-called lower and lowly. The fact that this text calls itself "the fifth Veda" (even if it is not the only text that aspires for this status), DK suggests, amplifies the volume of this protest.

On his journey, DK recalls the niṣādasthapati, the chief, or king of the Niṣāda tribe, mentioned in Jaimini's *Mīmāṃsāsūtra*. For him, this is an illustration of the breadth of the social fabric, above and beyond the varṇa or caste system. For me, any mention of the Niṣādas brings to mind Ekalavya, one of the *Mahābhārata*'s unforgettable characters. The son of the Niṣāda king (in the epic, the phrase is niṣāda-rāja), Ekalavya is eager to learn "the science of archery" (dhanurveda) from Droṇa, the famous archery guru, together with the kṣatriya princes at the royal court. But his attempt to cross over from tribe to caste ends with blood and tears. Ekalavya's blood and the readers' tears. Droṇa demands Ekalavya's right thumb as his teacher's fee (aṅguṣṭho dakṣiṇo dīyatāṃ, he commands harshly), and the Niṣāda, without a moment's hesitation, cuts off his thumb and hands it over to him. "In archery," S. Shankar explains,

> the thumb is an absolutely crucial digit. [. . .] Never again will Ekalavya be a challenge either to Droṇa and his favorite disciple Arjuna, or to the social order that they represent. (1994, 482 and 484)

And KD Vyas writes:

> The subaltern Ekalavya's bloodied thumb remains with us as a resonant smear of the truth of power. [. . .] The bloodied smear of the truth tells Ekalavya, overriding all ambiguities, who he is, who he is not, and what he never can hope to be.[1]

I have no clue who the writer of these lines is. Contemporary, political, razor-sharp, he (or she, or they) adopted the name of no other than the legendary author of the *Mahābhārata*, Kṛṣṇa Dvaipāyana Vyāsa (hence KD Vyas) as their pseudonym. But the point made here is loud and clear. Ekalavya's bloodied thumb is a painful reminder that (quoting Gopal Guru again) "exclusion, marginalization, ghettoization, and bracketing" are as much a syndrome of the present-day as they are of the past.

DK does not mention Ekalavya, but he does mention, both in "Socio-Political" and elsewhere, his Upaniṣadic double Satyakāma Jābāla. Satyakāma's story (narrated in *Chāndogya-Upaniṣad* 4.4.1-4.9.3) is again about caste and exclusion. Young and full of hope, Satyakāma does not allow his ambiguous family lineage to prevent him from living up to his name ("he whose desire is the truth") and manages to acquire knowledge of the Brahman (here, a synonym of truth) not from, but despite, his guru. Śaṅkara, the authoritative commentator of the *Upaniṣad*, strives to solve the social difficulty interwoven in the narrative by "Brahmanizing" Satyakāma, a move that grants him the adhikāra, or entitlement for the knowledge he seeks. According to Śaṅkara, Satyakāma's mother, Jabālā, was not "serving, that is, servicing men," as implied in the *Upaniṣad* (see CU 4.4.2). This explicit articulation is Ananya Vajpeyi's. Vajpeyi further suggests that "in all likelihood, the son of such mother would be treated as a śūdra" (2011, 349). But in Śaṅkara's alternative narrative, Jabālā was in fact a devoted wife, taking care of guests and visitors in her husband's household. "I was not in a state of mind to think of gotra etc." (gotrādi smaraṇe mama mano nābhūt), Śaṅkara imagines her telling her son. She was too busy, he implies, absorbed in her devoted work, to think or ask about their gotra. But gotra, namely, the record of one's family lineage, is a prerequisite if one wishes to be guided by a guru.

DK is disappointed by Śaṅkara's interpretive move. According to DK, the role of the commentator, or the intellectual at large, is to reveal, not to conceal social injustice. In his paper "The Vedic Corpus and the two Sūtra-Texts: The Mīmāṃsāsūtra and the Brahmasūtra," DK asserts that "the profound and far-reaching insight of the Upaniṣadic quest is twisted and perverted to suit narrow sectarian caste-interests of a society." "That a person writing in the eighth century [Śaṅkara]," DK adds, "should underwrite the partisan and prejudicial opinion of the author of a text written at least 500 years earlier [the *Brahmasūtra*, which claims to convey the gist of the *Upaniṣad*, but "opts against all reason for the exclusion of śūdras from the right to the knowledge of Brahman"] speaks volumes for what had happened to orthodox Vedic Hinduism during this period" (2011, 263). Neither Bādarāyaṇa, the author of the *Brahmasūtra*, nor Śaṅkara, who commented on both the *Upaniṣad* and the *Brahmasūtra*, stood against exclusion. In his paper "The Mīmāṃsaka versus the Yājñika: Some Further Problems in the Interpretation of *Śruti* in the Indian Tradition" (1995), DK pays another visit to Satyakāma's story. Here he quotes from this Upaniṣad at length, in the original Sanskrit, and remarks:

> Now this is simple and straightforward Sanskrit, requiring no philological expertise for its understanding. And yet, Śaṅkara comments on it in the following manner. (1995, 74)

Otherwise a minimalist when it comes to quoting, DK now quotes from Śaṅkara's commentary, again in the original, again at length, as if to imply that otherwise—unless he shows his readers the text—they will not believe, as he did not, that this is indeed how Śaṅkara works with the Upaniṣad. Having quoted text and commentary, DK writes:

> The turns and twists which Śaṅkara introduces to make the story respectable, and the so-called śruti [the scriptures] acceptable to the social prejudices of his time, would have been laughable if they did not also have a tragic aspect to them. Imagine! The great ācārya [Śaṅkara] making the poor Jabālā [Satyakāma's mother] not only a slave, entertaining her husband's guests all the twenty-four hours every day of the year, but he had to kill her husband so that she may be provided an excuse for not knowing what the gotra of her son's progenitor is. [. . .] Moreover, Śaṅkara gives no reason why she did not try to get the information after her husband's death, particularly when she must have known that such information would be required at the time of her son's marriage, if not at the time of his studies. She did not try to find because she knew that the information sought for could not be found. And this is what she is trying to say in so many plain words, whose simple and obvious meaning Śaṅkara is willfully trying not to understand, for that will destroy his private personal conception of what the śruti ought to say, or be. Or else, he is afraid of the undesirable consequences of the truth on society and public morality of his times. In either case, Śaṅkara is not being true to the śruti, nor displaying an attitude to it which one would expect to be displayed to a text deemed as revelatory. But then, did he not know what he was doing? Did he not see the absurdity of the hypotheses he had postulated to hide the truth? (1995, 74–5)

According to DK, Śaṅkara strips the Upaniṣadic story of its courageous social message. In the *Upaniṣad*, the teacher's reluctance to teach Satyakāma does not prevent the latter from solving the riddle of the Brahman. In the forest, he is enlightened by a bull (ṛṣabha), the fire (agni), a goose (haṃsa), and a diver-bird (madgu). I would suggest that it is Satyakāma's "otherness," which Śaṅkara aims to conceal, that enables him to acquire knowledge of the Brahman, which from a daily-worldly perspective is the "ultimate otherness." Moreover, he acquires this knowledge through "other" sources of knowledge (the animals and the fire instead of a standard guru). His success in achieving his spiritual goal despite his social background is seen by DK as an indication that for the author of the *Upaniṣad*, unlike his commentators, the Brahman is not and should not be excluded from anyone, whatever his caste is.

Back in "Socio-Political," DK suggests that "the first issue of debate among social theorists," as far as caste is concerned, was whether "a person belongs to these categories [the castes] by birth or by virtue of his acquired capacities to perform those functions?" (1997, 239). "The great empires known in India," he offers a reply of his own,

> from the Mauryan times onwards, were seldom founded by a person belonging to the kṣatriya varṇa [the warrior-ruling caste], or to a jāti [sub-caste] which is supposed to belong to this varṇa. (1997, 240)

Hence in practice, in history, virtue overcomes birth. The second issue of debate was the ideal relationship between the varṇas, or castes. "The conflict between power and knowledge and wealth," DK continues to narrate the story of "the history and thought about society and polity in India", "is writ large on the history of all civilizations, but it took a peculiar turn in India." This peculiar turn has to do with the fact that the Brahmins made a constant attempt to ensure that the rulers comply with "the norms that were expected of them" (1997, 240). DK depicts a sociopolitical reality with checks and balances, which enabled the state to function not merely at the whims and fancies of the ruler. To protect freedom of expression, DK further writes, the Brahmins were granted the status of adaṇḍya and avadhya, that is, given immunity from punishment and especially death penalty. The narrative sketched by DK is very different from the one usually presented about Indian philosophy. No duḥkha, mokṣa, or Brahman here, but social and political issues, such as freedom of speech, relevant and burning to this very day.

DK continues to portray a world of relations. He touches on the conflict between Brāhmaṇa and Śramaṇa, namely, between the Brahmins, in charge of "the norm-establishing function" of the society, and the Buddhist and Jain traditions of renunciation. DK's portrayal of the social role of the Brahmins sits well with Johannes Bronkhorst's claim that Brahmanism (his phrase) reinvented itself in the first centuries CE, after the decline of the "Vedic sacrificial tradition," as a "socio-political ideology" (I draw on his paper "Brahmanism: Its place in ancient Indian society," 2017). Bronkhorst further suggests that the Brahmins became advisers to ruling kings in matters of governance and were instrumental in running the state. The Buddhist and Jain monks could not provide such services to the king owing to their position as world-renouncers (I draw on his lecture "Rethinking India's Past").[2]

DK further touches on the relationship between the kṣatriya, or rājanya, and the śramaṇa, namely between kings and renouncers. "Right from the earliest Buddhist and Jain texts recounting the lives of the Buddha and the Mahāvīra [the founding fathers of the two traditions]," DK writes,

> it was a point of special emphasis that the ruling kings in those times not only paid visits to these outstanding spiritual personalities, but showed proper respect by getting down from their elephants and chariots, and walking on foot to the abode of the master. Many of the Mughal paintings display continuity in this respect. (1997, 242)

Paintings no less that written texts tell the historical story. DK further suggests that in the Buddhist and Jain canons, we hear of kings who converted into these traditions, and who sometimes even renounced their kingdoms and opted for the spiritual path. However, the king-renouncer relationship was not always idyllic. By their very renunciation, the renouncers form an alternative to the "normative life" in the world that the king epitomizes. By definition, they pose a threat to social structures and worldly frames.

The next issue raised in DK's discussion is the formation of parallel social and political patterns in renouncer communities. The very phrase "renouncer community" looks paradoxical. Is not renunciation a solitary pursuit? Romila Thapar explains that "institutionalized renunciation," namely, the creation of renouncer sects, served both for "preaching the message," since "those who believed that they had found the way wished to enlighten others," and to provide protection for the otherwise defenseless wandering ascetic (1988, 292). She agrees with DK that "the joining of an order by the renouncer often brought him back into performing a social role" (1988, 274). According to DK, "the Buddhist Bhikṣu, or the Jain Muni, is an integral member of a large community that dictates and determines the shape of his life and spiritual quest in the most detailed manner imaginable" (1997, 244). The establishment of these renouncer communities, DK notices, created a "large-scale dependence on the ruler, on the one hand, and on the wealthy trading community on the other, right from the time of the Buddha and Mahāvīra." "The Buddhist and the Jain formation of large-scale organizations," he adds, "became the dominant model to be revived later by Śaṅkara, and followed by later ācāryas [spiritual leaders] in the Indian tradition." DK lets the cat out of the bag, further suggesting that "the large-scale support that such organizations required from the society and the polity exerted at least some influence on the spiritual pursuit itself." Here and elsewhere, DK insists that the spiritual quest cannot be divorced from its worldly—social, political, and economic—foundation. Just like in current debates about academic (un)freedom, DK openly suggests that even in the spiritual realm, the sponsors have a say. DK touches here on the economy of mokṣa and the politics of spirituality. He further writes that these "societies of renouncers," as he puts it, and the "internal organization of discipline and hierarchies within them" need to be reflected upon closely, "as these societies began to have both an economic and political aspect to them, mirroring all the problems of the society and polity that their members left" (all quotes from 1997, 244). It is implied that the human being is a social and political animal, even the renouncer.

Toward the end of "Socio-Political," DK raises an issue that bothered him over time, and that is discussed in several of his essays. "The political theorist," he writes, "was also interested in theoretically countering the radically individualistic implication of the theory of karma, which almost led to moral monadism" (1997, 246). What is "moral monadism," and how and why would the theory of karma lead to moral monadism? DK explains in his early Shimla Lectures (delivered in 1967 and first published in 1969):

> The doctrine of karma in traditional Hindu thought reflects the basic presupposition that it would be an immoral world if one were to reap the fruits of someone else's actions. The monadic morality of the Hindu is thus conceived of in an essentially asocial manner. It does not derive from an other-centered consciousness in which the consequences of one's actions on others are the subject of one's focus of attention. Rather, it is the consequences of one's actions upon oneself which provide the main ground for morality in Hindu thought, and thus pave the way for a very different kind of perspective on the entire issue of action and one's relations with others. At the deepest level, not merely does what one does have consequences upon oneself but, conversely whatever happens to one could *only* be the result of one's own actions. Thus, not only do one's own actions have consequences on oneself, but also, if the world is to be a moral world, *nothing* else could. (*Civilizations: Nostalgia and Utopia*, 2012, 13–14)[3]

According to the theory of karma, one's present position in the world is the causal result of one's actions in the past. In the same way, one's present actions will determine one's future position. It is implied, and this is DK's concern, that the karma theory leaves no place for the other, for you. The other, at best, is instrumental to enable me to bring to fruition the karmic baggage that I carry along, and hopefully to acquire—owing to my attitude toward him—puṇya, merit, "good karma" that will have positive future consequences. One can hardly effect the other. One's actions determine one's own karma and one's future born of this karma. Morally speaking, then, each to his own. Therefore, DK speaks of "monadic morality" or "moral monadism." In "Socio-Political," he works with the notion of responsibility. "Strangely," DK writes,

> neither the political nor the social theorists [of classical India] moved forward to develop a full-fledged theory of karma in which collective responsibility could become the center of theoretical concern in reflection on human action. It is only the king who was supposed to share in the merit and demerit of his subjects, but as far as his subjects were concerned, there was no sharing in the fruits of action. (1997, 246).

DK's critique of "the prison house of I-centricity" and the illusion of "In the beginning there was the self" (see Chapter 3) now takes a social turn. Social, since action is at the heart of the social realm. DK does not hesitate to reveal a flaw in one of the inalienable assets of the Indian culture—the theory of karma. But this is not all. How does this "moral monadism," DK wonders, fit with the entire procedure of the Vedic yajña (sacrifice, ritual)? In the yajña, the yajamāna, the "patron" of the ritual, hires the services of a ṛtvika, a priest, to perform the ritual for him. The labor, the craft, the doing are all the priest's; hence according to the theory of karma, the fruits should be his. But surprisingly, it is the yajamāna who enjoys, or is supposed to enjoy, the fruits of this action. The whole ritual is formed to enable him to reap the fruits.

In light of this alleged contradiction between karma and yajña, DK appealed to an ensemble of pandits of the Mīmāṃsā tradition, and asked them if Jaimini, author of the *Mīmāṃsāsūtra*, "accepts the principle that whoever does the karma [the ritual, the action], its phala [fruit, result] goes to him only, [. . . or] does Jaimini have a different theory of karma?" (2003, 204 and 209). Why Jaimini of the *Mīmāṃsāsūtra*? Since the Mīmāṃsakas are interested in the ritual. Or as Johannes Bronkhorst more accurately puts it,

> Strictly speaking, and seen from their own theoretical perspective, the Mīmāṃsakas were not interested in the ritual. They studied the eternal Veda, using refined tools of interpretation, and it turned out that the Veda told them to perform rituals. Their ritual activities were not the result of their interest in ritual, but the outcome of their study of the infallible Veda. Had their interpretational efforts convinced them that the Veda told them to play tennis, they would then have played tennis, whether they liked it or not. (2014, 467)

Since they do not play tennis, but know the ins and outs of the Vedic ritual, DK addresses his query to the Mīmāṃsakas, the present-day descendants of Jaimini. This query was the starting point of another round of Saṃvād under the title "Does Mīmāṃsā treat the theory of karma as a pūrva-pakṣa [counter position]?" that appeared on the pages of the *JICPR* and later in DK's *Discussion and Debate in Indian Philosophy* (2004, 203–22). DK's query was translated into Sanskrit for the pandits, and their response translated back into English. DK insisted that the original Sanskrit is published together with its translation, to demonstrate that "Sanskrit still is a living all-Indian language of intellectual discourse," as he puts it in his Shimla Lectures (2005).

In search of a remedy for the monadic implications of the theory of karma, DK appeals to the Vedic yajña. The Vedic ritual is traditionally seen as the paradigmatic human action, resonating in every other action.

Svargakāmo yajeta ("whoever wishes to reach heaven, should sacrifice") is the basic formula of human action. Action is projected as the connecting thread between desire and fruit, or between desire and the achievement of the object, or objective of desire. As always, DK sees what others do not, namely, a contradiction between karma and yajña, the two central theoretical frames of action in classical India. According to the former, one's actions, and no one else's, have consequences on oneself and on no one else. In the latter, the actions of one person have consequences on another. But the pandits, in this round of Saṃvād, do not seem to grasp the broader picture at the horizon of DK's query. Instead, they provide him with a samādhāna, a solution to his query based on classical texts. DK asks them whether Jaimini accepts the karma theory, which appears to contradict the foundation of the yajña. "No contradiction" is their unanimous answer and solution, as the following lines will show. But DK, we already know, is hardly interested in "solutions." Of course, he is interested to be enlightened about the position of the *Mīmāṃsāsūtra* and its commentarial body. But his attempt is more far-reaching. He aspires to think with and from these source texts, and to formulate a new theory of action based on reciprocity between self and other, other and self.

No less than eight pandits responded to DK's query. The first of them, N. S. R. Tatacharyaswami, writes (I quote from the English translation by Kalanath Shastri):

> Jaimini accepts the theory that whoever does the karma [action] gets the phala [fruit, result]. Now if the yajamāna [the sponsor of the ritual] is unable to do the whole karma himself, he hires the ṛtvikas [priests] who help him in the karma. Thus in the main karma, the yajamāna is the doer (kartā). Therefore, the phala goes to him. The karmas of hired adhvaryus [the adhvaryu is in charge of the physical details of the ritual] reap fruit not to them, but to the yajamāna. (2003, 209)

This is the standard position, to be repeated by every other respondent, each in his own way. The yajamāna is the doer, it is his ritual; the priests are mere assistants, hence the fruit of the ritual belongs to him. But if the ritual is a collaborative undertaking, why should the fruits not be shared? For the pandits, the ritual is collaborative only in a technical sense. Pandit Surya Prakash Shastri explains:

> The Bhāṣya [Śabara's commentary on the *Mīmāṃsāsūtra*] clearly says that since the yajamāna does the utsarga [the act of offering the sacrifice to the deity], by that deed he does the whole thing. Therefore,

> we cannot say that the yajamāna is not the doer. There is no kartṛtva's abhāva [absence of doership] in the yajamāna. This is the samādhāna [the solution to the DK's query]. (2003, 2010).

"The yajamāna, is the causer (prayojaka) kartā [doer]," Pandit E. S. Varadacharya further elucidates. As the causer, the effect belongs to him; hence the theory of karma remains intact.

But a prayojaka is also an employer. And indeed, he employs the priests who physically perform the ritual. Pandit Laxminarayan Murti Sharma explains that the yajamāna gives dakṣiṇā to the ṛtvikas who assist him in performing the ritual. Romila Thapar explains that "dakṣiṇā is a gift or a donation made to a priest, or a sacrificial fee" (1979, 95). She further suggests that,

> in the study of the society and economy of ancient India, information has often to be ferreted out from seemingly unlikely sources. What is often associated with apparently non-economic activity such as religious rituals, can sometimes provide insights into social and economic concerns. (1979, 94)

DK would sign on every word. Like Thapar, he is interested in society and economy. Like her, he pays attention to the socio-economic foundation of the "apparently non-economic" spiritual quest and religious practice. Thapar speaks of valuable gifts that the priests would receive as dakṣiṇā for their sacrificial work, like the chariot of the yajamāna, the golden seats on which they sat, or a certain number of cows (1979, 101). But they did not share the fruits of the ritual. As a matter of fact, the pandits of our Saṃvād do speak of "auxiliary" or "intermediary" fruits of ritual that the priests did receive in the course of the ritual. This is not the final phala, fruit, aspired for by the yajamāna, but midway merits, or blessings of the gods, which contribute to the ritual procedure itself—merits needed for the operation of the yajña. For DK, this is crucial information, since it is a sign of shareability, subsidiary and midway as much as these fruits are.[4] For the pandits, this is just a footnote to the ritual, nothing more. The ṛtvikas and the yajamāna, Pandits N. S. Ramanuja Tatacharya and Sampat Narayana tell DK, are like soldiers and their king. They fight for him, but "the victory belongs to the king" writes Tatacharya (2003, 214). "The king enjoys the kingdom, not the warrior," Narayana agrees. For them, the hierarchy is clear. But why can there be no sharing of victory and kingdom?

It is a fact of life that people often work together, collaborate, cooperate, and enjoy the fruits of their action together. Rajendra Swaroop Bhatnagar goes as far as suggesting that every human action is a collaboration carried out in a setting that enables, or at least does not prevent, its performance; hence the idea of "my action" is a misnomer (personal communication, August 2019). It is also a fact of life that people share the pain and pleasure of others around them, the fruits of their karma if you wish. But why this shareability does not find adequate expression and is not duly discussed at the theoretical level, either in karma or yajña?[5]

In his answer to DK's query, Sampat Narayana further maintains that "here too," namely, with reference to the Vedic ritual and its fruits, "the Vedic injunction is the deciding factor, and not logic" (2003, 218). This remark marks the difference between insider and outsider. For DK, the Vedic injunction is not the final word, and his insistence on shareability, which he was hoping to find in a more pronounced fashion in the Mīmāṃsaka reading of the Vedic ritual, as against the "moral monadism" that he diagnosed in the theory of karma, is a central leitmotif of his social thinking. It goes back to his early Saṃvād with the Asian economists and his ardent query about the individual kisān, the particular farmer, within the broader picture of "welfare" and "development." DK pleads for shareability of fruits from the Vedic ritual to postcolonial economy. But then, as Romila Thapar shows, perhaps the two, economy and ritual, are not as far apart as they may seem.

3 The Active and the Contemplative Values

In an intriguing passage of his commentary on the *Bṛhadāraṇyaka-Upaniṣad*, Śaṅkara writes:

> A resident of Kashi who wishes to reach Gangadvara does not travel eastward. (na hi gaṅgā-dvāraṁ pratipitsuḥ kāśī-deśa-nivāsī pūrvābhimukhaḥ prati, BU-bhāṣya 4.4.22, *Ten Principal Upaniṣads with Śāṅkarabhāṣya*, 2007, 132)

Kashi and Gangadvara are the present-day cities of Varanasi and Haridwar, central pilgrimage sites then and now. But Śaṅkara's statement consists of more than travel instructions for the perplexed pilgrim. It is part of a broader discussion in which he argues that whoever has a desire for the external world has no adhikāra, entitlement, or suitability, for pārivrājya, "wandering mendicancy" that leads to mokṣa or "ultimate freedom." The geographical metaphor works in the service of this argument. Gangadvara stands for mokṣa. Whoever wishes to reach Gangadvara does not travel eastward, for the obvious reason that it is located north-west of Kashi. But this is not all. We can assume that the seeker of mokṣa would travel north-west in a boat on river Gaṅgā (Ganges). The river connects Gangadvara and Kashi. But as anyone who ever visited any of the two cities or has a sense of geography knows, the Gaṅgā flows from Haridwar to Varanasi. Therefore, to row toward mokṣa is a matter of rowing against the stream. And whoever ever rowed a boat knows how difficult it is to row against the stream.

But DK, with whom I read this paragraph from Śaṅkara almost twenty years ago, was hardly taken by the metaphor. As always, he was more fascinated with the here, with the reality of the everyday. He believed that there is a lot to discover and to achieve, even if the resident of Kashi does travel eastward or otherwise decides to stay at home, in Kashi. Rowing against the stream of mokṣa, DK insists that the external world, that Śaṅkara so sweepingly dismisses, needs to be attended to and taken care of. "Ātman-centricity," DK warns his listeners in his early Shimla Lectures,

> leads a people's attention away from an active concern with society and its betterment [. . .] when a society's best brains are concerned with a pursuit of something which is essentially a-social or trans-social, and which requires an active withdrawal from the institutions that sustain it, then the road is prepared for the inevitable take-over either by those who are interested in their own gain, or by those who are bent on transforming the world in the image of their own good. The immoralists from within and the messiahs from without rule the social realm alternately, after the ātman-centricists have withdrawn into their own pursuit of trans-social reality. (1969, 22)

Spiritual pursuit, DK repeats again and again, must not come at the expense of the world and the worldly. If the best brains all go to Gangadvara, Kashi will be taken over (if not taken already) by immoralists and messiahs. DK strives to prevent this dystopic reality. According to him, the Brahman [beyondness, Gangadvara] can wait. The social domain comes first.

"The realm of values," DK opens his paper "The Active and the Contemplative Values" (1969/1989),

> is disclosed to man by a perpetual dissatisfaction with things as they are, accompanied with the feeling that they can and ought to be different. These "things," with respect to which continuous dissatisfaction is felt, include one's own self, other persons and both the natural and social states of affairs. This dissatisfaction provides the dynamics for change, exploration and experimentation. (1989, 211)

Like the writings of the spiritualists, his perennial philosophical opponents, DK's present move begins with duḥkha, which he renders as dissatisfaction, as the catalyst for change. But change, in DK, is as much a change in the world as it is a change of one's own self. For the spiritualists, self comes before the world. For DK, it is the other way around. "The problems that arise with respect to the other," he continues to write,

> whether in the form of persons, or natural, or social states of affairs, seem essentially different from those that arise with respect to the individual's own self. (1989, 211)

The "active values" relate in DK's present formulation to the problems of the former kind, between self and other; "contemplative values" to problems of the latter kind, between one and oneself. I will shortly explain what these values—active versus contemplative—are and what role they play, but first, the river again.

"That which is called the river of the mind," Vyāsa, the *Yogasūtra* commentator, famously writes (in his bhāṣya on YS 1.12),

> flows in two directions. It flows toward the good (kalyāṇāya) and toward evil (pāpāya). That which is inclined toward the domain of viveka [distinction between self and world] and leads to kaivalya [disengagement as freedom] flows to the good. That which is inclined toward the domain of aviveka [non-distinction] and leads to saṃsāra [worldliness] flows to the evil. [cittanadī nāma ubhayatovāhinī vahati kalyāṇāya vahati pāpāya ca. yā tu kaivalyaprāgbhārā vivekaviṣayanimnā sā kalyāṇavahā. saṃsāraprāgbhārā avivekaviṣayanimnā pāpavahā.] (Aranya, 2012, 34–5, my translation)

In Śaṅkara, we saw earlier, it is up to the seeker to decide in which direction to turn his boat. Vyāsa's metaphor is different. He likens the human mind to a river flowing in two directions, and suggests that taking the route to Haridwar (if I may interweave the two metaphors) is "good" but taking the other, worldly direction is "evil," or leads to "evil." He equates worldliness, or what Śaṅkara refers to as the external world, with evil, whereas detachment from the world is depicted by him as leading to "the good." These two equations take us back to DK's discussion of nivṛtti and pravṛtti, the inward-facing and outward-facing modes of consciousness (see Chapter 3), and his protest against the fact that the former is traditionally regarded as "intrinsically desirable," the latter as "something undesirable in itself." We saw that according to DK, these two modes are complementary, and that he opts for a free travel between withdrawal and return, worldlessness and worldliness. In "The Active and the Contemplative Values," DK focuses not on these consciousness-modes, but on two sets of values—the active and the contemplative, which are the ethical expression of the inner flow of consciousness toward and away from the world. Working here at the ethical level, DK sees a measure of antagonism between these value-sets. He depicts each of them in detail before raising the question about the possible integration between them despite their opposite directions. The active values, DK writes, pertain to the social domain. In this respect, he speaks of cooperation that contributes to the establishment of a community, and of what he refers to as collective responsibility and collective decision-making. "There are many things," he suggests,

> that one would never do in an individual or personal capacity but which, in the context of a family, or nation, or institution, become right, or are even felt as imperatives for one's actions. (1989, 216)

This paragraph marks the metamorphosis from "I" to "we." As a part of "we," one sees things differently, and acts-behaves in a "we-mode." DK continues to write that the active values work for and within a "super-individual collective," and that they lead to "essential involvement in temporality, historicity and sociality." Contemplative values, on the other hand, lead in a different direction altogether. Here, "it is being itself that is at the center of attention," and

> what matters is the achievement of a state of consciousness, valuable, meaningful and free in itself. It is the stilling of time, the withdrawal from society, the transcending of history, that is the essence of the matter. (1989, 217)

The two sets of values are depicted by DK as inverted mirror images of one another. And he continues to write that "the contemplative values basically take one away from the other." Such is the case, DK suggests, both with regard to the mystic and the drug addict. This is an interesting observation. "They both have a minimal relationship to the world of objects, the world of the other." The addict depends on "the physical availability of his chosen drug, this is his limitation." The mystic "requires nothing in the world, his will and imagination suffice him for all that he longs for." But as he proceeds on the path, "ultimately, even the prop of the imagined object is given up," and will alone takes him forward. "God is the last imaginary object in this process," DK writes (all quotes from 1989, 217–18). Yes, even God is finally given up.

This is the transition from saguṇa-Brahman to nirguṇa-Brahman (Brahman with and without qualities or epithets), or from saguṇa-bhakti to nirguṇa-bhakti (worship of God and devotion toward, or in light of a formless totality).

Detour: In his chapter on Bhakti in *Indian Philosophy: A New Approach*, his alternative textbook of Indian philosophy, DK suggests that nirguṇa-bhakti was born of the challenge posed by the ideal of nirguṇa-Brahman, "the impersonal and abstract nature of the ultimate reality," to the bhakti tradition that sees emotion as the sole means of reaching the divine, or the sublime. DK mentions Kabīr, the fifteenth-century mystic-poet, and his contemporary Guru Nānak, the first of the Sikh gurus, as "the greatest exemplars" of nirguṇa-bhakti. In both cases, he wonders about the impact of Islam, besides the significance of the notion of nirguṇa-Brahman, on their "emphasis on the non-representational character of the ultimate reality and the denunciation of any attempt to symbolize it in any visible form" (1997, 151).

DK continues to meditate on the concept of nirguṇa-bhakti in his paper "Did the Gopīs Really Love Kṛṣṇa? Some Reflections on bhakti as a Puruṣārtha in the Indian Tradition" (2001/2012). The title is thought-provoking. How can anyone ask if the gopīs, the cowgirls, really loved Krishna? Their love is supposed to be paradigmatic for every devotee and worshiper of god Krishna. But DK, as usual, raises the "impossible question." In this paper, an appendix to the Saṃvād with traditionalists in Vrindavan on philosophy and the emotions, he reads closely the *Bhāgavata Purāṇa*, the eleventh- or twelfth-century treatise of bhakti (at least in his estimation),[6] which portrays the alleged life-story of god Krishna. Connecting the notions of bhakti and rasa (the devotional and the aesthetic emotions respectively), and drawing on KCB's essay "The Concept of Rasa," DK calls attention to KCB's "interesting suggestion" that "in feeling, the experiencing consciousness wants to become totally free of the object, so that it does not depend on it for its being what it is." In other words, bhakti as a rasa, as "feeling par excellence" (KCB's articulation, 2008, 349 and 355), necessitates a measure of distance from the object. Such distance, of the gopīs from Krishna, DK finds in the *Purāṇa* narrative, when "eternal dalliance" is replaced with "eternal memory," which must finally also be given up. "If the puruṣārtha of bhakti [devotion as a human goal] is to become completely free of the object," DK writes,

> even in its imagined form [...] to free oneself even from that bondage, one would like to live in a world of feelings which is completely autonomous, self-subsistent and self-sufficient. This is the puruṣārtha which the ideal of bhakti seems to seek, and the gopīs seem to symbolize to the fullest possible extent. (2012, 284)

For DK, the gopīs epitomize pure, free, objectless love. KCB would remind him that rasa, the essential aesthetic feeling, is not just objectless but also "impersonal," related merely to "the felt-person-in-general [who] may be called the Heart Universal" (2008, 353–4). Hence in nirguṇa-bhakti, both object and subject dissolve (the subject in its everyday sense, in relation with objects, not KCB's "pure subject" that draws on the notion of the ātman). Feeling alone prevails.

Back to the main road: DK continues to depict the active and the contemplative values as antithetical. When one is absorbed in action, he writes, there is simply no time "to stand and stare." Moreover, in the eyes of the kartā, the doer, the contemplative values seem "shadowy and vague, hallucinatory creations of self-hypnotized minds, creatures of imagination lost in themselves" (1989, 219). This type of accusation is often heard today in the current debate about the future of humanities in higher education. DK, a master of contemplation—in the philosophical, not the spiritual, sense of the word—hardly endorses this one-sided perspective, or the other-sided ivory-tower view that looks down at everything practical and corporeal. He is well aware of the burning need for action, and he dedicates a long paragraph in "The Active and the Contemplative Values" to the difficulty of life in the slum. A concrete window to the "real life" in the midst of a purely theoretical or contemplative discussion. DK provides his readers with a vivid description of the "smoke and smog that hangs in the air" and "the dirt and the stink [which] get into one's mind." The effort "to open pathways to the moon and the stars," he writes poetically, can seem Sisyphean, but no more than not engaging with this painful reality (1989, 213). I read this paragraph as an urgent call for action.

How to integrate the active and the contemplative? DK closes his paper with this open question. Kamalchand Sogani, his colleague and friend, takes up the challenge and writes in response:

> The great contemplatives like Mahavira, Buddha, Christ, Gandhi etc., were neither nonactivist, nor did they regard activity as a necessary evil. Daya Krishna does not seem to distinguish between a pure action and action done by affective prejudices. In my view, he who has opted for contemplative values will perform the actions more devotedly and efficiently than the man who is dedicated only to active values, inasmuch as, in the former, the duty-consciousness is supreme. (1971, 264)

Sogani denies any contradiction, or even tension, between the active and the contemplative values. This is the standard formula. Whenever DK raises a problem, or points out a difficulty, paradox, or anomaly, the traditionalist would deny that there is an anomaly, paradox, difficulty, or problem. But for DK, we already know, questions and problems are the fuel of philosophy, of thinking at large. Sogani, an insider of the Jaina tradition, believes that action of the best kind (he makes a distinction between "pure action" and action born of egotistic motives) is undertaken by "contemplatives," and he mentions world-changers like Mahāvīra, Buddha, Christ, and Gandhi. I am not sure that Gandhi fits well with the other three. They are all spiritual leaders, and, at least the first two, out and out renouncers and proponents of world renunciation. Gandhi, for me, is no less an "activist" than he is a "contemplative," and besides his spiritual tendencies that capture Sogani, he is a politician; an ethical, even spiritual politician, but a politician committed to social and political goals in and for the world, for India. Sogani draws on stellar figures. DK's discussion is more down to earth. In his Shimla Lectures (2005), he speaks of Gandhi, Tagore and Sri Aurobindo, and says:

> They were great people, not pigmies like us! They stood straight. Their spine was not bent. (2012, 112)

But (and in DK, there is always a "but") DK does not wish to cling to the past and to indulge in nostalgia. These greats are inspiring, and they surely contributed as much as they could, but there is still a lot of work to be done, and now it is our turn to make our contribution. Moreover, he implies at Shimla, times have changed as they always do, hence not everything that these great figures did, said, or believed in, is still relevant today. Furthermore, and here I return to "The Active and the Contemplative Values," the question of integration applies not just to a Gandhi but even to "pigmies like us." The question is whether integration is possible now and here, in Jaipur, in the slum, imperfect as one is and as one's actions are bound to be.

4 The Conscience Keepers

I would like to suggest that the answer to the question of integration is given by DK in practice, in life. Besides his numerous publications in hardcore philosophical journals and books, he used to write regularly for venues that appeal to a broader readership, such as *Quest: A Quarterly of Inquiry, Criticism and Ideas*, edited by Abu Sayeed Ayyub and Amlan Datta, that was shut down by the editors in 1976 during "the Emergency" in refusal to abide to the new censorship regulations. DK was also a frequent contributor to the *Economic and Political Weekly* (*EPW*). In *Quest*, *EPW*, and other public venues, DK raised a voice for social equality in India and for a dialogue between equals at the international level. He would criticize the fact that in world politics, and in the academia, the standards are always primarily Western. He would aim his arrows at what he saw as the hypocrisy of the West, and more broadly of the mighty and powerful everywhere, that hardly see and listen to the weak and the weakened in society, or in the world. He would appeal for multivocality, for the inclusion of new players in the political arena, every political arena. He was an exponent of critical thinking. Critical thinking above all. And a sharp opponent of guruism of any kind. Authority on one hand, and subservience and subjection on the other, were hardly his cup of tea. DK's political writings are not a separate corpus. There is a clear continuity between DK the professional philosopher and DK the social and political activist writer. The contemplative and the active converge both in his academic writings and in his out-of-the-ivory-tower essays.

In his article "Encounters between Civilizations: The Question of the Centre and the Periphery" (1997, henceforth "Encounters"), published in *New Quest*, the post-Emergency avatar of *Quest*, edited by A. B. Shah, DK reminds his readers that "we may have a Plato, an Aristotle, a Kant and a Hegel," but "we also have a Shankar, a Ramanuja and a Gangesh" (DK reserved the diacritical marks for his more academic writings). This is his usual appeal to his Indian readers, to expand their intellectual horizons and discover the potency of Indian thinking. These lines, the final lines of *Daya Krishna and Twentieth-century Indian Philosophy*, are written at the library of the University of Rajasthan, Jaipur. I met a PhD student of philosophy earlier today. He is writing his dissertation on the notion of despair in Kierkegaard and Sartre. What about an Indian twist, I asked him, a visit, say, to the *Mahābhārata*, or a philosophical exploration in the writings of DK and Ramchandra Gandhi? His surprise at my suggestion and his obvious reluctance to broaden the scope of his work show that even today, even here, many still believe that "the West is the best." Moreover, it shows that Indian philosophy, classical and contemporary, is still awaiting "discovery" not just in the West but initially in India. On Shankar (Śaṅkara), Gangesh (Gaṅgeśa), Kant, and the others, DK further writes that "one may continuously return to the task of understanding and perpetuating their thought, as if they achieved a finality in the philosophical enterprise of a civilization." But for him, we already know, thinking is an open-ended process, and finality in the realm of ideas is a misnomer. "Perhaps we could think of Kant in another way," DK writes elsewhere,

> not as a philosopher to be "understood" by other thinkers in the last two hundred years, but as a starting point for carrying the

> Kantian enterprise further. This can be done in the context of other philosophers also, instead of wasting time in "understanding" what they "really" said. We might profit from their insights and carry them further to the best of our ability. This would bring diverse and multiple aspects of a thinker to our notice, which are seldom seen, and other strains which exist only as a tendency in his thought. (I quote from a letter written by DK to his friend and colleague Bhuvan Chandel in February 2006).[7]

DK writes along similar lines in "Encounters" that,

> a Buddha, a Mahavira, or a Gandhi, or a Vivekananda, or an Aurobindo were merely what may be called "stops," or "markers" in the march of civilization. (1997, 263–4)

And the march continues.

Still in "Encounters," DK is surprised at the irrational fear in the West of anything non-Western. It should be the other way around, he suggests, since "all non-Western civilizations have been put on defense for at least the last 300 years, if not more, and the West is today both politically and economically dominant" (1997, 262). I often wonder what DK would say of the present-day world of immigration, relocation, dislocation, and displacement; a world of migrants, refugees, exiles, escapees, and homeless, where the primordial fear of the other plays a central role.

DK's critique of the West is sharp and lucid. Here is another example:

> The history of the way human rights have been sought to be applied in the last fifty years shows not only that it can be manipulated as a political weapon by states, to serve their interests, but also that the choice of the areas in which it is applied is highly selective in character. [. . .] The case of powerful pharmaceutical industries who "freely" dump drugs banned in many Western countries in the so-called "Third World" without protest from anybody is not even mentioned by anybody. (I quote from DK's article "A Radical Revision of Human Rights: the Need for Rethinking in a Universal Perspective," 1998, 149)

DK's arrows are directed here at those who condemn the violation of human rights but violate human rights in their backyard, away from the limelight of the media (the case of Guantánamo comes to mind). Double-standard and hypocrisy are the name of the game, and DK pulls out the penetrating example of medicines banned in the so-called First World that are sold and distributed ("dumped," he angrily writes) in the "Third World." In the name of medical aid, yet another round of exploitation takes place.

In his article "Peace: The Enemy of Nations" (2007, unpublished), DK adds the notions of "peace" and "terrorism" to the list of empty words, like "human rights" or "medical aid," that are manipulated and used politically by almost every player at the world arena. It is too easy, DK reminds his readers, to divide the world into "good guys" and "bad guys." It takes us away from dealing with reality as it is—complex and challenging—behind flat slogans. DK protests against language-laundering (in the same lines of money-laundering), searching for a measure of ethics in the political realm, more often than not in vain. "But few care or dare to accuse the powerful," he further writes in "Encounters," "who determine what shall be talked about, and what ignored, or forgotten." And he adds that "unless intellectuals in the non-Western world, including India, become aware of the situation, the emerging world will be completely shaped by the Western perception of what the global situation ought to be" (1997, 262). This wake-up call corresponds with DK's appeal to his fellow classicists, almost a decade later, in his Shimla Lectures, to step out and come down from the realm of "pure reason" and become involved in the vyavahāric, worldly domain.

An activist with a pen in hand, we saw that DK reflects not just on pressing issues, global and local, social and political, but also on the role of the intellectual. In his article "The US-Iraq Conflict and the Global Intellectual Community: Some Unasked Questions" (1998), DK writes:

> The intellectuals are supposed to be the conscience keepers of the world, and vigilant critics of those who are in power. [. . .] The "Brahmanical" function of the intellectual class, vis-à-vis those who exercise the ruling function in any society or polity, is one of the crucial factors in restraining those who rule from departing too much from the path of "dharma" or righteousness. To be an intellectual means just this: that one is not completely governed by considerations of wealth and power, hence not afraid of displeasing those who may withhold patronage because of their overwhelming power. [. . .] If freedom has any intellectual content, then the acts of the mighty and the powerful have to be scrutinized on the bar of rightness, which itself, of course, is not easy to determine. (1998, 1515)

The "Brahmanical" function of the intellectual, in DK, has nothing to do with caste, hierarchy, and politics of exclusion. In correspondence with the abovementioned historical role of the Brahmins as keepers of norms and values, restricting the powerful and the mighty, and safeguarding the checks and balances of state and society, it was DK's conviction that the task of the intellectual, as the keeper of conscience, is to tell the truth in the face of power, without fear or favor—to tell the truth, to expose hypocrisy and injustice, and to protect the path of dharma. But what is dharma? Here again, DK picks and chooses from a long history of meanings, and comes up with his own definition of this salient notion. Adhikāra, or entitlement, or exclusion, or casteism, are of course out of the question. Instead, DK suggests that dharma "involves awareness of the other, the multiple others, and the obligation towards them" (2005, 174). This quote is from his paper "Eros, Nomos and Logos." A comparative philosopher without borders (I borrow this phrase from Chakrabarti and Weber, 2015), DK weaves together the Greek notion of "nomos" and "dharma" as its Indian counterpart. Dharma, then, is my obligation toward the other. "This," he writes,

> is perhaps what the *Gītā* meant when it said "parasparaṃ bhāvayantaḥ śreyaḥ param avāpsyatha" ["through reciprocity, the highest good can be achieved," BG 3.11]. The key terms are "paraspara" and "śreyas," the former implying a relation of perfect equality between self and other, while the latter involves an element of universality and objectivity, or at least inter-subjectivity. (2005, 175)

Here again, DK—the alleged heretic—quotes from memory half a verse from the *Bhagavadgītā*, as classical commentators often do (the other half, dealing with the relationship between humanity and divinity, is besides his present argument). And if this is not enough, he further offers his own bhāṣya, or commentary. "No-one trashed Indian philosophy as Daya Krishna did," a famous Sanskritist told me in Delhi, just a couple of weeks ago. "Trashed" is the word that he chose to use. What a misconception! DK did not trash. He loved Indian philosophy. He injected life into Indian philosophy. Dharma, according to DK, is a matter of "perfect equality between self and other," supported by a sense of "universality and objectivity, or inter-subjectivity." Usually translated as "the good," DK implies that the notion of śreyas in the abovementioned verse from the *Gītā* hardly stands for what is good for me. If anyone is to be prioritized, it is not me but the other, always the other.

In a recent visit to JNU (Jawaharlal Nehru University), Delhi, I passed by Kaveri Hostel, and saw this graffiti writing on the wall:

> Education divorced from life and politics is lies and hypocrisy; laḍo paḍhāī karne ko, paḍho samāj badalne ko! [Fight for the right to study, study to change the society!].

This demand for convergence between the contemplative and the active reminds me of DK. For me, this graffiti is a living, breathing version, young and furious, of DK's emphatic plea at Shimla: "But Friends, the *vyavahāra* matters!"

Notes

Introduction

1 I wish to thank Ramesh Chandra Shah for his kind permission to quote from these letters.
2 Ramesh Chandra Shah's book *Ancestral Voices: Reflections on Vedic, Classical and Bhakti Poetry* (2006).
3 I quote from *The New Yorker* (September 19, 2008) https://www.newyorker.com/books/page-turner/this-is-water
4 Salman Rushdie translates the chorus of the hit song "Mera Joota Hai Japani," from Raj Kapoor's iconic film *Shree 420* (1955), including the line I quoted:

> O, my shoes are Japanese; these trousers English, if you please. On my head, red Russian hat; my heart's Indian for all that. (*The Satanic Verses* 1989, 5) https://www.penguinrandomhouse.ca/books/158937/the-satanic-verses-by-salman-rushdie/9780676970630/excerpt

5 Lévi-Strauss (1966).
6 Lévi-Strauss as quoted by Daya Krishna (1989), xvi; Daya Krishna quotes from Lévi-Strauss (1966), 126.
7 Daya Krishna (1989), xv; Lévi-Strauss (1966), 126.
8 See, for instance, Diane Lewis's paper "Anthropology and Colonialism," published in *Current Anthropology* (December 1973), the same journal in which Lévi-Strauss's paper appeared seven years earlier.

Chapter 1

1 Kant's comments on the Chinese culture are not better informed or less racist than his remarks on the Indian culture. See Van Norden (2017), 22–3.
2 Ganeri (2011), introduction, p. 10 footnote #13
3 http://ndpr.nd.edu/news/minds-without-fear-philosophy-in-the-indian-renaissance/
4 I am thankful to Professor Sachchidanand Mishra of Banaras Hindu University who provided me the original paper in Sanskrit, which is now available at www.dayakrishna.org
5 See also Jonardon Ganeri's paper "Sanskrit Philosophical Commentary" (2010).
6 On the question which texts were written by Śaṅkara (and which are ascribed to him traditionally but were not necessarily composed by him), see Karl Potter's paper "Śaṅkarācārya: The Myth and the Man," *Journal of the American Academy of Religion* 48 (1982), 111–25. On the dispute about

the authorship of the *Yogasūtra-bhāṣya-vivaraṇa*, see the introduction of my book *Exploring the Yogasūtra: Philosophy and Translation* (Raveh 2012).

7 I wrote to Mukund Lath, and asked him about Vedic śākhās that DK spotlights in his Ṛgveda Project. This is what he wrote back:

> The Veda was learnt—which meant a recitation to begin with—in somewhat different readings by different groups, or you may say, schools or gharānās—gharānās of different Brahmin families (as in musical gharānās today). This meant different readings of the same text. Dayaji's question was, how can it be called the same text? In older times, and, orally speaking, even today, the "same" text can be put in different words. (Personal communication, June 2019).

The śākhās are these schools of recitation, each with its "somewhat different reading".

8 On the category of abhāva, DK further writes in his paper "Some Problems Regarding Thinking about Abhāva" (2011). His initial thoughts in his textbook came to fruition in this later paper.

Chapter 2

1 On rasa, I would recommend Arindam Chakrabarti's paper "Play, Pleasure, Pain: Ownerless Emotions in Rasa-Aesthetics" (2009), Lawrence McCrea's paper "Resonance and its Reverberations: Two Cultures in Indian Epistemology of Aesthetic Meaning" (2018), and of course Sheldon Pollock's *A Rasa Reader: Classical Indian Aesthetics* (2016).

2 Mukund Lath suggests that there are two aspects to rasābhāsa, the ethical dimension (social violation resulting in a "false feeling," as in Pollock) and a purely aesthetic dimension, for example, in music. A rāga, he illustrates can be too "flat" or "watery," hence arouse in the listener a correspondingly "flat" or "watery" rasa, which according to him is another instance of rasābhāsa. (Personal communication, January 2019)

3 These quotes from Rushdie's *The Enchantress of Florence* are from the *LA Weekly* (May 28, 2008), https://www.laweekly.com/arts/salman-rushdie-an-excerpt-from-the-enchantress-of-florence-2153684

4 These quotes are from the chapter "Playing the English Gentleman" in Gandhi's autobiography. The full text of Gandhi's autobiography is easily accessible online.

Chapter 3

1 "The Cosmic" is open for reading at www.dayakrishna.org

2 *Towards a Theory of Structural and Transcendental Illusions* is a hardly known and hardly discussed work of DK. Prasanjit Biswas's lucid paper "Daya Krishna's 'Presuppositionless Philosophy': Sublimity as the Source of Value and Knowledge" (2014) is a rare exception.

3 I wish to thank D. P. Chattopadhyaya for his kind permission to quote from this letter.
4 Eyal's introduction can be accessed here: https://books.google.co.il/books?id=dsz5AwAAQBAJ&pg=PT5&dq=habit+forming+products&lr=&source=gbs_toc_r&cad=4#v=onepage&q=habit%20forming%20products&f=false
5 Paulson (2016).

Chapter 4

1 A Dossier Concerning the KD Vyas Correspondence (Vol.1) RAQS Media Collective, #14 "Concerning Ekalavya" https://www.academia.edu/4094134/A_DOSSIER_CONCERNING_THE_KD_VYAS_CORRESPONDENCE_VOL.1_
2 The 5th C. R. Parekh Memorial Lecture, "Rethinking India's Past" by Johannes Bronkhorst, India International Centre, Delhi, August 7, 2019.
3 DK's *Civilizations: Nostalgia and Utopia* includes both series of lectures, the 1967 and the 2005 Shimla Lectures.
4 Apropos shareability and the Vedic ritual, Y. Krishan (2001) adds to the discussion of the Saṃvād, and mentions another example of shareability, hardly midway or subsidiary—the Śrāddha Karma, or Śrāddha ritual, performed for the sake of the ancestors by their descendants. Here the descendants perform the ritual (or in fact, again, the ritual is performed by priests hired by the descendants), but the benefit, or the fruit of the ritual, goes not to the living descendants but to "the unembodied souls of the deceased," as Krishan puts it. What could be a more tangible example of shareability at the heart of the ritual?
5 Here I refer the readers to Y. Krishan's paper "Collective Karmas" (1989), which is about shareability of karma. "Collective karmas," Krishan writes, "are to be defined in terms of (a) the authors or persons who perform the karmas [actions], and (b) the retribution of karmas, when it affects simultaneously a large number of persons," as in "mass tragedies, both natural and munmade" (179). Krishan seeks to formulate the concept of "collective karma," drawing on two main sources. First, on the Buddhist doctrine of anātmavāda, which sees interconnectivity (or if you wish, intersubjectivity) at the very level of selfhood. Since there is no "separate self," but instead a network of relations, karma cannot be perceived as belonging to any separate self. "In other words," Krishan writes, "there is a universal, undifferentiated corpus of karmas, as against corpora in severalty (181). And second, Krishan draws on the writings of contemporary thinkers from Swami Vivekananda to Mahatma Gandhi and Sri Aurobindo, who like DK see the need for shareability. Aurobindo, for instance, refers (in *The Problem of Rebirth*) to karma of the family, of the nation, and of humankind as a whole, but at the same time insists that "what matters supremely is what

I make of my heredity and not what my heredity makes of me" (Krishan, 187). "The Hindus," Krishan agrees with DK, "firmly believed in the doctrine of personal responsibility of a man for his moral acts," and, moreover, "the concept of collective karma [which he endeavors to develop] is foreign to the Indian religious tradition, and in fact is a negation of the classical doctrine of karma" (189 and 193).

6 Dating the *Bhāgavata Purāṇa* is no easy task. In this respect see Edwin Bryant's paper "The Date and Provenance of the *Bhāgavata Purāṇa* and the Vaikuṇṭha Perumāl Temple," *Journal of Vaishnava Studies* 11.1: 51–80.

7 I wish to thank Bhuvan Chandel for her kind permission to quote from this letter.

Bibliography and Further Reading

Prepared with Elise Coquereau-Saouma

I Books by Daya Krishna (English and Hindi, in chronological order)

The Nature of Philosophy, Calcutta: Prachi Prakashan, 1955.

Planning, Power and Welfare, Delhi: The Office for Asian Affairs, Congress for Cultural Freedom, 1959.

Considerations towards a Theory of Social Change, Bombay: Manaktalas, 1965.

Social Philosophy: Past and Future, Shimla: Indian Institute of Advanced Study, 1969.

Political Development: A Critical Perspective, Delhi: Oxford University Press, 1979.

Gyāna Mīmāṃsā, Jaipur: Rajasthan Hindi Granth Academy, 1980.

with Fred W. Riggs, *Development Debate*, Jaipur: Printwell Publishers, 1987.

The Art of the Conceptual: Explorations in a Conceptual Maze over Three Decades, Delhi: Indian Council of Philosophical Research in association with Munshiram Manoharlal Publishers, 1989.

Indian Philosophy: A Counter Perspective, Delhi: Oxford University Press, 1991, 1996. Revised Edition by Sri Satguru Publications, Delhi, 2006.

The Problematic and Conceptual Structure of Classical Indian Thought about Man, Society and Polity, Delhi: Oxford University Press, 1996.

Indian Philosophy: A New Approach, Delhi: Sri Satguru Publications, 1997.

Prolegomena to Any Future Historiography of Cultures and Civilizations, Delhi: Munshiram Manoharlal Publishers, 1997.

New Perspectives in Indian Philosophy, Delhi and Jaipur: Rawat Publishers, 2001.

Developments in Indian Philosophy from the Eighteenth Century Onwards: Classical and Western, Vol. X Part. 1 of *History of Science, Philosophy and Culture in Indian Civilization*, General Editor D. P. Chattopadhyaya, Delhi: Centre for studies in Civilizations, 2002.

Bhārtīya Darśana: Eka Nayī Dṛṣṭi, Delhi and Jaipur: Rawat Publishers, 2004.

The Nyāya Sūtras: A New Commentary on an Old Text, Delhi: Sri Satguru Publications, 2004.

Bhāratīya Evaṃ Pāścātya Dārshanik Paramparāṃ, UGC ASIHSS Program, Department of Philosophy, Rajasthan University and Literary Circle, Jaipur, 2006. (Indian and Western Philosophical Traditions: Collected Essays by Daya Krishna in Hindi, ed. Yogesh Gupta.)

Contrary Thinking: Selected Essays by Daya Krishna, eds. N. Bhushan, J. L. Garfield and D. Raveh, New York: Oxford University Press, 2011.
Civilizations: Nostalgia and Utopia, Delhi: SAGE, 2012.
Towards a Theory of Structural and Transcendental Illusions, Delhi: Centre for Studies in Civilizations & Munshiram Manoharlal Publishers, 2012.
Agenda for Research in Indian & Western Philosophy, Vols. 1 & 2, eds. R. S. Bhatnagar and Yogesh Gupta, Jaipur: Department of Philosophy, University of Rajasthan and Literary Circle, 2013.
Bhārtīya Ciṇtan Paraṃparāeṇ: Nae Āyām, Naī Diśāeṇ, ed. Krishna Dutt Paliwal, Delhi: Sasta Sahitya Mandal, 2013.

II Books edited by Daya Krishna

Daya Krishna (ed.), *Modern Logic: Its Relevance to Philosophy*, Delhi: Impex India, 1969.
Daya Krishna (ed.), *Indian Education Today: Prospects and Perspectives*, Jaipur: Rajasthan University Press, 1970.
Daya Krishna (ed.), with A. M. Ghose, *Contemporary Philosophical Problems: Some Classical Indian Perspectives*, Poona: Indian Philosophical Quarterly Publications, 1978.
Daya Krishna (ed.), with B. V. Kishan, *What Is Living and What Is Dead in Indian Philosophy*, Waltair: Andhra University Press, 1978.
Daya Krishna (ed.), with A. M. Ghose and P. K. Srivastava, *The Philosophy of Kalidas Bhattacharyya*, Poona: Indian Philosophical Quarterly Publications, 1985.
Daya Krishna (ed.), *India's Intellectual Traditions, Attempts at Conceptual Reconstructions*, Delhi: Indian Council of Philosophical Research in association with Motilal Banarsidass, 1987. The book includes, besides other contributions, two essays by Daya Krishna, "The Search for a Conceptual Structure of the Nāṭyaśāstra" and "India's Intellectual Tradition: An Overview".
Daya Krishna (ed.), *Paschimi Darshan Ka Itihas*, I & II, Jaipur: Rajasthan Hindi Granth Academy, 1987.
Daya Krishna (ed.), with K. L. Sharma, *The Philosophy of J. N. Mohanty*, Delhi: Indian Council of Philosophical Research, 1987.
Daya Krishna (ed.), with M. P. Rege, R. C. Dwivedi, and Mukund Lath, *Saṃvāda, A Dialogue between Two Philosophical Traditions*, Delhi: Motilal Banarsidass, 1991.
Daya Krishna (ed.), with K. Satchidananda Murty, *History, Culture and Truth: Essays Presented to Professor D. P. Chattopadhyaya*, Delhi: Kalki Prakashan, 1999.
Daya Krishna (ed.), with Mukund Lath and Francine E. Krishna, *Bhakti: A Contemporary Discussion—Philosophical Explorations in the Indian Bhakti Tradition*, Delhi: Indian Council of Philosophical Research, 2000.

Daya Krishna (ed.), *Discussion and Debate in Indian Philosophy: Vedānta, Mīmāṃsā and Nyāya*, Delhi: Indian Council of Philosophical Research, 2004.
Daya Krishna (ed.), *The Jaipur Edition of the Ṛgveda*, 2007, Unpublished.

III Articles by Daya Krishna (articles republished in essay-collections are marked with *)

Daya Krishna, "The Experiential Standpoint in the Philosophy of Sri Aurobindo," *The Sri Aurobindo Annual*, Pondicherry, 1948, 58–65.
Daya Krishna*, "An Attempted Analysis of the Concept of Freedom," *Philosophy and Phenomenological Research* 12, no. 4 (June 1952): 550–6.
Daya Krishna*, "Some Considerations on F. S. C. Northrop's Theory of Concepts," *The Philosophical Review* 61, no. 3 (July 1952): 392–9.
Daya Krishna*, "Assumptions in the Social Sciences," *Ethics* 63, no. 2 (January 1953): 137–9.
Daya Krishna, "An Experiment in Democracy," *Quest* (1954).
Daya Krishna*, "Mysticism and the Problem of Intelligibility," *The Journal of Religion* 34, no. 2 (April 1954): 101–5.
Daya Krishna, "Social Change - An Attempt at a Study in Conflicting Patterns of Social Action," *Philosophy and Phenomenological Research* 14, no. 4 (1954): 567–73.
Daya Krishna, "Investment, Priorities and Planning," *The Eastern Economist* (September 23, 1955).
Daya Krishna*, "Surplus Value, Profit and Exploitation," *The Review of Economic Studies* 22, no. 2 (1954–1955): 96–108.
Daya Krishna*, "Arthur Lewis Looks at Economic Growth," *The Economic Weekly* 8, no. 35 (September 1956): 1041–3.
Daya Krishna, "Financial Stability, Inflation & Economic Growth," *The Eastern Economist* (July 20, 1956).
Daya Krishna*, "Invariants of the Human Situation: Valuations and Limitations," *Prabuddha Bharata* 61, no. 4 (April 1956): 185–8.
Daya Krishna*, "Mechanisation and Agriculture," *Commerce*, Bombay (April 1956).
Daya Krishna*, "Planning & Democratic Freedom," *The Eastern Economist* (August 1956).
Daya Krishna, "Socialism, Private Enterprise and Democracy," *The Eastern Economist* (September 7, 1956).
Daya Krishna*, "The Moral and the Axiological 'Ought' – An Attempt at a Distinction," *The Journal of Philosophy* 53, no. 21 (October 1956): 634–41.
Daya Krishna, "The Pursuit of Excellence - A Critical Reflection on the Education Commission Report," in *Higher Education in India*, ed. A. B. Shah (1956).

Daya Krishna*, "Two Types of Appearance and Two types of Reality," *Revue Internationale de Philosophie* 10, no. 37 (October 1956): 332–9.
Daya Krishna, "Was Ist Philosophie?," *Studium Generale* 8 (August 1956).
Daya Krishna, "An Attempt towards a Theory of Ethics," *Sagar University Research Journal* (1957).
Daya Krishna, "Decadence and Literature: Some Considerations," *Banking* (November 1957).
Daya Krishna*, "Investment, Inflation and Employment," *The Eastern Economist* (1957).
Daya Krishna*, "Law of Contradiction and Empirical Reality," *Mind, New Series* 66, no. 262 (April 1957): 250–7.
Daya Krishna, "Sense and Superstition in the Social Sciences," *Banking* (February 1957).
Daya Krishna, "Action and Contemplation," *Visva-Bharati Quarterly* 24 (1958–59): 1–11.
Daya Krishna, "Des Coefficients Politiques," Extrait du *Contrat Social* 2, no. 5 (September 1958): 299–302.
Daya Krishna, "Is Philosophy Linguistic Analysis?" *Proceedings of the Indian Philosophy Congress* (1958).
Daya Krishna*, "The Nature of Value Judgements," *Australasian Journal of Philosophy* 36, no. 1 (May 1958): 18–24.
Daya Krishna*, "Some Considerations on Morris Lazerowitz's 'The Structure of Metaphysics,'" *Mind* 67, no. 266 (April 1958): 236–43.
Daya Krishna, "Some Suggestions Towards the Formation of Political Index Numbers," *Le Contrat Social*, Paris (September 1958).
Daya Krishna, "The State and the Writer," *VAK* (1958).
Daya Krishna*, "Symmetry, Transitivity and Reflexivity," *Analysis* 19, no. 1 (October 1958): 7–11.
Daya Krishna, "Use and Abuse of the Concept of 'Determination' in the Social Sciences," *Quest* (April–June 1958).
Daya Krishna, "On the Evaluation of Creative Literature," *Quest* (April–June 1959). Republished in *New Letters Magazine* 48, nos. 3 and 4 (Spring–Summer 1982).
Daya Krishna, "Science and Reality," in *Entretiens: International Institute of Philosophy and Indian Philosophical Congress*, ed. N. A. Nikam, Mysore, 1959.
Daya Krishna, "What Is Democracy" (a paper written for the International Seminar on Representative Government and Public Liberties in the New States, held in the Isle of Rhodes, Greece, October 1958; published in *New States Congress for Cultural Freedom* (May 1959).
Daya Krishna, "Des Valeurs Essentielles en Politique," *Le Contrat Social*, Paris (July 1960).
Daya Krishna, "K. C. Bhattacharyya on Indian philosophy," *Visva-Bharati Quarterly* 26, no. 2 (1960): 1–8.

Daya Krishna*, "Pitirim A. Sorokin and the Problem of Knowledge," *The Indian Journal of Philosophy* 10 (1960): 175–84.

Daya Krishna*, "Symmetry, Transitivity and Reflexivity – A Further Discussion," *Journal of the Philosophical Association* (July 1960).

Daya Krishna*, "Types of Coherence," *The Philosophical Quarterly* 10, no. 40 (July 1960): 193–204.

Daya Krishna, "Yoga: Immortality and Freedom by Mircea Eliade," Review Article, *Philosophy East and West* 10, no. 3/4 (October 1960–January 1961): 173–5.

Daya Krishna, "Colour, Incompatibility and Language-Games," *Indian Journal of Philosophy* 3 (August 1961): 55–60.

Daya Krishna, "Endymion and Keats's Later Poems," *The Literary Criterion* (1961).

Daya Krishna*, "Lying and the Compleat Robot," *The British Journal for the Philosophy of Science* 12, no. 46 (August 1961): 146–9.

Daya Krishna*, "Religious Experience, Languages and Truth," A Symposium on *Religious Experience and Truth*, ed. Sidney Hook, New York: New York University Press, 1961.

Daya Krishna*, "The Synthetic a-Priori: Some Considerations," *Philosophy* 36, no. 137 (April–July 1961): 211–15.

Daya Krishna, "Democracy and Traditional Values," in *A New Survey of the Social Sciences*, ed. B. N. Verma, Bombay: Asia Publishing House, 1962.

Daya Krishna, "'The Intellectual on the Dissecting Table', Review of Edward Shils's *The Intellectual between Tradition and Modernity*," *Quest* 34 (July–September 1962): 56–60.

Daya Krishna, "Sources of Indian Tradition, compiled by Wm. Theodore de Bary, Stephen Hay, Royal Weiler, and Andrew Yarrow," Review Article, *Philosophy East and West* 13, no. 2 (July 1963): 159–65.

Daya Krishna* "On the Distinctions between the Natural Sciences, Social Sciences and the Humanities," *International Social Sciences Journal* 16, no. 4 (1964): 513–23.

Daya Krishna*, "Reflections on an Alleged Anecdote in Śaṅkara's Life, *Quest* 43 (October–December 1964): 31–5. Republished in *Contrary Thinking: Selected Essays by Daya Krishna*, eds. Bhushan et al., 2011, 285–90.

Daya Krishna, "Report on the Object, Scope and Methods of a Study on the Main Trends of Research in the Social and Human Sciences," UNESCO Export Committee Report, Paris (June 22–7, 1964).

Daya Krishna*, "Adhyāsa: A Non-Advaitic Beginning in Śaṅkara's Vedānta," *Philosophy East and West* 15, no. 3/4 (July–October 1965): 243–9.

Daya Krishna, "Science and the Humanities," in *Climbing a Wall of Glass: Aspects of Educational Reform in India*, eds. J. W. Airan, T. Barnabas and A. B. Shah, Bombay: Manaktalas, 1965.

Daya Krishna*, "Three Conceptions of Indian Philosophy," *Philosophy East and West* 15, no. 1 (January 1965): 37–51.

Daya Krishna*, "Value and Reality," *Visva-Bharati Journal of Philosophy* (February 1965).
Daya Krishna*, "Three Myths about Indian Philosophy," *Diogenes* 14, no. 55 (September 1966): 89–103.
Daya Krishna*, "Vedānta – Does It Really mean Anything?" *Conspectus* 2, no. 2 (1966): 20–8.
Daya Krishna, "Government Operations in Foodgrains—A Comment," *Economic and Political Weekly* 2, no. 48 (December 9, 1967): 2131–2.
Daya Krishna, "The Pursuit of Excellence," *Quest*, Special Number (March 1967): 15–23.
Daya Krishna, "Is Īśvara Kṛṣṇa's Sāṁkhya-Kārikā really Sāṁkhyan?" *Philosophy East and West* 18, no. 3 (July 1968): 194–204.
Daya Krishna*, "The Active and the Contemplative Values," *Philosophy and Phenomenological Research* 29, no. 3 (March 1969): 414–22.
Daya Krishna, "Alienation, Positive and Negative," *Diogenes* 18, no. 72 (December 1970): 39–55.
Daya Krishna, "Philosophy in India (1955–66)," in *Contemporary Philosophy – A Survey*, ed. R. Klibansky, 1971, 564–77.
Daya Krishna*, "The Self-Fulfilling Prophecy and the Nature of Society," *American Sociological Review* 36, no. 6 (1971): 1104–7.
Daya Krishna*, "Appearance and Reality," In *Current Trends in Indian Philosophy*, eds. K. Satchidananda Murty and K. Ramakrishna Rao, Andhra University Press, 1972.
Daya Krishna*, "It Can't Be Said So What?" *Indian Review of Philosophy* 1, no. 4 (1972): 269–82.
Daya Krishna, "Political Thought in the US—A Case Study of Academic Escapism," *Quest* 78 (September–October 1972): 35–40.
Daya Krishna, "The Concept of Political Development in American Political Science in the Sixties," in *Foreign Values and South East Asian Scholarship*, eds. Joseph Fischer, University of California Press, 1973.
Daya Krishna*, "The Concept of Revolution: An Analysis," *Philosophy East and West* 23, no. 3 (July 1973): 291–7.
Daya Krishna*, "Logic and Ontology," in *Contemporary Indian Philosophy*, ed. M. Chatterjee, Delhi: Motilal Banarsidass Publishers, 1974, 1998, 21–41.
Daya Krishna, "Philosophy: Influence of Theory on Practice," in *Philosophy: Theory & Practice – Proceedings of the International Seminar on World Philosophy*, Madras, December 7–17, 1970, ed. T. M. P. Mahadevan, Madras: The Centre for Advanced Study in Philosophy, University of Madras, 1974, 307–23.
Daya Krishna, "Reply to Raj Krishna," *Economic and Political Weekly* (1974).
Daya Krishna*, "Shall we be Diffracted? A Critical Comment on Fred Riggs's Prismatic Societies and Public Administration," *Administrative Change* (June 1974).
Daya Krishna, "Technology and Meaningful Patterns of Life," U.G.C. Seminar Report, 1975, 31–4.

Daya Krishna, "Contemporary India - A Crisis of Identity and Dilemmas of Development," *Quest* 97 (September–October 1976).
Daya Krishna, "Kalidas Bhattacharyya and the Logic of Alternation," *Indian Philosophical Quarterly* 3, no. 2 (January 1976): 195–208.
Daya Krishna, "Science, Technology and Value," *Diogenes* 24, no. 95 (September 1976): 29–40.
Daya Krishna*, "Towards a Saner View of Development: A Comment on Fred W. Riggs's Comment," *Administrative Change* (January 1976).
Daya Krishna*, "Arts and the Cognitive Enterprise of Man," *Visva-Bharati Quarterly* 41, nos. 1–4 (May 1977): 216–29.
Daya Krishna*, "Culture - A Field of Interdisciplinary Study," *International Social Science Journal*, UNESCO 29, no. 4 (1977): 651–70.
Daya Krishna, "Religion and the Critical Consciousness," *New Quest* 10 (July–August 1978): 241–8.
Daya Krishna*, "Some Reflections on Professor Riggs' Clarifications of Development," *Administrative Change* (July–December 1979).
Daya Krishna, "God and the Human Consciousness," *Diogenes* 117, no. 30 (March 1982): 1–10.
Daya Krishna*, "Anthropology – The Bonded Science?" *New Quest* (May–June 1983).
Daya Krishna*, "The Upaniṣads: What Are They?" *Journal of Indian Council for Philosophical Research* 1, no. 1 (Autumn 1983).
Daya Krishna*, "Indian Philosophy and Mokṣa: Revisiting an Old Controversy," *Journal of Indian Council of Philosophical Research* 2, no. 1 (Autumn 1984): 49–68.
Daya Krishna, "Philosophical Theory and Social Reality," in *Philosophical Theory and Social Reality*, ed. Ravinder Kumar, Delhi: Allied Publishers, 1984, 28–44.
Daya Krishna, "God and the Nation State," paper written for the Conference "God and Global Justice," Puerto Rico, 1984. Published in *Diogenes* 33, no. 129 (March 1985): 91–100.
Daya Krishna*, "Self and Its Representations in Literature," *The Literary Criterion*, 20, no. 3 (1985).
Daya Krishna*, "The Vedic Corpus: Some Questions," *Journal of Indian Council of Philosophical Research* 3, no. 1 (Autumn 1985): 103–28.
Daya Krishna*, "Comparative Philosophy: What It Is and What It Ought to Be?", *Diogenes* 34, no. 136 (December 1986): 58–69. Republished in *Interpreting Across Boundaries, New Essays in Comparative Philosophy*, eds. G. J. Larson and E. Deutsch, Delhi: Motilal Banarsidass Publishers, 1989, 71–83. Republished in *Contrary Thinking: Selected Essays by Daya Krishna*, eds. Bhushan et al., 2011, 59–67.
Daya Krishna*, "The Myth of the Puruṣārthas," *Journal of Indian Council of Philosophical Research* 4, no. 1 (Autumn 1986). Republished in *Pathways to Literature, Art and Archeology, Pt. Gopal Narayan Bahura Felicitation*

Volume, Vol. II, eds. Chandramani Singh and Neelima Vashishtha, Publication Scheme, Jaipur (1991); and published again under the title "The Myth of the Ethics of Puruṣārtha or Humanity's Life Goals," in *Indian Ethics: Classical Traditions and Contemporary Challenges*, eds. P. Bilimoria, J. Prabhu, and R. M. Sharma, Hampshire: Ashgate, 2007, 103–15.

Daya Krishna, "Overview of Country Reports," in *Teaching and Research in Philosophy: Asia and the Pacific* (Studies on Teaching in Philosophy throughout the World, II), Paris: UNESCO, 1986, 1–16.

Daya Krishna, "Communication, Identity and Self-Expression: Essays in Memory of S. N. Ganguly, eds. S. P. Banerjee and Shefali Moitra," Review Article, *Philosophy East and West* 38, no. 4 (October 1988): 431–6.

Daya Krishna*, "Thinking vs. Thought: Strategies for Conceptual Creativity," *Journal of Indian Council of Philosophical Research* 5, no. 2 (1988): 47–57. Republished in *Thinking Across Cultures: The Third International Conference on Thinking*, eds. Donald M. Topping, Doris C. Crowell and Victor N. Kobayashi, New York: Routledge, 1989, 195–204. Republished again in *Contrary Thinking: Selected Essays by Daya Krishna*, eds. Bhushan et al., 2011, 27–36.

Daya Krishna, "Knowledge, Reason and Human Autonomy," *Journal of Indian Council of Philosophical Research* 7, no. 1 (September–December 1989): 121–38.

Daya Krishna*, "Yajña and the Doctrine of Karma: A Contradiction in Indian Thought about Action," *Journal of Indian Council of Philosophical Research* 6, no. 2 (January–April 1989): 61–74.

Daya Krishna*, "The Text of the Nyāya-Sūtras – Some Problems," *Journal of Indian Council of Philosophical Research* 7, no. 2 (January–April 1990): 13–40.

Daya Krishna, "Secularism: Sacred and Profane," in *Culture and Modernity: East-West Philosophic Perspectives*, ed. E. Deutsch, Honolulu: University of Hawaii Press, 1991, 548–59.

Daya Krishna*, "The *Varṇāśrama* Syndrome of Indian Sociology," *Contributions to Indian Sociology* 26, no. 2 (1992): 281–98.

Daya Krishna, "Emerging New Approaches in the Study of Classical Indian Philosophy," in *Contemporary Philosophy: A New Survey*, ed. Guttorm Fløistad, Vol. 7, Netherlands: Kluwer Academic Publishers, 1993, 69–82.

Daya Krishna*, "Mīmāṃsā Before Jaimini: Some Problems in the Interpretation of Śruti in the Indian Tradition," *Journal of Indian Council of Philosophical Research* 9, no. 3 (1993): 103–11.

Daya Krishna, "Religion and Science: Reflections from Indian Perspectives," *The Journal of Religious Studies* 25, no. 2 (1994): 3–13.

Daya Krishna*, "The Mīmāṃsaka versus the Yājñika: Some Further Problems in the Interpretation of *Śruti* in the Indian Tradition," *Journal of Indian Council of Philosophical Research* 12, no. 2 (1995): 63–79. Republished in *Contrary Thinking: Selected Essays by Daya Krishna*, eds. Bhushan et al., 2011, 228–44.

Daya Krishna, "New World Order and Indian Intellectuals," *Economic and Political Weekly* 30, no. 2 (January 1995): 93–6.

Daya Krishna, "Realms of Between: Some Reflections on Murty's *The Realm of Between*," in *The Philosophy of K. Satchidananda Murty*, eds. S. Bhattacharyya and A. Vohra, Indian Council of Philosophical Research, Delhi, 1995, 169–76.

Daya Krishna*, "Indian Philosophy in the First Millennium A.D.: Fact and Fiction," *Journal of Indian Council of Philosophical Research* 13, no. 3 (May–August 1996): 127–35.

Daya Krishna, "Potter's New Bibliography of Indian Philosophy: One Step Forward and Three Steps Backwards," *Journal of Indian Council of Philosophical Research* 13, no. 3 (1996): 162–8.

Daya Krishna*, "Vedānta in the First Millennium A.D.: The Case Study of a Retrospective Illusion Imposed by the Historiography of Indian Philosophy," *Journal of Indian Council of Philosophical Research*, Special Issue (June 1996): 201–7.

Daya Krishna, "Encounters between Civilizations: The Question of the Centre and the Periphery," *New Quest* 125 (September–October 1997): 262–9.

Daya Krishna, "Socio-Political Thought in Classical India," in *A Companion to World Philosophies*, eds. E. Deutsch and R. Bontekoe, Malden: Blackwell, 1997, 237–47.

Daya Krishna*, "The Plurality of Civilizations and the Question of Identity," in *Science, Philosophy and Culture, Multi-disciplinary Explorations* (Part 2), eds. D. P. Chattopadhyaya and Ravinder Kumar, *Project of History of Indian Science, Philosophy and Culture*, Delhi: Centre for Studies in Civilizations, 1997.

Daya Krishna*, "Where Are the Vedas in the First Millennium AD?" *Journal of Indian Council of Philosophical Research* 15, no. 1 (1997): 77–82.

Daya Krishna, "Have the Neo-Naiyāyikas been Leading Us Up the Garden Path? A comment on the Kroḍapatras by D. Prahlada Char," *Journal of Indian Council of Philosophical Research* 15, no. 3 (1998): 121–41.

Daya Krishna*, "Is Tat Tvam Asi the Same Type of Identity Statement as The Morning Star Is the Evening Star?" *Indian Philosophical Quarterly* 25, no. 1 (1998): 1–13. Republished in *Contrary Thinking: Selected Essays by Daya Krishna*, eds. Bhushan et al., 2011, 75–85.

Daya Krishna*, "The Myth of the Prasthāna Trayī," *Journal of Indian Council of Philosophical Research* 16, no. 1 (September–December 1998): 85–91.

Daya Krishna, "A Radical Revision of Human Rights: The Need for Rethinking in a Universal Perspective," in *Taking Action for Human Rights in the Twenty-First Century*, ed. F. Mayor, Paris: UNESCO, 1998, 148–51.

Daya Krishna*, "Towards a Field Theory of Indian Philosophy: Suggestions for a New Way of Looking at Indian Philosophy," *Journal of Indian Council of Philosophical Research* 15, no. 2 (1998): 81–7.

Daya Krishna, "US-Iraq Conflict and Global Intellectual Community: Some Unasked Questions," *Economic and Political Weekly* 33, no. 25 (June 20, 1998): 1515–16.

Daya Krishna*, "How Anekāntika is Anekānta? Some Reflections on the Jain Theory of Anekāntavāda," *Journal of Indian Council of Philosophical Research* 16, no. 2 (January–April 1999): 121–8.

Daya Krishna*, "Thinking Creatively about the Creative Act," *Punjab University Research Bulletin* 30, nos. 1 and 2 (1999): 18–26. Republished in *Contrary Thinking: Selected Essays by Daya Krishna*, eds. Bhushan et al., 2011, 39–45.

Daya Krishna, "Time, Truth and Transcendence," in *History, Culture and Truth: Essays Presented to D. P. Chattopadhyaya*, eds. Daya Krishna, K. Satchidananda Murty and Bhuvan Chandel, Delhi: Kalki Prakash, 1999, 323–36.

Daya Krishna*, "Was Ācārya Śaṅkara Responsible for the Disappearance of Buddhist Philosophy from India?" *Journal of Indian Council of Philosophical Research* 17, no. 1 (1999): 127–30.

Daya Krishna, "The New Tribal States," *Economic and Political Weekly* 35, no. 46 (November 11, 2000): 3997–8.

Daya Krishna*, "The Shock-Proof, Evidence-Proof, Argument-Proof World of Sāmpradāyika Scholarship of Indian Philosophy," *Journal of Indian Council of Philosophical Research* 17, no. 2 (2000): 143–59. Republished in *Contrary Thinking: Selected Essays by Daya Krishna*, eds. Bhushan et al., 2011, 191–205.

Daya Krishna*, "Can the Analysis of Adhyāsa ever Lead to an Advaitic Conclusion?" in Daya Krishna, *New Perspectives in Indian Philosophy* (2001): 150–63. Republished in *Contrary Thinking: Selected Essays by Daya Krishna*, eds. Bhushan et al., 2011, 206–16.

Daya Krishna*, "Did the Gopīs Really Love Kṛṣṇa? Some Reflections on Bhakti as a Puruṣārtha in the Indian Tradition," in Daya Krishna, *New Perspectives in Indian Philosophy* (2001): 175–88. Republished in *Contrary Thinking: Selected Essays by Daya Krishna*, eds. Bhushan et al., 2011, 275–84.

Daya Krishna, "Is the Doctrine of Arthavāda Compatible with the Idea of Śruti?" in Daya Krishna, *New Perspectives in Indian Philosophy*, Jaipur and Delhi: Rawat Publications, 2001, 115–26.

Daya Krishna, "Kant's Doctrine of the Categories: Some Questions and Problems," *Journal of Indian Council of Philosophical Research* 18, no. 4 (October–December 2001): 1–11.

Daya Krishna*, "Nyāya: Realist or Idealist? Has the Debate Ended, the Argument Completed?" *Journal of Indian Council of Philosophical Research* 18, no. 1 (January–March 2001): 161–3.

Daya Krishna, "Possible Worlds," *Journal of Indian Council of Philosophical Research* 18, no. 2 (April–June 2001): 181–92.

Daya Krishna, "A Short Note on the Inner Sense and the Three (or Four) Notions of Self in Kant," *Journal of Indian Council of Philosophical Research* 19, no. 4 (October–December 2002): 129–36.

Daya Krishna, "Fichte – The Forgotten Philosopher," *Journal of Indian Council of Philosophical Research* 19, no. 4 (October–December 2002): 29–36.

Daya Krishna, "Grammar, Logic and Mathematics: Foundations of the Civilizations Man Has Built," *Journal of Indian Council of Philosophical Research* 19, no. 3 (July–September 2002): 65–74.

Daya Krishna, "Identity, Difference and the Problem of Reflexivity and Explanation," *Journal of Indian Council of Philosophical Research* 19, no. 1 (January–March 2002): 1–18.

Daya Krishna, "India's Civilizational Enterprises in the Third Millennium AD: Maintenance, Renewal and New Directions," in *Antaral: End-Century Meditations*, ed. K. Satchidanandan, Delhi: Sahitya Akademi, 2002.

Daya Krishna, "Sign, Sense and Reference: Reflections on Problems in the Philosophy of Language," *Journal of Indian Council of Philosophical Research* 19, no. 2 (April–June 2002): 129–38.

Daya Krishna, "Polity, Economy and Society: Structural Contradictions and the Dynamics of History," *Journal of Indian Council of Philosophical Research* 20, no. 2 (April–June 2003): 31–46.

Daya Krishna*, "Freeing Philosophy from the prison House of I-Centricity," *Journal of Indian Council of Philosophical Research* 20, no. 3 (July–September 2003): 135–43. Republished in *Contrary Thinking: Selected Essays by Daya Krishna*, eds. Bhushan et al., 2011, 293–8.

Daya Krishna*, "Illusion, Hallucination and the Problem of Truth," *Journal of Indian Council of Philosophical Research* 20, no. 4 (October–December 2003): 129–46. Republished in *Contrary Thinking: Selected Essays by Daya Krishna*, eds. Bhushan et al., 2011, 165–77.

Daya Krishna, "Praśastapāda's Mapping of the Realm of Qualities: A Neglected Chapter in Indian Philosophy," *Journal of Indian Council of Philosophical Research* 20, no. 1 (October–December 2003): 115–24.

Daya Krishna*, "Madness, Reason and Truth," *Journal of Indian Council of Philosophical Research* 21, no. 2 (January–March 2004): 89–100. Republished in *Contrary Thinking: Selected Essays by Daya Krishna*, eds. Bhushan et al., 2011, 157–64.

Daya Krishna*, "Negation: Can Philosophy Ever Recover from It?" *Journal of Indian Council of Philosophical Research* 21, no. 2 (April–June 2004): 179–92. Republished in *Contrary Thinking: Selected Essays by Daya Krishna*, eds. Bhushan et al., 2011, 115–24.

Daya Krishna*, "Rasa – The Bane of Indian Aesthetics," *Journal of Indian Council of Philosophical Research* 21, no. 3 (July–September 2004): 119–35. Republished in *Contrary Thinking: Selected Essays by Daya Krishna*, eds. Bhushan et al., 2011, 89–102.

Daya Krishna*, "Reality, Imagination and Truth, *Journal of Indian Council of Philosophical Research* 21, no. 4 (October–December 2004): 115–28. Republished in *Contrary Thinking: Selected Essays by Daya Krishna*, eds. Bhushan et al., 2011, 178–87.

Daya Krishna*, "Definition, Deception and the Enterprise of Knowledge," *Journal of Indian Council of Philosophical Research* 22, no. 1 (January–March

2005): 75–89. Republished in *Contrary Thinking: Selected Essays by Daya Krishna*, eds. Bhushan et al., 2011, 144–54.

Daya Krishna*, "Eros, Nomos and Logos," *Journal of Indian Council of Philosophical Research* 22, no. 2 (April–June 2005): 165–82. Republished in *Contrary Thinking: Selected Essays by Daya Krishna*, eds. Bhushan et al., 2011, 309–21.

Daya Krishna*, "Thinking with Causality about Causality: Reflections on a Concept Determining All Thought about Action and Knowledge," *Journal of Indian Council of Philosophical Research* 22, no. 3 (July–September 2005): 123–38. Republished in *Contrary Thinking: Selected Essays by Daya Krishna*, eds. Bhushan et al., 2011, 46–56.

Daya Krishna*, "Knowledge: Whose is It, What Is It, and Why has It to Be True?" *Indian Philosophical Quarterly* 32, no. 3 (2005): 179–87. Republished in *Contrary Thinking: Selected Essays by Daya Krishna*, eds. Bhushan et al., 2011, 137–43.

Daya Krishna*, "Substance: The Bane of Philosophy," *Journal of Indian Council of Philosophical Research* 22, no. 4 (October–December 2005): 181–93. Republished in *Contrary Thinking: Selected Essays by Daya Krishna*, eds. Bhushan et al., 2011, 103–11.

Daya Krishna*, "Apoha and Samavāya in a Kantian Perspective," in Daya Krishna, *Indian Philosophy: A Counter Perspective* (Revised and Enlarged Edition), Delhi: Sri Satguru Publications, 2006, 250–61. Republished in *Contrary Thinking: Selected Essays by Daya Krishna*, eds. Bhushan et al., 2011, 68–74.

Daya Krishna, "Bondages of Birth and Death: Emerging Technologies of Freedom on the Horizon and the Hope of Final Release from the Foundational Bondage of Mankind," in Daya Krishna, *Indian Philosophy: A Counter Perspective* (enlarged and revised edition), Delhi: Sri Satguru Publications, 2006, 509–29.

Daya Krishna, "Law, Logic and Ethics: Issues at the Heart of Society and Polity," *Journal of Indian Council of Philosophical Research* 23, no. 1 (January–March 2006): 147–68.

Daya Krishna*, "Ṛgveda: The Mantra, the Sūkta and the Maṇḍala or The Ṛṣi, the Devatā, the Chanda: The Structure of the Text and the Problems Regarding It," *Journal of Indian Council of Philosophical Research* 23, no. 2 (April–June 2006): 1–13. Republished in *Contrary Thinking: Selected Essays by Daya Krishna*, eds. Bhushan et al., 2011, 247–56.

Daya Krishna, "Chance, Probability, Indeterminacy and Knowledge," *Journal of Indian Council of Philosophical Research* 23, no. 3 (July–September 2006): 91–110.

Daya Krishna, "The Cosmic, Biological and Cultural Conditionings, and the Seeking for Freedom," *Journal of Indian Council of Philosophical Research* 23, no. 4 (October–December 2006): 133–60.

Daya Krishna, "The Undeciphered Text: Anomalies, Problems and Paradoxes in the Yogasūtra," in Daya Krishna, *Indian Philosophy: A Counter Perspective* (enlarged and revised edition, 2006), 204–23. Republished in Daniel Raveh, *Exploring the Yogasūtra: Philosophy and Translation*, 2012, 90–104.

Daya Krishna*, "The Vedic Corpus and the Two Sūtra Texts Concerned with it, the Mīmāṃsāsūtra and the Brahmasūtra," in Daya Krishna, *Indian Philosophy: A Counter Perspective* (enlarged and revised edition, 2006), 151–80. Republished in *Contrary Thinking: Selected Essays by Daya Krishna*, eds. Bhushan et al., 2011, 257–71.

Daya Krishna, "How Empirical is the Empirical: Some Reflections," *Journal of Indian Council of Philosophical Research* 24, no. 1 (January–March 2007): 193–9.

Daya Krishna, "Some Reflections on the Knowledge Called Mathematics," *Journal of Indian Council of Philosophical Research* 24, no. 1 (January–March 2007): 1–20.

Daya Krishna*, "Freedom, Reason, Ethics and Aesthetics," *Journal of Indian Council of Philosophical Research* 24, no. 2 (April–June 2007): 1–12. Republished in *Contrary Thinking: Selected Essays by Daya Krishna*, eds. Bhushan et al., 2011, 299–306.

Daya Krishna, "Some Problems Regarding Thinking about Abhāva in the Indian Tradition," *Contrary Thinking: Selected Essays by Daya Krishna*, eds. Bhushan et al., 2011, 125–33.

IV Unpublished Articles by Daya Krishna (written in 2006-2007)

"Anumāna"

"Art and the Mystic Consciousness"

"Conversation, Dialogue, Discussion, Debate and the Problem of Knowledge"

"Experience, Dubitability and Certainty"

"Knowledge, Predictability and Truth"

"Narrative, Meta-Narrative and No Narrative"

"Peace, Polity and Ethnicity"

"Peace: The Enemy of Nations"

"The Formative Period of Indian Civilization: The Vedic, the Śramaṇa, the Āgamic Traditions; the Interactions Between them and the Reflexive Reflections on Them"

"The Sources, the Texts, the Subsidiaries, the Supportive, the Exegetical Literature: The Puzzle and the Problem of the Veda in the Indian Tradition"

"The Yajurveda Text - The Heart of the Veda Yajña: One, Two, or Too Many?"

"Thinking Without Things, Without Identity, without Non-Contradiction and Yet Thinking Still"

Literature on Daya Krishna

I Edited Volumes

Chandel, B. and Sharma, K. L. (eds.), *The Philosophy of Daya Krishna*, Delhi: Munshiram Manoharlal Publishers, 1996.

Mayaram, S. (ed.), *Philosophy as Saṃvāda and Svarāj, Dialogical Meditations on Daya Krishna and Ramchandra Gandhi*, Delhi: Sage, 2014.

Sharma, K. L. and Bhatnagar, R. S. (eds.), *Philosophy, Society and Action, Essays in Honour of Prof. Daya Krishna*, Jaipur: Aalekh Publishers, 1984.

II Selected Articles

Bhushan, N. and Garfield, J. L., "Can Indian Philosophy be Written in English? A Conversation with Daya Krishna" (2008). https://www.academia.edu/2833422/Can_Indian_Philosophy_Be_Written_in_English_A_Conversation_with_Daya_Krishna_Nalini_Bhushan_Smith_College

Biswas, Prasanjit, "Daya Krishna's 'Presuppositionless Philosophy': Sublimity as the Source of Value and Knowledge," in *Philosophy as Saṃvāda and Svarāj, Dialogical Meditations on Daya Krishna and Ramchandra Gandhi*, ed. S. Mayaram, Delhi: Sage, 2014, 139–60.

Brandner, R., "Should One Try to Understand Indian Philosophy on the Western Model? Fundamental Defect in Daya Krishna's Approach to the 'Understanding' of Indian Philosophy," *Journal of Indian Council of Philosophical Research* 16, no. 2 (January–April 1999): 141–5.

Chakrabarti, A., "New Stuff: on the Very Idea of Creativity in Philosophical Thinking," introduction to N. Bhushan, J. L. Garfield and D. Raveh (eds.), *Contrary Thinking: Selected Essays by Daya Krishna*, New York: Oxford University Press, 2011, 4–24.

Chattopadhyaya, D. P., "Reflections on Daya Krishna's Concept of Action," in *The Philosophy of Daya Krishna*, eds. Bhuvan Chandel and K. L. Sharma, Delhi: Munshiram Manoharlal Publishers, 1996, 162–81.

Coquereau, E., *Intercultural Dialogues and Creativity of Knowledge: A Study of Daya Krishna*, Doctoral Dissertation submitted to the University of Vienna, January 2019.

Coquereau, E., "Seeking Values in Daya Krishna's Philosophy," in *Kontexte des Leiblichen, Contexts of Corporality*, eds. C. Nielsen, K. Novotny, and T. Nenon, Nordhausen: Traugott Bautz, 2016, 125–49.

Dallmayr, F., "Reason and Lifeworld: Two Exemplary Indian Thinkers," in *Integral Pluralism, Beyond Culture Wars*, Lexington: The University Press of Kentucky, 2010, Chapter 8, 43–165.

Freschi, E., "Unveiling Indian Philosophy: An Obituary for Daya Krishna," *Rivista di Studi Sudasiatici* II (2007): 265–70.
Freschi, E., Coquereau, E., and Ali, M., "Rethinking Classical Dialectical Traditions: Daya Krishna on Counter-position and Dialogue," *Culture and Dialogue* 5, no. 2 (2017): 173–209.
Garfield, J. L., *Love, Law and Language: Continuing to Think with Daya-ji*, Jaipur: The Daya Krishna Annual Lecture, 2018.
Garfield, J. L. and Chakrabarti, A., "Remembering Daya Krishna and G. C. Pande: Two Giants of Post-Independence," *Philosophy East and West* 63, no. 4 (October 2013): 458–64.
Krishan, Y., "Comments on the Article Entitled Yajña and the Doctrine of Karma: A Contradiction in Indian Thought and Action by Daya Krishna," *Journal of Indian Council of Philosophical Research* 18, no. 1 (January–March 2001): 227–34.
Malkani, G. R., "A Discussion of Daya Krishna's Views on Advaitic Adhyāsa," *Philosophy East and West* 16, no. 1/2 (January–April 1966): 81–3.
McGhee, M., "Learning to Converse: Reflections on a Small Experiment," *Philosophy East and West* 63, no. 4 (October 2013): 530–42.
Miller, D., "Reading Derrida with Daya Krishna: Postmodern Trends in Contemporary Indian Philosophy," *Sophia* 57, no. 3 (2018): 425–42.
Mohanty, J. N., "Some Thoughts on Daya Krishna's Three Myths," in *The Philosophy of Daya Krishna*, eds. Bhuvan Chandel and K. L. Sharma, Delhi: Munshiram Manoharlal Publishers, 1996, 68–80.
Potter, K. H., "Are All Indian Philosophers Indian Philosophers?" *Journal of Indian Council of Philosophical Research* 2, no. 2 (1985): 145–9.
Prasad, R., "Daya Krishna's Therapy for Myths of Indian Philosophy," *Journal of Indian Council of Philosophical Research* 1, no. 2 (December 2015): 1–14.
Raveh, D., "Text as a Process: Thinking with Daya Krishna," *Sandhān, Journal of Centre for Studies in Civilizations* 7, no. 2 (July–December 2007): 191–205.
Raveh, D., "Knowledge as a Way of Living: A Dialogue with Daya Krishna," *Philosophy East and West* 58, no. 4 (October 2008): 431–7.
Raveh, D., "Philosophical Miscellanea: Excerpts from an Ongoing Dialogue with Daya Krishna," *Philosophy East and West* 63, no. 4 (October 2013): 491–512.
Raveh, D., "Thinking Dialogically about Dialogue with Martin Buber and Daya Krishna," *Confluence: Journal of World Philosophies* 4 (2016): 8–32.
Sen, P. K., "Daya Krishna on Some Indian Theories of Negation: A Critique," *Philosophy East and West* 63, no. 4 (October 2013): 543–61.
Shalya, Y., "Daya Krishna Ka Samaaj-Darshanik Vimarsh," in *Bhartiya Darshan ke 50 Varsh*, ed. Ambika Datta Sharma, Sagar: Vishvavidyalaya Prakashan, 2006, 181–202.
Sjödin, A.-P., "Conceptualizing Philosophical Tradition: A Reading of Wilhelm Halbfass, Daya Krishna, and Jitendranath Mohanty," *Philosophy East and West* 61, no. 3 (July 2011): 534–46.

Sogani, K. C., "Some Comments on Daya Krishna's Essay The Active and the Contemplative Values," *Philosophy and Phenomenological Research* 32, no. 2 (December 1971): 264–66.

Tiwari, D. N., "Reflections on Dayakrishna's Philosophy," *Indian Philosophical Quarterly* 25, no. 3 (July 1998): 373–87.

Xavier, C. J., "Saṃvāda as Successful Communication: Daya Krishna's Ideas on Dialogue in Communication," *Indian Philosophical Quarterly* 43, nos. 1–4 (April 2017): 197–212.

Other Cited Sources

Ten Principal Upaniṣads with Śāṅkarabhāṣya (Īśā, Kena, *Kaṭha, Praśna, Muṇḍaka, Māṇḍūkya, Taittirīya, Aitareya, Chāndogya, Bṛhadāraṇyaka*), Works of Śaṅkarācārya in the original Sanskrit (2007) Delhi: Motilal Banarsidass.

* * *

Aranya, Swami Hariharananda (2012) *Yoga Philosophy of Patañjali*, translated from the original Bengali into English by P. N. Mukerji, Kolkata: University of Calcutta.

Aurobindo, Sri (1998) [1914-1916] *The Secret of the Veda*, Pondicherry: Sri Aurobindo Ashram.

Aurobindo, Sri (2005) [1939-1940] *The Life Divine*, Pondicherry: Sri Aurobindo Ashram.

Bader, Jonathan (2000) *Conquest of the Four Quarters: Traditional Accounts of the Life of Śaṅkara*, Delhi: Aditya Prakashan.

Bandyopadhyay, Sibaji (2014) "Of Gambling," in *Mahabharata Now: Narration, Aesthetics, Ethics*, eds. Arindam Chakrabarti and Sibaji Bandyopadhyay, Delhi: Routledge, 3–28.

Bandyopadhyay, Sibaji (2018) "Aesthetic of Theft," in *The Bloomsbury Research Handbook of Indian Aesthetics and the Philosophy of Art*, ed. Arindam Chakrabarti, London and New York: Bloomsbury, 195–214.

Benjamin, Walter (1999) "The Task of the Translator: An Introduction to the Translation of Baudeair's *Tableaux Parisiens*" (first published in 1923), in Benjamin's *Illuminations*, translated by Harry Zohn, London: Pimlico, 69–82.

Benjamin, Walter (1999) "The Work of Art in the Age of Mechanical Reproduction" (first published in 1935), in Benjamin's *Illuminations*, London: Pimlico, 217–52.

Bhatt, Bansidhar (1978) "Interpretation of Some Crucial Problems in Śaṅkara's Adhyāsa-Bhāṣya," *Journal of Indian Philosophy* 5, no. 4: 337–53.

Bhattacharyya, Krishnachandra (1954) "Svarāj in Ideas," *Visva Bharati Journal* 20: 103–14. Republished in the *Indian Philosophical Quarterly* 11, no. 4: 383–93 (1984).

Bhattacharyya, Krishnachandra (2008) [1958] *Studies in Philosophy*, ed. Gopinath Bhattacharyya, Delhi: Motilal Banarsidass.

Bhattacharyya, Krishnachandra (2008) "The Concept of Rasa," in his *Studies in Philosophy*, 347–63.

Bronkhorst, Johannes (2014) "Mīmāṃsāsūtra and Brahmasūtra," *Journal of Indian Philosophy* 42, no. 4: 463–9.

Bronkhorst, Johannes (2017) "Brahmanism: Its Place in Ancient Indian Society," *Contributions to Indian Sociology* 51, no. 3: 361–9.
Chakrabarti, Arindam (1983) "Is Liberation (*mokṣa*) Pleasant?" *Philosophy East and West* 33: 167–82.
Chakrabarti, Arindam (1995) "Kant in India," in *Proceedings of the Eighth International Kant Congress*, ed. Hoke Robinson, Milwaukee: Marquette University Press, 1: 1281–6.
Chakrabarti, Arindam (2002) "Disgust and the Ugly in Indian Aesthetics," in *La Pluralita Estetica: Lasciti e irradiazioni oltre il Novecento, Associazione Italiana Studi di Estetica*, Turin: Trauben, 345–63 (I work with the author's original version, pp. 1–19).
Chakrabarti, Arindam (2009) "Play, Pleasure, Pain: Ownerless Emotions in Rasa-Aesthetics," chapter 14 of *Science, Literature and* Aesthetics, ed. Amiya Dev, Vol. XV Part 3 of the series *History of Science, Philosophy and Culture in Indian Civilization*, General Editor D. P. Chattopadhyaya, Delhi: Centre for Studies in Civilizations.
Chakrabarti, Arindam (2018) "Contemporary Indian Aesthetics and Philosophy of Art," Introduction to *The Bloomsbury Research Handbook of Indian Aesthetics and the Philosophy of Art*, ed. Arindam Chakrabarti, London and New York: Bloomsbury, 1–24.
Chakrabarti, Arindam and Weber, Ralph, eds. (2015) *Comparative Philosophy without Borders*, London: Bloomsbury Academic.
Chandra, Vikram (1995) *Red Earth and Pouring Rain*, New York and Boston: Little, Brown and Company.
Chatterjee, Margaret (1974) *Contemporary Indian Philosophy: A Reader*, London: George Allen and Unwin.
Derrida, Jacques (1983) "The Principle of Reason: The University in the Eyes of Its Pupils," trans. Catherine Porter and Edward P. Morris, *Diacritics* 13, no. 3: 2–20.
Derrida, Jacques (1986) "Title (To Be Specified)," in *Parages*, ed. J. P. Leavey, trans. T. Conley, J. Hulbert, J. P. Leavey, and A. Ronell, Stanford: Stanford University Press.
Derrida, Jacques (2004) *Eyes of the University: Right to Philosophy 2*, Stanford: Stanford University Press.
Deshpande, Sharad, ed. (2004) "200 Years of Kant," Special Number of the *Indian Philosophical Quarterly* 31, no. 1–4, http://www.unipune.ac.in/snc/cssh/ipq/english/vol31_1-4.htm
Doniger, W. and Kakar, S., trans. (2002) *Kamasutra*, Oxford: Oxford University Press.
Eyal, Nir (2014) *Hooked: How to Build Habit-Forming Products*, New York: Portfolio Publishers.
Fuller, Steve (2018) *Post-Truth: Knowledge as a Power Game*, London: Anthem Press.
Gandhi, M. K. (1968) [1927] *An Autobiography or The Story of My Experiments with Truth*, Ahmedabad: Navajivan Publishing House.

Gandhi, Ramchandra (1981) "On Meriting Death," *Philosophy East and West* 31, no. 3: 337–53.
Gandhi, Ramchandra (2011) [1984] *I am Thou: Meditations on the Truth of India*, Delhi: Academy of Fine Arts and Literature.
Gandhi, Ramchandra (1992) *Sītā's Kitchen: A Testimony of Faith and Inquiry*, Albany: State University of New York Press.
Gandhi, Ramchandra (2002) *Svarāj: A Journey with Tyeb Mehta's Shantiniketan Triptych*, Delhi: Vadehra Art Gallery.
Gandhi, Ramchandra (2003) "Mokṣa and Martyrdom," a lecture delivered at the National Institute of Advances Studies, Bangalore on November 14, 2003; https://www.youtube.com/watch?v=NPYb3BsoCI0; "Mokṣa and Martyrdom" was transcribed and is included in *The Seven Sages: Selected Essays by Ramchandra Gandhi*, ed. A. Raghuramaraju, Delhi: Penguin Books, 2015, 121–41.
Ganeri, Jonardon (2010) "Sanskrit Philosophical Commentary," *Journal of Indian Council of Philosophical Research* 25, no. 1: 107–27.
Ganeri, Jonardon (2011) *The Lost Age of Reason: Philosophy in Early Modern India* (1450–1700), Delhi: Oxford University Press.
Ganeri, Jonardon (2016) "Why Philosophy Must Go Global: A Manifesto," Comprised of the text of "Manifesto for a Re:emergent Philosophy," and "Reflections on Re:emergent Philosophy," *Confluence: An Online Journal of World Philosophies* (June 2016): 134–41, and 164–86, https://philarchive.org/archive/GANWPM
Garfield, Jay (2017) "Solving Kant's Problem: K.C. Bhattacharyya on Self-Knowledge," in *Indian Epistemology and Metaphysics*, ed. Joerg Tuske, London: Bloomsbury, 355–77.
Garfield, Jay and Bhushan, Nalini, eds. (2011) *Indian Philosophy in English: From Renaissance to Independence*, New York: Oxford University Press.
Garfield, Jay and Bhushan, Nalini (2017) *Minds Without Fear: Philosophy in the Indian Renaissance*, New York: Oxford University Press.
Grinshpon, Yohanan (2011) *The Secret Śaṅkara: On Multivocality and Truth in Śaṅkara's Teaching*, Leiden: Brill.
Guru, Gopal (2000) "Dalits from Margin to Margin," *India International Centre Quarterly* 27, no. 2: 111–16.
Guru, Gopal (2018) "Aesthetic of Touch and Skin: An Essay in Contemporary Indian Political Phenomenology," in *The Bloomsbury Research Handbook of Indian Aesthetics and the Philosophy of Art*, ed. Arindam Chakrabarti, London and New York: Bloomsbury, 297–316.
Halbfass, Wilhelm, ed. (1995) *Philology and Confrontation: Paul Hacker on Traditional and Modern Vedānta*, Albany: State University of New York Press.
Hiriyanna, M. (1932) *Outlines of Indian Philosophy*, London: George Allen and Unwin.
Horgan, John (1993) "The Death of Proof," *Scientific American*, October 1993: 92–103.

Iveković, Rada (1997) "The Politics of Comparative Philosophy," in *Beyond Orientalism: The Work of Wilhelm Halbfass and Its Impact on Indian and Cross-Cultural Studies*, eds. E. Franco and K. Preisendanz, Amsterdam and Atlanta: Rodopi, 221–33.

Iveković, Rada (2000) "Coincidence of Comparison," translated by Penelope Deutscher, *Hypatia* 15, no. 4: 224–35.

Krishan, Y. (1989) "Collective Karmas," *East and West* 39, no. 1/4 (December 1989): 179–94, Istituto Italiano per l'Africa e l'Oriente.

Kwan, Tze-wan (2008) "The Overdominance of English in Global Education: Is an Alternative Scenario Thinkable?" in *Educations and their Purposes: A Philosophical Dialogue among Cultures*, eds. Roger Ames and Peter Hershock, Honolulu: University of Hawaii Press, 54–71.

Lath, Mukund (1992) "Aristotle and the Roots of Western Rationality," *Journal of Indian Council of Philosophical Research* 9, no. 2: 55–68.

Lath, Mukund (1998) *Transformation as Creation: Essays in the History, Theory and Aesthetics of Indian Music, Dance and Theatre*, Delhi: Aditya Prakashan.

Lath, Mukund (2003) "Identity Through Necessary Change: Thinking about Rāga-bhāva, Concepts and Characters," *Journal of Indian Council of Philosophical Research* 20, no. 1: 85–114; reproduced in the *Journal of World Philosophies* 4 (winter 2018): 6–23.

Lath, Mukund (2004) *Dharmasaṃkat: kiṃ karma kim akarmeti kavayo'py atra mohitāḥ*, Allahabad: Raka Prakashan for Darshan Pratishthan Jaipur.

Lath, Mukund (2018) "Thoughts on Svara and Rasa: Music as Thinking/Thinking as Music," in *The Bloomsbury Research Handbook of Indian Aesthetics and the Philosophy of Art*, ed. Arindam Chakrabarti, London and New York: Bloomsbury, 93–106.

Lévi-Strauss, Claude (1966) "Anthropology: Its Achievements and Future," *Current Anthropology* 7, no. 2: 124–7.

McCrea, Lawrence (2018) "Resonance and its Reverberations: Two Cultures in Indian Epistemology of Aesthetic Meaning," chapter 1 of *The Bloomsbury Research Handbook of Indian Aesthetics and the Philosophy of Art*, ed. Arindam Chakrabarti, London and New York: Bloomsbury, 25–41.

Mohanty, J. N. (1997) "A History of Indian Philosophy," in *A Companion to World Philosophies*, eds. Eliot Deutsch and Ron Bontekoe, Malden: Blackwell, 24–48.

Oinam, Bhagat (2018) "Philosophy in India or Indian Philosophy? Some Post-Colonial Questions," *Sophia* 57, no. 3: 457–74.

Okri, Ben (2011) *A Time for New Dreams*, London: Rider.

Olivelle, Patrick, trans. (2008) *The Life of the Buddha by Ashva-ghosha*, Clay Sanskrit Library, New York: New York University Press.

Patnaik, Priyadarshi (1999) "Text as a Process," *Journal of Indian Council of Philosophical Research* 16, no. 3: 99–106.

Paulson, Steve (2016) "Critical Intimacy: An Interview with Gayatri Chakravorty Spivak," https://lareviewofbooks.org/article/critical-intimacy-interview-gayatri-chakravorty-spivak/#

Peng, Wen-Shien (2008) "A Critique of Fred W. Riggs' Ecology of Public Administration," *Public Administration Quarterly* 32, no. 4: 528–48.

Pollock, Sheldon (2001) "The Social Aesthetic and Sanskrit Literary Theory," *Journal of Indian Philosophy* 29, no. 1/2: 197–229.

Pollock, Sheldon (2016) *A Rasa Reader: Classical Indian Aesthetics*, Historical Sourcebooks in Classical Indian Thought series, New York: Columbia University Press.

Potter, Karl H. (1995) [1970, 1983] *Encyclopedia of Indian Philosophies, Vol. 1: Bibliography*, https://faculty.washington.edu/kpotter/

Potter, Karl H. (2004) "The Development of Advaita Vedānta as a School of Philosophy," in *Discussion and Debate in Indian Philosophy: Vedānta, Mīmāṃsā and Nyāya*, ed. Daya Krishna, Delhi: Indian Council of Philosophical Research, 3–38.

Radhakrishnan, Sarvepalli (2008) [1923] *Indian Philosophy*, Vol. 1, Delhi: Oxford University Press.

Raghuramaraju, A. (2006) *Debates in Indian Philosophy, Classical, Colonial and Contemporary*, Delhi: Oxford University Press.

Raghuramaraju, A. (2012) *Enduring Colonialism: Classical Presences and Modern Absences in Indian Philosophy*, Delhi: Oxford University Press.

Raghuramaraju, A. (2013a) "Buddhism in Indian Philosophy," *India International Centre Quarterly* 40, no. 3/4 (Winter 2013–Spring 2014): 65–85.

Raghuramaraju, A. (2013b) *Philosophy and India: Ancestors, Outsiders, and Predecessors*, Delhi: Oxford University Press.

Raghuramaraju, A. (2017) *Modern Frames and Premodern Themes in Indian Philosophy: Border, Self and the Other*, London and New York: Routledge.

Ramanujan, A. K. (1991) "Three Hundred Rāmāyaṇas: Five Examples and Three Thoughts on Translation," in *Many Rāmāyaṇas: The Diversity of a Narrative in South Asia*, ed. Paula Richman, Berkeley: University of California Press, 22–49.

Raveh, Daniel (2012) *Exploring the Yogasūtra: Philosophy and Translation*, London and New York: Continuum.

Raveh, Daniel (2016) *Sūtras, Stories and Yoga Philosophy: Narrative and Transfiguration*, London and New York: Routledge.

Rushdie, Salman (2010) [1981] "Imaginary Homelands," in his *Imaginary Homelands*, London: Vintage, 9–21.

Rushdie, Salman (2006) [1982] *Midnight's Children*, New York: Random House.

Rushdie, Salman (1989) *The Satanic Verses*, New York: Viking Penguin.

Rushdie, Salman (2008) *The Enchantress of Florence*, London: Jonathan Cape.

Sarma, Pandit R. Thangaswami (1980) *Advaita Vedānta Literature: A Bibliographical Survey*, Madras: University of Madras (Madras University Sanskrit Series, 36).

Sarma, Pandit R. Thangaswami (1985) *Darśanamañjarī*, Madras: University of Madras.

Sarma, Pandit R. Thangaswami (1996) *Mīmāṃsāmañjarī*, Delhi: Munshiram Manoharlal.

Shah, K. J. (1988) "Of Artha and the Arthaśāstra," in *Way of Life: King, Householder, Renouncer*, ed. T. N. Madan, Delhi: Motilal Banarsidass, 55–74.

Shah, Ramesh Chandra (2006) *Ancestral Voices: Reflections on Vedic, Classical and Bhakti Poetry*, Delhi: Motilal Banarsidass.

Shankar, S. (1994) "The Thumb of Ekalavya: Postcolonial Studies and the 'Third World' scholar in a Neocolonial World," *World Literature Today* 68, no. 3: 479–87.

Sharma, Ambika Datta (2017) *Yashdev Shalya Samagra*, Vols. 1–4, Delhi: DK Printworld.

Shukla, Badrinath (1988) "Dehātmavāda or the Body as Soul: Exploration of a Possibility Within Nyāya Thought," translated from the original Sanskrit by Mukund Lath, *Journal of Indian Council of Philosophical Research* 5, no. 3: 1–17.

Shukla, Pandit Badrinath (1987) *Śataślokī* ("Hundred Verses on Emancipation"), Delhi: Indian Council of Philosophical Research Publications.

Spivak, Gayatri Chakravorty (1996) *The Spivak Readar*, eds. Donna Landry and Gerald Maclean, London and New York: Routledge.

Suhrud, Tridip (2013) "Emptied of all but Love: Gandhiji on 30 January 1948," Nehru Memorial Museum and Library, History and Society Series, Occasional Paper #18, pp. 1–15.

Thapar, Romila (1979) "Dāna and Dakṣiṇā as forms of Exchange," in her *Ancient Indian Social History: Some Interpretations*, Hyderabad: Orient Longman, 94–108.

Thapar, Romila (1988) "Householders and Renouncers in the Brahmanical and Buddhist Traditions," in *Way of Life: King, Householder, Renouncer: Essays in Honour of Louis Dumont*, ed. T. N. Madan, Delhi: Motilal Banarsidass, 273–98.

Thibaut, G., trans. (1994) *The Vedānta Sūtras with the Commentary of Śaṅkarācārya* (Parts I and II), in *Sacred Books of the East*, ed. Max Muller, Vols. 34 and 38, Delhi: Motilal Banarsidass.

Tola, Fernando and Dragonetti, Carmen (2009) "Coincidences between Indian and Western Theories of Categories," *Annals of the Bhandarkar Oriental Research Institute* 90: 11–41.

Vajpeyi, Ananya (2011) "The Śūdra in History: From Scripture to Segregation," in *South Asian Texts in History: Critical Engagements with Sheldon Pollock*, eds. Y. Bronner, W. Cox, and L. McCrea, Asia Past & Present: New Research from the Association for Asian Studies, No. 7, 337–58.

Van Norden, Bryan (2017) *Taking Back Philosophy: A Multicultural Manifesto*, New York: Columbia University Press.

Weiner, Sonia (2012) *f-e-n-c-e-s*, Gallery Text for the exhibition FENCES, June 2012, Zilum Ba'am, Tel Aviv.

Whaling, Frank (1979) "Śaṅkara and Buddhism," *Journal of Indian Philosophy* 7, no. 1: 1–42.

Žižek, Slavoj (2009) "Philosophy Is NOT a Dialogue," in Alain Badiou and Slovoj Žižek, *Philosophy in the Present*, trans. Peter Thomas and Alberto Toscano, Cambridge: Polity Press, 49–72.

Index

Note: Page numbers followed by "n" refer to notes.